Cry Out and Write

CRY OUT AND WRITE

A FEMININE POETICS
OF REVELATION

Edward Peter Nolan

◇   ◇   ◇

CONTINUUM • NEW YORK

1994
The Continuum Publishing Company
370 Lexington Avenue, New York, NY 10017

Printed in the United States of America

Library of Congress Cataloging-in-Publication Data

Nolan, Edward Peter, 1937–
    Cry out and write : a feminine poetics of revelation in Vibia
Perpetua, Hildegard of Bingen, and Julian of Norwich / Edward Peter
Nolan.
        p.   cm.
    Includes bibliographical references and index.
    ISBN 0-8264-0684-X (alk. paper)
    1. Christian literature, Medieval and modern—Women
authors—History and criticism—Theory, etc.   2. Christian
literature, English (Middle)—Women authors—History and criticism-
-Theory, etc.   3. Christian Literature, Latin—Women authors-
-History and ciriticism—Theory, etc.   4. Hildegard, Saint,
1098–1179—Style.   5. Julian, of Norwich, b. 1343—Style.
6. Perpetua, Saint, d. 203—Style.   7. Femininity (Psychology) in
literature.   8. Authorship—Sex differences.   9. Revelation in
literature.   10. Women and literature.   11. Poetics.   I. Title.
PA8030.C47N65   1994
870.9'9287'0902—dc20
                                                                        94-19544
                                                                        CIP

Contents

Acknowledgments 7

Preface: Toward a Feminine Poetics 9

Chapter 1: The "Gendered" Style: Perpetua's Waterjug, Hildegard's Womanish Times, and Julian's Hazelnut 15

Chapter 2: Vibia Perpetua Martyr and a Feminine Style of Revelation 32

Chapter 3: Hildegard of Bingen and the *Via Affirmativa* 46
  Legitimacy of Voice 55
  The Affair of Richardis von Stade 73
  Letter to the Prelates of Mainz 94
  In vera visione: Beginning, Middle, and End 111
      Scivias 114
      Liber Vitae Meritorum 119
      Liber Divinorum Operum: The End of Time 123

Chapter 4: Julian of Norwich and the *Via Negativa* 136
  The Kenosis of Christ and Julian's Field of Play 140
  Reading the Westminster *Shewings* 148
      The Unpublished Westminster Manuscript 148
      The Text, with Gloss and Commentary 151

Afterword: Conclusions, Contexts, and Open Questions 204

Select Bibliography: Works Cited and Suggestions for Further Reading 209

Index 213

Acknowledgments

First, my gratitude to Justus George Lawler, editor and friend. And for many years of sustaining conversations my thanks to: D.C. Baker, Howell Chickering, Sister Julia Bolton Holloway, John Leo Murphy, Elizabeth Robertson, and R.J. Schoeck. I am also extremely grateful to the President's Office, the Chancellor, the Vice-Chancellor for Academic Affairs, the Dean of Arts and Sciences, The Graduate Committee on Arts and Humanities, and the Council on Research and Creative Work, all at the University of Colorado, for a semester's research leave and various travel grants that enabled me to complete this project. I owe many thanks to Barbara Newman, Nicholas Watson, and Dorothy Clayton, who were generous with their helpful suggestions and wise warnings. Finally I wish to take this opportunity to express my immeasurable indebtedness to Traute and Esther Maass, to my mother Charlotte Nolan, to my beloved daughter Charlotte Catherine Elisabeth, and to that fountain of laughter, my grandson Dakota.

And as for my wife Liesel, center and light of life for me now and always—this book is hers.

Preface: Toward a Feminine Poetics

*I*t is my hope that this book can provide two things: access to some intriguing visionary texts that are seldom if ever available elsewhere, along with some additional contexts in which to read them with due confidence and pleasure.

To expand on that a bit, the primary intention here is to make it possible for readers with other than philological interests to engage in an adventure usually reserved for specialists and scholars of Latin and Middle English: the close reading of the visionary literature of three early Christian women. To help accomplish that goal, fresh translations are presented of the autobiographical section of the martyrology of Vibia Perpetua, who died in the gladiatorial games of early third-century Carthage, several key passages from the letters and visionary writings of Hildegard of Bingen, an influential twelfth-century abbess of the Rupertsberg, her own religious foundation overlooking the Rhine, and a specially designed version of a still unpublished manuscript of the *Shewings* of Julian of Norwich, a fourteenth-century English anchoress. The chief focus and emphasis of this study will center on the work of Hildegard and Julian; the textual legacy of Vibia Perpetua will function primarily as a starting point from which to frame the major issues we shall be investigating throughout the study.

The texts that I have specially prepared of these women are nested in what I hope will prove to be an enabling fabric of essayistic commentary, which should provide not only greater insight into the writings of these extraordinary women from a medieval point of view, but also a means of relating their work to more contemporary issues involving the poetics as well as the politics of gender, along with other domains of human experience that are the shared subjects of psychology, literary theory, and religious studies.

The works of these visionary women have remained so inaccessible to so many for so long not just because they have been inadequately disseminated, but also because an important but recalcitrant doublet of issues resides at their core. Just as each of these visionaries perceived and wrote about what they saw in fundamentally diverse ways, each shared, over vast gaps in time and culture, a keen sense of being a woman caught up and isolated within a male-dominated world. The difficulties involved in this cultural configuration are not new to any of us, but they are intensified in this case by another complicating commonality: although each text provides its own illuminating avenue into a particular seer's visitation by dream or holy vision, all of the accounts we now have of the personal experiences of these women have been written down by men.

The challenge is to seek additional leverage into these visionary works that will help us better sense the nature and function of the originating contributions made by the women, as well as the mediating contributions made by the men. As we learn to hear more clearly these women's voices as midwived into written discourse by men, we learn to appreciate more deeply how both sexes worked in sometimes adversative, but ultimately in collaborative ways to ensure that the private and unique experiences of these women got saved—how their voices, what St. Augustine called the "sacrifice" of their tongues, were converted and woven into stable and sharable texts for all of humanity to hear and read over time.

To get a better sense of the double en/gendering of these texts we must, despite real and inescapable conceptual and methodological difficulties, agree to attempt a siege against the fortifications that time and pen have built up around the originating female voices. In the hope of hearing some genuine echo of a particular woman crying out of the grip of recollected holy vision, we have to work from the textual legacy crafted by a male scribe, back through a process of transmission and dictation, to a voice that cannot, by the very nature of that process, be reconstructed with full confidence.

It is precisely because this goal cannot be accomplished directly that some scheme of indirection is required: we need to engage our capacities of imaginative sympathy as fully as possible, in order to reconstruct what might have been the kind of existential situation in which the women found themselves, even as we attempt to recuperate a sense of the literary processes of inscription in which the men were engaged. Then, with a healthy dose of skepticism regarding the reliability of our own procedures, we must read again the actual texts and try to extrapolate some general principles of discourse formation that will help account for the language we have in front of us. To do that, we need a reasonable model for assessing the impact of gender on the ways the discourse was put together in these works. In speaking of the impact of gender, we are not talking about biological determinism, of course, but as we shall briefly discuss below, patterns of gender identification and participation that were at least partly shaped by cultural as well as personal history.

In a search for a heuristic lens through which we can imagine seeing doubly en/gendered principles of composition at work in discourse formation, I propose we examine two of the general ordinating principles of discourse as we find them deployed in our particular texts: the syntax of word and the syntax of image.

Medieval scribes were primarily responsible for guaranteeing accuracy of textual transmission from one generation to another; they worked, for the most part, in monastic communities made up mostly of men, but also, and not that infrequently, important contingents of women, all of whom were drawn, at times, from the most distant corners of Europe. It was, however, the men who performed the scribal functions of reliable textual transmission over time as well as place; they could provide such a guarantee of linguistic accuracy because they were learned in Latin as well as fluent in their own particular vernacular languages, and knew the difference. This made them as useful for us as for their contemporary masters.

The high middle ages was a time in which the Latin language as written was under theological protection as the language of divine revelation, as well as the institutional protection of both state and church as a conservative factor in maintaining collective stability. At the same time, there is irony in the fact that Latin as spoken was in fact, like all other languages, undergoing constant change, change rapid enough to appear to many speakers and writers of it, such as Dante Alighieri, as a living mirror of cultural deterioration.[1]

My primary assumption is, I hope, reasonable: that a scribe engaged in the process of writing down the recollected revelations of a woman's vision, from manuscript, or from the more fugitive marks of the stylus on wax tablets, or from the even more ephemeral sounds of oral dictation, would be much more likely to emend the "grammaticality" of the language than the order of the images. My hypothesis based on this assumption is this: **if the order of words in the text was subject to the editorial functions of the male scribe, the order of the images that we find there can be attributed, with reasonable safety, to the originating "voice" of the female seer.**

I have to stipulate at the start that there is no way I can think of to

---

1. Dante is especially illuminating as he views the strengths and weaknesses of one language through the prism of the other: See his *De volgare eloquentia* (a work in Latin concerned with the vernacular) and relevant sections of the *Convivio* (concerned with Latin, but written in the vernacular).

present this hypothesis as scientifically verifiable. Yet for me that fact does not constitute a compelling reason to abandon considering these texts from the dual vantage points of word and image. After all, we are not talking about modes of discourse formation that are actually separable in the real world of speaking, listening, writing, and reading. Such principles of composition can only be clearly separated in the discourse we use to talk about them. In real time, any such impulses driving the composition and decoding of language combine in an integrative psycho-motor process that results in a discourse that turns out to be extremely resistant to any precise analysis of its own formation. Therefore any "truth" to be won by employing my hypothesis of double en/gendering will be a matter of heuristic rather than of scientific verifiability.

Given that fact, I have attempted no systematic linguistic analyses of the visionary discourse before us in the hope of providing rigorous, "scientific" testing of our model. I have rather tried to show that certain tensions between the syntax of words and the ordering of images can be sometimes modestly, sometimes quite stunningly, illuminating. But it doesn't always have to happen in the same ways, nor even all the time. In actual fact, I believe we gain a great deal with very little methodological investment in working with this hypothesis of double en/gendering. As long as no fundamental claims are made that are contingent upon the verifiable truth of the hypothesis, there is no need to create any special additional apparatus for linguistic, rhetorical, structural, or thematic analyses of texts.

In sum, it is more important that this working hypothesis regarding the feminine ordination of image be true insofar as it proves useful in achieving greater understanding of the texts at hand, than that it be true insofar as reaching scientifically verifiable assertions. It should be clear that I linger over this distinction, not only because I feel that it is valid, but also because I wish it could be otherwise.

Finally, I am more than casually aware of an additional overlay of personal and inescapable irony that surrounds this project. Even as I speculate on ways in which the very texts that mediate the originating voices of these women have become—insofar as they were written down by men—a barrier that also separates us from them, I construct, by the very presence of my translations, yet another layer of textual barrier between ourselves and the feminine source we seek to find. For by the very nature of the process, I inevitably traduce the voices of these medieval women even as I try to carry them across into our own time and mores, remaining only too aware that this is a *translatio* across a real abyss of incalculable distance. But as that is the fundamental burden deriving from the nature of any historical investigation, there seems little more to do about it than to keep the eyes and ears—as well as the mind—wide open.

But one is not necessarily doomed to complete passivity in these situations. For instance, in order to make more porous the additional barrier unavoidably created by my own translations, I have kept, within the translations themselves, some of the more difficult, and/or characteristic words and phrases to be found in the original manuscripts. This way the textual echo of the voices of these medieval women can act as both check and gloss on my own.

CHAPTER 1

The "Gendered" Style: Perpetua's Waterjug, Hildegard's Womanish Times, and Julian's Hazelnut

As a first pass at gathering a preliminary inventory of features that we might wish to associate with a gendered style, we begin with a quick analysis of some typical passages of narrative description that belong to the medieval domain of sacred reportage. We start by looking at an example of an early, yet typical hagiographic narrative as exemplary of the "middle" style of medieval Latin discourse, the anonymous "Martyrdom of Marian and James." We then glance at particularly telling moments of the narrative modes of Perpetua, Hildegard, and Julian. The goal here is not to supplant any earlier readings with a more "correct" reading: the goal is merely to call into question the underlying assumptions driving earlier readings. Here are the opening moves made by the narrator of the "Martyrdom of Saints Marian and James":

> [**Nam pergebamus in Numidiam**] We were on our way to-gether to Numidia, having embarked in friendly and equal comradeship (as we always had done) on that journey which would lead me to the welcome duties imposed by faith and religion, but would bring them to heaven. Thus we arrived at a town called Muguae. . . . .Here, because of the blind madness of the pagans and the action of military officials, the onslaught of persecution surged like the waves of this world, and the fury of the ravening Devil gaped with hungry jaws to weaken the faith of the just.
> Thus the blessed martyrs Marian and James possessed the

signs that they had always desired that the divine choice had fallen on them: for led as they were when the time was now ripe into that area in which the storm of persecution was raging with special fury, they realized that their footsteps had been guided by the providence of Christ to the very spot where they would receive their crown. For the madness of a blind and bloodthirsty prefect was hunting out all of God's beloved by means of bands of soldiers with a vicious and savage spirit. Indeed his viciousness was exercised not only against those who were living freely for God and had remained undisturbed by the earlier persecutions; but the Devil stretched forth his insatiate hand as well against those who, though earlier driven out into exile, had become martyrs in spirit though not yet by blood[1]

This narrator is a male friend of the soon-to-be martyrs, Marian and James. He describes people, events, situations and intentions in an easy, often seamless alternation of reporting the facts and interpreting those very facts. He thereby creates embracing grammatical and thematic structures and contexts of relational intelligibility. His style of reportage is quite close to the *modus praedicandi,* a preaching style of that epochal threshold in which late antiquity abutted early medieval culture, and we should be able to stipulate for the moment that this mode of discourse reflects the dominating narrative style of the Latin Middle Ages. It is the "male" style of a speaker who is perhaps even more eager to tell you what things mean in terms of his (or another's) **program of intention,** than to dwell at any length on what those things in fact **actually are.** It is a linear, but richly metaphoric style that is both linguistically and imagistically hypertactic: thus it provides ample signals of a system of hierarchy and subordination for the creation of an imaginable order of contextuality between and among the words and images, as well as the events and the implied themes of the discourse.

Turning now for contrast to three variations of the "feminine" style, it seems wise to signal the inventory of what Hans Robert Jauss would call our "horizon of expectation."[2] To create or generate a counter-

---

1. "The Martyrdom of Saints Marian and James," *Acts of the Christian Martyrs,* introductions, texts and translations by Herbert Musurillo (Oxford: Clarendon Press, 1972, 195–97).

2. My use of "feminine" is a considered attempt to defuse a bit of the inevitable polemics that arise with the use of the word "feminist." "Feminist" indexes for this writer more a mode of approach than a subject under observation. "Feminine" in this study will address the subject of inquiry, i.e. ways of ordinating words and images that reflect more fluid and synthetic, than linear and analytic, modes of organizing discourse and images.

voice with which to speak both within and against a dominating male style, the hypothetical insurgent/resistant female must be cunning; she must speak a discourse that is different enough to be heard, even as it appears close enough to that of the "male" dominator to be intelligible. We will therefore look for a reading of these women's texts that embodies an imaginable feminist point of view in which women are NOT assumed to be hopelessly exploited, victimized, and marginalized. My "feminist" point of view here rather assumes that women can be, and in fact often are, represented as intellectually, psychologically, and ethically daring, powerful, and creative in the face of the overwhelming forces of male political and physical authority that they all too often have to face.

The assumption that women in literature will, if observed carefully enough, appear marginalized and thus weak in voice and only strong in silence, has evoked a litany of reader response over the past decade or so that may well be part of the current horizon of expectation of certain feminist approaches, but it also reverberates in my ear far too loudly with earlier, patriarchal attitudes that both created and maintained the dominating antifeminist tradition for well over two thousand years of western cultural history. My assumption is that if you expect to hear strength, and you do hear strength, you may in fact be sounding strength. I am also well aware of the dangers of circularity inherent in such assumptions, but know no way to deal with these dangers except to employ constant vigilance in the face of them.

We begin by "listening" to Vibia Perpetua's report of an encounter with her father. Early on in her *Passio*, Vibia Perpetua, in a fortuitous anticipation of Gertrude Stein, tells us what she told her father: that a jug is a jug is a jug.

> [**Pater, inquio, vides verbi gratias vas hoc jacens, urceolum sive aliud?**] 'Father,' I asked, 'Do you see, for example, this pot lying here? this jug or whatever?' And he said 'I see it.' And I said to him, 'Is there any other name you can call it other than that which it is?' And he answered, 'No.' 'And so I cannot call myself anything other than what I am: a Christian.' Then my father was angered by that word and bore down on

---

Hans Robert Jauss' term "horizon" provides a useful image of our psychological threshold of reception as readers of any text. Both our horizon of expectation as well as our horizon of experience get mutually and reciprocally stretched and enriched by encountering previously unknown facts and relationships as we read. Better understanding those horizons in others as well as ourselves helps us understand more deeply both what texts meant to others in historical time, as well as who we really are in the context of our own contemporary situations.

me as if to rip out my eyes, but his anger alone sufficed him, in fact he and his devil's arguments were vanquished, and then for a few days I was parted from my father, thanks be to God, and I was refreshed [refrigeravi] by his absence.'

Many an English teacher might be tempted to give Perpetua low marks for her addiction to the run-on sentence; and it is surely true that the most obvious thing about her narrative style is the proliferation of "ands" and the corresponding lack of subordinating language particles. The predilection for run-on syntax, along with an inner lexicon significantly less varied, and arguably less sophisticated than that of the male narrator of the martyrdom of Marian and James, for example, led Erich Auerbach to expose his own "masculinist" predilections, even as he prepared the grounds of his real admiration for the lady:

> There is no rhetorical art in Perpetua's narrative. The careful education she had received is hardly reflected in her style. Her vocabulary is limited; her sentence structure is clumsy, the connectives are not always clear. A specialist cannot help noting the many vulgarisms (such as *mittit se* for *ruit*) and typically Christian locutions (such as *refrigerare*). The language in general is brittle, quite unliterary, naive, almost childlike. And yet Perpetua is expressive. She speaks of things that do not occur elsewhere in ancient literature . . . the first hours in prison, in the stifling darkness, among the soldiers, with her famished child . . .[3]

In his phrase, "the careful education she had received is hardly reflected in her style," Auerbach more or less unwittingly conflates ideological values he associates with class and perhaps to some extent with gender; he admires her, but notes first and foremost that her "talk," to borrow a telling phrase of John Berryman's, is not "spiffy." The deeply humane Auerbach also reveals himself as a conventional, even fastidious, class-conscious academic of his time. Another humanist scholar, E.C.E. Owen, sometime fellow of New College, Oxford, as well as assistant master at Harrow, also let slip a similar conflation of attitudes. In addressing the other first-person narrative of martyrdom in the *Passio*, Perpetua's fellow-martyr Saturus, he too criticized the

---

3. *Literary Language*, 63. Auerbach goes on to speak of the way in which Perpetua's use of the *sermo humilis* actually presents reality with an almost unprecedented dignity and elevation; he even compares her, in terms of heroic stature, to Sophocles' figure of Antigone.

grammar and rhetoric of the writer, this time a male, and in ways that run counter to his express intention. He actually links the style of Saturus to that of Perpetua—all in a diction thoroughly seasoned with late victorian and edwardian shibboleths of education:

> His two most striking peculiarities are (a) his use of the words 'I said', 'he said', 'they said' without variation, and (b) a love for vague, indeterminate phrases, e.g. 'like as it might be' ('talis quasi') . . . and the use of 'the other' ('ceteri') five times in the same chapter. These two peculiarities are suggestive of an education inferior to that of Perpetua. We all know how fond uneducated people are of phrases like 'in a manner of speaking', 'sort of', 'as you might say' . . .[4]

However suggestive these two peculiarities are of an education inferior to Perpetua's, it is undeniable that she makes frequent uses of precisely such locutions herself.

As we shall see in the next chapter, there is in fact much more of interest to Perpetua's style than a reduced lexicon (which we will show is in fact highly charged) or a penchant for the run-on sentence, and her avoidance of metaphor. In fact we will discover how important it is to note that in the implied calculus of her rhetoric Perpetua does NOT link waterjugs to Christians. On the contrary, she insists on insularity, that jugs are jugs and Christians are Christians. She puts her words together in an order of clearly severed juxtapositions and so, in her mind and in her discourse, she arranges the world. As she does so she insists, however obliquely, not on the spirit, but on the letter of reality: on the literal quiddity of things as they are, prior to any relation that may obtain between them and other things.

I shall argue that this allegiance to the literal betrays a centripetal impulse: **that Perpetua's way of making her words and images point inward onto themselves protects the autonomy of the image *qua* image, of the letter *qua* letter.** This impulse is, I believe, a crucial aspect of an essentially feminine mode of ordination. It is not a biologically feminine mode, of course, and certainly not an erotically feminine mode; but rather a mode that can be described and defended as syntactically and rhetorically feminine. I argue in this way most of all because I wish to refresh for a moment precisely our sense of that capacity of language to focus the crucial direction of signification inward, a capacity that works with and among the many disparate vectors determining

---

4. Owen, *Authentic Acts*, 75.

meaning. We tend to overlook or even forget it in our search for connection, interface, overview, for the big picture.

In her last great visionary work, the *Liber Divinorum Operum*, Hildegard notes a universal waning of *viriditas*, her own Latin coinage for the greening power of the world, and attributes the cause of what she calls "feminine debilitation" [muliebrem debilitatem] to the presence of a "judge-of-royal-name" [judex nominis regalis]:

> [**Tunc viriditas virtutum arvit**] Then the greening power of the natural forces dried up, and Justice itself tipped toward downfall. In accord with that the greening power of the earth drew back into all seeds as the upper domains of air became transformed in ways to counter the tendencies of their genesis. Summer wore a contradictory chill, and Winter a paradoxical warmth. Such a dryness arose in some places on the earth, and such a moistness in others with so many of all the other anticipatory signs that the Son of God predicted to his disciples concerning the Second Coming, that many began to believe the end of the world was at hand.[5]

Scholars have identified this tyrannical *judex* as Henry IV, and have recently found previously unknown documentation to further evidence such an identification.[6] But there is a limit to the real use for us now of decoding such an image as standing for an eleventh century political figure and event. However important it may have been for Hildegard and her contemporaries to read in this apocalyptic imagery the "presence" of a particular political danger, the reverse may well be more important for us. We may prefer instead to exchange, say, our present sense of being caught in what seems a Brownian movement of unceasing and trivializing politics, in order to enter into a revisioning of our own world as undergirded by a significant pattern, a pattern whose implied perdurability can conceivably provide us with some brief relief, if not actual consolation.

We have our own horizons of experience and expectation, a mixture of memory and desire drawn from hundreds of years of individual and collective reality streaming from Hildegard's time to our own. It has created an aggregate of collective experience from which we cannot expect to escape and still remain ourselves. It is we alone who shall determine what value images from the past finally have for us. And so

---

5. *LDO*, pars III, Visio X, 7. *PL* 1005C–D.
6. Hans Liebeschutz cites A. Borst, in *Deutsches Archiv,* 13 (1959): 319 (*Das allegorische Weltbild,* 182).

the question of "what did she mean" cannot be determined or evaluated solely by asking what her own momentary intention was, or even what her most penetrating contemporaries understood her to mean, although as responsible readers we must reach as far in that direction as we can. Ultimately we must ask what it means for us.

In our reading of Hildegard's haunting visionary and prophetic imagery, it does little for many of us to know that the judge with the royal name was or was not actually Heinrich, sometime Caesar of the Holy Roman Empire of the Germanic Nation. We may well rather view the identity of the *judex regalis nominis* as generic, as completely substitutable in time, always already a somebody/nobody coming or going. What really concerns us is not the identity of the judge, but the image Hildegard gives us of the metamorphic power which his rhythmic alternation of presence and absence always seems to have on the seasons. It is not then the particular *judex* that matters, but the way time feels "womanishly debilitated" when we find him there, and the way that feeling brings us once again the knowledge that "now there is a diminishing of the greening power of the world." This style of ordinating images is characteristic of Hildegard; it is also anti-exegetical at the core, a style resistant to interpretation beyond its own imagery. It is therefore an essential aspect of the inventory of the feminine style.

The unforgettable image of the hazelnut in the *Shewings* of Julian of Norwich has captivated many of her readers. But upon examination of the actual text, we suddenly realize that whatever we have, it is NOT the image of a hazelnut at all:

> And so in this sight I saw that he is everything that is good, according to my understanding. And in this he shewed me a little thing that was the quantity of a hazelnut lying in the palm of my hand as it seemed, and it was as round as any ball. I looked upon it with the eye of my understanding, and I thought what may this be. And it was answered generally thus. It is all that is made. I marveled how it might last, for I thought it might suddenly have fallen to nought [fallen to nothing, into nothingness] for littleness. And I was answered in my understanding. It lasts & ever shall for God loves it, and so has every thing its beginning by the love of God. In this little thing I saw three properties. The first is that God made it, the second is that God loves it, and the third is that God keeps it. But what is this to me? Truly, the maker, the keeper & the lover.[7]

---

7. My modernization of Sister Julia Holloway's transcription of the unpublished Westminster Manuscript of Julian's *Shewings* (fols. 74r–74v).

Any identification of the thing Julian seems to see in her hand as a hazelnut is false. Part of the point is to begin to see that the thing, round as a ball, is not a hazelnut but rather something that has the apparent quantity of a hazelnut. The thing that is so round and small is Creation itself. She is not asserting an unfathomable equation, but a proportion that is more or less imaginable: as God to the world, so the world to the hazelnut. Difference does not get eaten up by metaphoric assertion here. Julian, like Perpetua and Hildegard before her, takes great care to protect the autonomy of the images she is juxtaposing to one another by the rhetorical processes of similitude. We shall shortly see how the simile also functions as a major weapon of the feminine style.

We shall explore these gendered differences in more detail as we examine the style of Perpetua in the next chapter. At the moment perhaps we can summarize these preliminary hunches by suggesting that the feminine style has at least the following central features, broadly construed. It privileges the presence of words and images rather than their referential power to point outward and away to "meanings." It is essentially anti-metaphoric: it shies away from fables of false identity and prefers to maintain as a value the autonomy of things, words and images even as it juxtaposes them with one another in similitudes in order to create a structure of intelligibility by emphasising difference as well as similarity. In the service of such an embracing and clarifying kind of protection, the feminine style reveals itself not as linear, but as curvilinear in its self-forwarding. It is self-reflexive, and is characterized by an additive, paratactic grammar of words and images that returns and loops back upon itself.

* * * * *

Any such hypothesis that insists on a gendering of styles raises an obvious question: Are these male and female styles biologically en/gendered? and the answer is of course equally obvious: No. Any such idea of en/gendering, in order to be intelligible, must be seen as culturally shaped: both by the individual will, as well as by the personal, social, and political contexts of history.

In terms of personal history, all of our women were fundamentally sequestered in one way or another. Perpetua marginalized herself (and was also all too eagerly marginalized by her culture) as a member of that subversive minority known as Christians. All we really know of her is embedded in her *Passio*.

Hildegard was "dedicated" to the Church as a tithe by her parents, and at the age of eight was delivered by them to Jutta of Spanheim to be enclosed as a pupil with her in her anchorage. Later, as the anchorage developed into a monastic community, Hildegard was elected abbess, and thus transmuted herself into a very public figure. But that simply shifted the terms of her isolation; she appropriated the lonely representative functions of abbess: both as a woman and as an administrator. And that aloneness sounds out of all her writing.

At some unknown juncture, Julian became an anchoress and apparently remained one all her life, in a kind of self-imposed exile from community. That isolation may help, at least partially, to account for the powerful feminine style to which they each contributed. But there were of course other and more general collective pressures operating as well.

One source of such pressure came from the awareness of the existence and tradition embodied in the work of other writers. This aspect of things appears historically almost irrecoverable in the case of Perpetua, but, in the cases of both Hildegard and Julian, surely quite central and to some extent recuperable. Although I must postpone discussion of such "anxieties of influence" until the conclusion of my companion inquiry into related visionary writing, the names we shall need to conjure with are surely clear now at the outset. Most of the names are of men, but some important ones are of women: Perpetua's not altogether silent fellow martyr, Felicitas, St. Augustine, Aetheria, Pseudo-Dionysius the Areopagite, Catherine of Sienna, the Victorines, Alan of Lille, Elizabeth of Schoenau, Dante, Brigitta of Sweden, Walter Hilton, Richard Rolle, William Langland, the authors of *Pearl* and *The Cloud of Unknowing*, and Margery Kempe.

But an even more fundamental source of pressure on the development of the feminine style stems from medieval modalities of literacy, modalities that are deeply and inextricably linked to the kinds of education available to women.[8] Again, this is not the place for extended discussion of such a vast, complex and crucial topic, yet a few observations seem mandatory.

Before turning to our three particular women, I had better disclose a particular bias. In the current debates regarding medieval literacy and education, I find both terms often far too narrowly construed, resulting in a set of exclusionary definitions that must be met by a "literate" individual that are not in fact historical, socially, or civilly realistic or responsible.

There is far more to literacy than the mere ability to read and write down letters of the alphabet in a discourse intelligible to one's neigh-

---

8. See Select Bibliography for a short bibliographic note on sources for further reading on women's education in the middle ages and on the issues surrounding women and literacy.

bors. And there is a great deal "less" to literacy than a complete training in all available genres of writing and a demonstrated ability to replicate all these modes. For the term "literate" to be useful to us, we must be able to stipulate that a person does not have to have the capacity to be a professional reader or writer in order to be elevated into the stratosphere of the "literate." On the other hand, we probably should be able to ask of the literate that they reflect in their thinking, speaking, and whatever kinds of exposition they engage in, the rich interplay of words and images that are common to the culture in which they live. In order for us to become more aware of, and sympathetic to, the medieval social reality, we need to recuperate a way of reading that has all but disappeared from our current sense of things.

We are so fraught with the history of our own individual encounters with texts in our own educations that we lose sight of a central modality of textual interchange that thrived throughout the middle ages: the now lost art of reading aloud. We must remember that before the printing press, almost everyone's access to written work was limited to listening to others reading aloud: from the rhapsodes reciting Homer to assembled Athenians, to Virgil himself reading Aeneid Six to the court of Caesar Augustus. St. Augustine recalls in his *Confessions* how amazed he was to find that Ambrose read silently to himself; it is also revealing that in his own crisis of conversion, a "chance" reading of St. Paul in the Garden, he felt it necessary to tell us explicitly that he read silently. An obvious conclusion is that normal people in normal situations did in fact read aloud. One read for the many, and the many listened to and talked with one another, forming a literate community of discourse. And surely it was not necessary that everyone in it had to acquire the competence of professional readers and interpreters to be a viable member of such a community of discourse. To deny the honor badge of literacy to everyone in the community but those assigned the tasks of reading and writing is to miss out on a central aspect of the private as well as public reality of peoples' lives.

In place after place, we get a sense of the lively commonality of a public discourse anchored in the oral sharing of texts. We note, for example, that references to hearing books read becomes nearly formulaic for the *Cloud* poet:

All those who read or hear the matter of this book be read or spoken, & in this reading or hearing think it a good & liking thing, they are not necessarily called by God to work through this work, but only read and hear for the pleasant stirring up that they feel during the time of the reading. For it's likely that this stirring comes more from a natural curiosity of wit than of any calling of grace.[9]

Having made these general and preliminary observations regarding the construction of the term "literacy," we proceed to the three women who are our central concern.

In the case of Perpetua, the male narrator is not the least unruffled by the fact that she was liberally educated [*liberaliter instituta*]—whatever that may have meant for a young matron living in Africa in the third century. The likelihood is that she was bilingual, speaking Latin in the family and Greek in the city. It seems certain she had learned at least a Latin sufficient to keep records and write a kind of diary or journal— which is the consensus of current scholarship on the matter. We cannot in any confidence go much further than that.

As for Hildegard we know a lot more, and consequently a lot less. Part of the difficulty in her case, a difficulty that we will see surfacing again in the case of Julian of Norwich, is that she herself asserts on several occasions that her mistress, Jutta of Spanheim, although having taught Hildegard the psaltery, was herself *indocta*, or untaught. She says the same about herself as well, even with a kind of self-asserting pride. But she also assures us that in her vision she was taught the "inner knowledge of the exposition of holy texts" [*in textu interiorem intelligentiam expositionis*]. And yet she also says that her mode of reading them was "direct and simple" [*in simplicitate*] and not by means of textual analysis [*non in abscisione textus*]. It is very difficult to know what to make of all that. One is tempted to say that she means she read synthetically, or holistically, and not in the developing analytic traditions of scholastic exegesis that were sweeping Europe as the schools of Paris and Chartres were hatching the kinds of intellectual fever that led to the development of universities and their new curricula.

While I am as concerned as anybody about the dangers of engaging in anachronistic bootlegging of later concerns into Hildegard's mid-twelfth century attitudes, something of that tension between synthesis and analysis does seem to be lurking in her discourse. However embryonic, such a tension would also correspond to the larger syndrome we are discussing. For the synthetic impulse can and should be at least tentatively classified as a characteristically feminine impulse, and the analytic habit of mind as male.

At the very least, it does seem fair to say that Jutta taught her a Latin sufficient to read the vulgate translation of the psalms, and the orders

---

9. See *The Cloud of Unknowing*, P. Hodgson, ed., EETS OS 218, London, 1944, 130–31. Quoted by B. A. Windeatt in Marion Glasscoe, *Exeter '80*, 55.

of the service at a fairly young age. It also seems clear, given her enormous energy and inner ambition, that as she grew, her intellectual
appetite grew as well, and as her personal power base also grew by her
election to *magistra*, we can surmise that she took the trouble to improve
her Latin significantly. And yet for all this, she may well have stopped
at the stage of Latin learning that current theorists of foreign language
acquisition rather grimly term as "terminal intermediate"—for she was
adamant all her life that she be provided with a monk who could act
as her provost and secretary and in whose control of the finer grammatical points of Latin she could fully trust. At the same time, she
knew enough to be equally careful to make sure that she kept control
over the editorial power and license of these amanuenses as they transcribed the notes that she incised in wax tablets into the more stable
forms of inked calligraphy inscribed on parchment.

As one reads more and more of Hildegard's work, one becomes
convinced that whatever the general cultural evidence regarding
women's limited access to the male-dominated educational establishment, she herself read widely and deeply. She has a wide-ranging and
richly allusive style, one in which she not only quotes almost directly,
but much more frequently enjoys setting up oblique verbal as well as
thematic resonances with a range of holy texts, usually books of the
Old Testament, undergirded and reinforced with frequent reverberations with the epistles of Paul. She also seems conversant with some of
the major aspects of neo-platonism in general and the dionysian light
metaphysics in particular. Thus her web of textual reference is, to my
view, far too deeply integrated within her aggressively out-reaching
style of mind to be accounted for by any theory of scribal peppering
that could have occurred in the conversions of inscription from her
wax tablets to her provost Volmar's parchment.

As for Julian of Norwich, part of the problem involved in establishing the degree of her education and literacy stems, as in the case of
Hildegard, from her own protestations. The colophon in the Long Text
reads: "Revelations to one who could not read a letter. Anno Domini,
1373." This self-deprecatory alert is followed in the text itself by "these
revelations were shewed to a simple creature that could no letter."[10]

So it is no wonder that the question of her literacy and formal education has proved vexing to scholars of cultural history; and the jury is
still out. Until the recent work of Nicholas Watson, Maggie Ross, and
Vincent Gillespie, among others, the scholarly forces concerned with
Julian have been divided into two camps. One must first mention the
decades of work accomplished by James Walsh and Edmund Colledge,

---

10. Glasscoe, *LS*, 1.

culminating in their editions of the short text and the Paris long text through the Pontifical Institute and the University of Toronto Press. The other leader is perhaps less well known to American readers, and that is Marion Glasscoe who has provided a crucial edition of the competing British Library manuscript of the Long Text, and fielded a regular and indispensable series of seminars on fourteenth-century English mysticism over the past decade at the University of Exeter.

Colledge and Walsh imply that Julian was deeply trained in classical rhetoric as well as deeply read in contemporary mystical writers. Their analysis of the astounding level of sophisticated uses of myriad tropes and figures, both of word as well as thought, that underlies Julian's apparently simple and straightforward style is not only impressive, but extremely compelling in its general power. It seems likely that a woman with such control over the tradition could dispense altogether with scribal assistance and write her texts herself. This idea is especially attractive, given the fact that Julian was visited by divine revelation only once in her life (not including two short "aftershocks" later on) and seems to have spent between twenty and forty years revising her textual reports of the visions she had, and her growing and developing ideas concerning what they meant. She has been likened to Langland, in the sense that she seems never to have been able to reach completely satisfactory closure in terms of capturing the textual embodiment of her vision, and the idea of her revising away for years, quite alone with her thoughts, may be an attractive one for those of a romantic persuasion. As for her more general education, Colledge and Walsh assert that it is "beyond any doubt that when young Julian had received an exceptionally good grounding in Latin, in scripture and in the liberal arts. . . . she was able and permitted to read widely in Latin and vernacular spiritual classics: Augustine, Gregory, William of St. Thierry, and even Chaucer's translation of Boethius."[11] However excessively optimistic this may sound, she does reveal a deep attraction for dionysian mysticism, specifically mentioning Deonise (Pseudo-Dionysius the Areopagite), as well as making more oblique reference to others.

However well-educated Julian may herself have been, Glasscoe thinks it "very probable that her account of the revelations was dictated to an amanuensis."[12] If this were so, it would put Julian on a par with Hildegard in terms of our need to assess the actual role of male midwifery in the generation of her texts. But Watson argues against this idea

---

11. *Book of Showings*, p. 43–45 (the translation, not the Toronto edition, as quoted by Watson, "Composition," 674 n87).

12. Glasscoe, *LS*, xv.

because it is "hard to imagine any (presumably clerical) amanuensis resisting the temptation to make his presence felt (as in continental modes as well as in her follower, Margery Kempe).[13] On the other hand, Lynn Staley Johnson, in a recent article, deals directly with the two Englishwomen and their "uses" of male scribes in a provocatively different way.[14] She finesses the question of whether Julian actually used a scribe by the intriguing means of suggesting that whether she actually used one or not, her references to herself in the third person (in both versions of the Long Text) imply she was composing her work **as if** it had been dictated to a scribe. And that fact alone adds strong evidence to the thesis that Julian felt there was a real advantage to the scribal process, that it could add legitimacy to her otherwise feeble claim to authority as a woman. There is something seductive as well as fundamentally slippery about this argument; and it is surely something to keep in mind.

Watson, above, falls into the trap of what I would argue is a far too narrow construction of the term "literacy," by suggesting that learning something by hearing a story somehow provides evidence of illiteracy. At first he stipulates conventional wisdom on the matter when he says that Julian's insistence that she "cowde [knew] no letter" could merely indicate she couldn't read Latin. But he goes on to suggest that Julian could also have meant that she couldn't read at all.

> "There are two statements with direct bearing on this issue. One is S's [the Short Text] early 'I harde a man telle in haly kyrke of the storye of Saynte Cecylle.' This reliance on priestly storytelling for one of the formative experiences of her early life . . . surely does not bear out Colledge and Walsh's picture of "young Julian" as a scholar, but could be taken to support the Sloane colophon."[15]

Watson then drags in as additional evidence of Julian's possible illiteracy a tediously old chestnut in Julian criticism: the fact that one of her manuscripts contains a minor howler: "Benedicite Dominus" (rather than "benedicite Domine," or "benedictus Dominus").[16]

---

13. Watson, "Composition," 674 n87. There is an intriguingly ironic set of gender stereotypes lurking underneath the surface of these critics, none of whom could possibly be labeled anti-feminist in terms of either their work or their general approaches to the issues.

14. "The Trope of the Scribe and the Question of Literary Authority in the Works of Julian of Norwich and Margery Kempe, *Speculum* 66 (1991): 820–38.

15. Watson, "Composition," 674 n87. It is the Sloane colophon that says: "revelations to one who could not read a letter."

16. Seldom has so much been made of so little in medieval literary criticism. Colledge and Walsh argue on her behalf in rather interesting ways, although their pitch is ulti-

But Watson's main contribution to the question of Julian's literacy remains extremely important. Because he argues for a really massive extension of the time frame for the composing of both S and L (he opens that window from the space of twenty to forty years), he also can and does argue that if indeed she was relatively unlearned early on, she became extremely learned later—especially during the early fifteenth century when so much material on Bridget of Sweden was inundating the coastal towns, including Norwich.[17]

In any case, the literacy issue is, in one of Julian's unforgettable coinages, "unparceable" from the gender issue. And Julian also adds another appropriate tickler of her own in the famous mix of self-deprecation and self-assertion with which she addresses the reader in the Short Text:

> But God forbid that ye should say or take it so that I am a teacher, for I mean not so, no I meant never so. For I am a woman, lewd, feeble, and frail. But I know well this about what I say: I have it from the shewing of him that is sovereign teacher. And true charity stirs me to tell you it, for I would that God were known and my fellow-Christians thus speeded on—as I would be myself—to the more hating of sin and loving of God. But because I am a woman, should I therefore believe that I shall not tell you the goodness of God—since I saw in that same time that it is his will that it be known? And that shall ye well see in the matter that follows after this, if it be well and truly taken.[18]

In this marvelously crusty passage, we hear very clearly the ground of Julian's motive, and the urgent sense of imperative she had that accompanied the recollection of her vision: "since I saw in that same time that it is his will that it be known." Yet it is still difficult to ascertain whether the protestations of the "inferiority" of her gender and her "lewedness"—which in Middle English means unlettered and uneducated (and not ill-mannered)—are here to be taken literally, or are in

---

mately less than fully convincing. See note 17 in their Toronto edition of the *Book of Showings*, Part I, 211.

17. Watson is really indispensable here, see especially the final pages of his *Speculum* article, "Composition." For Bridget in England, see *The Liber Celestis of St. Bridget of Sweden*, the ETTS edition (no. 291) of "the Middle English version in BL MS Claudius Bi, together with a life of the saint from the same manuscript," edited by Roger Ellis (Oxford: Oxford University Press, 1987).

18. 47.34–48.12. Cited by Watson, "Composition," 652.

fact to be taken as a rhetorical commonplace used rather to assert her power by showing that she knows the anti-feminist conventions of her male audience, and so has every right and intention to speak to them in parity, as well as charity.

Finally, she reveals another kind of literacy that is crucial to the full understanding of the relation of image and word in her *Shewings*. And that is her awareness of the iconographic legacy of the pictorial arts. The starting point of her series of revelations consisted of her seeing a crucifix suddenly beginning to bleed. In her recollection of what all that meant, she anticipates writers such as René Girard on the compelling power of the desire to imitate as a trigger of inner as well as outer action. She tells us that she had long wanted a "bodily sight" of Christ. As Watson cites:

> ... that I might have seen bodily the passion of our lord, that he suffered for me ... notwithstanding that I believed seriously all the pains of Christ as holy church shews and teaches, and also the paintings of crucifixes that are made by the grace of God after the teaching of holy church to the likeness of Christ's passion, as far as man's wit may reach. Notwithstanding all this true belief, I desired a bodily sight wherein I might have more knowing of bodily pains of our lord our savior, and of the companion of our lady. (39.11–24)

Literacy for Julian must include, clearly, the ranges of power embodied in the *imago* as well as in the *verbum*.

I hope this preliminary discussion of medieval literacy and women's education helps modify anything that might have at first appeared unseemly in the idea of gendering the styles. We must see these styles, male as well as feminine, as shaped partly by the free expression of individual will, temperament, and intelligence, and partly by the self-chosen missionary program as envisioned by these women. But they must also be seen as at least partially conditioned by the cultural impact of personal, social, literary and theological history and tradition.

With all these caveats on the table, we can now examine some crucial texts of these visionaries: Vibia Perpetua of Carthage, Hildegard of Bingen, and Julian of Norwich. In the course of that reading we shall attempt to trace, however fitfully, the development of two complementary "styles" of inscribing revelation: the "feminine" and the "male." At the same time we shall examine varying modes of mixing those styles to meet more particular psychological, literary, political, and theological needs. As we do that, we shall also entertain, however tentatively, the idea that "feminine" and "male" styles of putting the words together reflect differing, yet ultimately interdependent modes of putting the world together.

◇ ◇ ◇

CHAPTER 2

Vibia Perpetua Martyr and a Feminine Style of Revelation

HIC SUNT MARTYRIS SATURUS SATURNINUS REBOCATUS
SECUNDULUS FELICITAS PERPETUA PASSI NONES MARTIS
—inscription over the tomb of Ss. Perpetua
and Felicitas, discovered in the
Basilica Maiorum, at Carthage.[1]

According to hagiographic tradition, Vibia Perpetua, a young Roman citizen in her early twenties, who was living in Carthage and had just given birth, suffered martyrdom with a group of fellow Christians in the games of official persecution held under the procurator Hilarianus on the March, 7, 203 CE.

In the official record of her martyrdom, the *Passio Sanctarum Perpetuae et Felicitatis*, a major portion of the narrative of her experience, including some astonishing reports of dream and vision, is alleged to have been written by Perpetua herself in the form of a diary or journal, as put down in her own hand.[2] And although this document has hardly generated what one would call an industry of research and commentary, it has remained of fairly steady interest ever since Tertullian and St. Augustine mentioned it at some length in their writings during the foundational years of the Christian Church.

The *Passio* is itself a compilation of texts; in the center is a report

---

1. Transcribed from a photograph taken by Père A.L. Delattre of the Musée Lavigerie at Carthage in 1907, and printed as frontispiece by E.C.E Owen to his *Some Authentic Acts of the Early Martyrs* (London: Society for Promoting Christian Knowledge, Clarendon Press, 1927).

2. My translations and all quotations are drawn from the Latin text of the *Passio* printed in Migne's *Patrologia Latina*, vol. 3 (Paris: Garnier, 1886), pp. 14–62.

allegedly made by Perpetua, "narrated by herself, as she left it written in her own hand and in her own way [jam hinc ipsa narravit, sicut conscriptum manu sua et suo sensu reliquit]."[3] Perpetua's own text is followed by another report, allegedly written by a martyred male colleague, Saturus. Both of these first-person narratives of events leading to documented martyrdom are framed by yet a third narrator, who left no form of signature whatever[4]. Although the attribution to Tertullian is no longer part of scholarly consensus, the narrative frame, along with the two autobiographical texts embedded in the martyrologies it embraces, has impressed readers as early as St. Augustine with an aura of unimpeachable authority.[5]

One of the most intriguing aspects of the entire *Passio* is reflected in the radically differing lexical and grammatical styles of those three narrative voices, and it is that difference with which we will be centrally concerned. So it will be primarily for ease of reference, rather than from any confidence in actual historical identification, that I will refer to these voices as if written by Saturus, Perpetua, and Tertullian.

And it is precisely the close examination of these telling differences in style that leads me to hypothesize a revisioning of the grammar of Perpetua as driven by a poetics of revelation that I have already, though only heuristically, characterized as "feminine." I suggest we can just as usefully call the style of Tertullian "male," and that of Saturus "mixed."

In the first chapter, I stated that we shall proceed to examine the foundation of a feminine style of inscribing revelation in more detail by analyzing the *Passio* of Perpetua. But in the present case it seems only wise to first review the arguments for acknowledging the authenticity of the text. What is the range of evidence indicating that we are in fact dealing with a text written by a woman?

Auerbach, Dodds, and Dronke all address the question of authenticity and agree that the evidence is strong for accepting Perpetua's report as coming from a diary in her own hand. But Dodds writes that Eduard Schwartz "thought that both documents [those of Perpetua and Saturus] were forged by the redactor."[6] Peter Habermehl, in a recently

---

3. See Select Bibliography for a full list of editions, translations, etc. as well as for suggestions for further reading.

4. Since the middle of the seventeenth century, the writer of the *Passio* has at times been identified as Tertullian, a contemporary of Perpetua, and one of the greatest of early African theologians, as well as a leading representative of the Church in Carthage.

5. Augustine, in fact, worried in several sermons that readers who appropriately reverence the martyrdom itself might be in danger of equating the report of it as equivalent to canonical scripture (Sermons 280, ch.i, and 282, ch.ii). Owen argues deftly on behalf of the Tertullian attribution, suggesting that the very silence of anonymity coupled with the hints of montanist heterodoxy in the narrative actually evidence Tertullian's presence, 75–76; Erich Auerbach dismisses any such probability in a parenthetical aside, 60.

6. *Pagan and Christian*, 48.

published dissertation written at the Free University of Berlin, reviews in detail the evidence pro and con for attributing the Perpetua text to the hand of the martyred woman.[7] Habermehl, I am relieved to report, is completely convinced of the authenticity of the text, but the heat of that conviction belies the fact that the evidence, though strong, is nonetheless circumstantial. Let me summarize the kinds and levels of evidence he brings to bear.

He first reviews stylistics in search of lexical and rhetorical consistency sufficient to identify the writer. Unfortunately the naiveté of his analysis renders it nearly useless; I hope I can do better in my own analysis below. The second string of evidence is more intriguing. He makes a fairly strong case that certain experiences reported by Perpetua, particularly the kinds of pain suffered by women as they initiate and cease nursing their children, is a particular matter of the clinical experience of new mothers, and has no prior existence in literary tradition. He is working on the reasonable supposition that if this text is not by Perpetua, it is fake, and *pretends* to be by Perpetua, and thus belongs to the genre of pseudo-epigraphy, a fairly "respectable" sub-genre of counterfeited reports of religious martyrdom in both Jewish and early Christian traditions. Habermehl argues that since there is no prior use of the theme of nursing difficulties present in either the general Hellenistic tradition nor in this particular tradition of pseudo-epigraphy, its presence here speaks to the likelihood that the journal entry concerning it is the authentic record of maternal experience.

The third level of evidence focuses even more sharply on the hagiographic tradition in general and the pseudo-epigraphical tradition of "sacred" counterfeiting in particular. And here I agree with Habermehl that the evidence he brings forward has real power. The fulcrum of his argument is this: if one cannot find either previous uses of the images and themes in the tradition, what was the counterfeiter drawing on? A secondary kind of argument is more deductive, but just as powerful: we need to be able to posit what would be a reasonable motive for engaging in a counterfeit in the first place. Whose interests got furthered if the general populace were to believe that Perpetua really wrote this document, especially if in fact she didn't? I realize that at this juncture we seem close to the looking-glass threshold of Wonderland, but my hope is that we can avoid actual entry if we move quickly and with some cunning.

What is not in the tradition to draw on is the presence of dreams and visions, either in the traditions of general hagiography or pseudo-

---

7. *Perpetua und der Ägypter, oder Bilder des Bösen im Frühen Afrikanischen Christentum: ein Versuch zur Passio Sanctarum Perpetuae et Felicitatis* (Berlin: Akademie Verlag, 1992).

epigraphy; just as telling is that there is no use in that tradition of diaries or journals either, with or without dreams and visions. It is therefore difficult to imagine where the putative counterfeiter found his models; and therefore it is more likely that the *Passio* contains the authentic, auto-biographic experience of a real Perpetua. The final argument in this line of thinking is deductive: precisely because Perpetua has no particular theological or ideological axe to grind, other than to refuse to give into the demands to worship the Roman idols, what hidden agenda does she serve? I hope Habermehl would agree with the whole point of our analysis presented below: that Perpetua provides no interpretation of her revelations, but seems rather moved to tell us about them merely because they occurred. If they serve no overt nor hidden agenda in the first place, what would be the conceivable motive for constructing a fictive Perpetua to tell us about them?

Habermehl's final evidence is far more positive in nature: that the incidents narrated by Perpetua accord with what we know about the early history of the Christian church in Carthage. Several years after the massacre of Christians which took the young life of Vibia Perpetua, Tertullian referred directly both to her martyrdom and to her personal report of visionary experience: "Why did Perpetua, strong martyr, see, on the day of her suffering, only martyrs in her vision of paradise if it were not the case that the Sword raised up to bar entry there was lowered for those who died in Christ, but not for those who died in Adam?"[8] Tertullian is surely a more powerful witness in his undisputed role as a contemporary theologian in the city of Carthage than he would be in the more disputed role of author of the *Passio*. Thus, according to Habermehl, the record stands and can be declared authentic: "The diary that we read stems from the pen of Perpetua." Let us then stipulate its authenticity as well, though there is no particular need to do so with the ringing optimism of Peter Habermehl.

We begin our analysis of the *Passio* with the initial framing style of Tertullian, the male narrator who opens the narrative of martyrdom:

> **[Si vetera fidei exempla]** If ancient examples of faith, that both testified to the grace of God, and worked for the edification of man, have for these reasons been set down in words so that reading them may revivify those events so that God be honored and man comforted, why shouldn't new examples be equally suitable to both those ends? For in future these will

---

8. Quomodo Perpetua, fortissima martyr, sub die passionis in revelatione paradisi solos illic martyras vidit, nisi quia nullis romphaea paradisi ianitrix cedit nisi qui in Christo decesserint, non in Adam? (*De anima* 55.4).

also become old and useful for posterity, though at present, because of the veneration paid to a presumed antiquity, they have less authority ... Several young catechumens were arrested: Revocatus and fellow slaves Felicitas, Saturninus and Secundulus. Among them were Vibia Perpetua, well-born, liberally educated [liberaliter instituta], honorably married, having a father and a mother and two brothers, one also a catechumen, and an infant son at the breast. She was about twenty-two years old ...

As I suggested in the introduction regarding the narrator of the martyrdom of Marian and James, Tertullian describes people, events, situations and intentions in an easy alternation of facts and interpretation, within a grammatical matrix that establishes syntactic and ethical hierarchies; thereby creating embracing structures and contexts of relational intelligibility. His style of reportage is quite close to the *sermo praedicandi* of early medieval culture, the dominating descriptive style of the Latin Middle Ages. It is the "male" style of a speaker who is just as desirous to focus on what things **mean** as on what things **are**. It is linguistically and imagistically hypertactic, providing a linear system of implied subordination between and among the words and images in the discourse.

At the risk of repetition, let me quote once again Perpetua's recollection of the key interview with her father:

> [**Pater, inquio, vides, verbi gratia, vas hoc jacens, urceolum sive aliud?**] 'Father,' I asked, 'Do you see, for example, this pot lying here? this jug or whatever?' And he said 'I see it.' And I said to him, 'Is there any other name you can call it other than that which it is?' And he answered, 'No.' 'And so I cannot call myself anything other than what I am: a Christian.' Then my father was angered by that word and bore down on me as if to rip out my eyes, but his anger alone sufficed him, in fact he and his devil's arguments were vanquished, and then for a few days I was parted from my father, thanks be to God, and I was refreshed [refrigeravi] by his absence.'

As we have already noticed, perhaps the most obvious thing about her narrative style is the proliferation of "and's" and the corresponding lack of subordinating language particles.[9]

---

9. Owen quotes Bishop J. Armitage Robinson, then (1927) the Dean of Wells Cathedral, as pointing out that Tertullian's work is "that of a man accustomed to composition,

It was Peter Dronke who finally found ways to deal with Perpetua's narrative mode as an effective tool for, rather than as a barrier to, the expression of a hard, clear and vibrant intelligence in the face of a hostile world. Both Dronke and I center on ways that Perpetua's style resists allegoresis, but where Dronke is strongest in his psychological analysis of Perpetua's dream narratives, I wish to focus more on the ways her impulses for linkage and severance range across her syntaxes of language and image.[10]

But there is much more to Perpetua's style than a penchant for what we now think of as the run-on sentence. In fact there is a richly suggestive range with which she ordinates language and image in her own segment of her *Passio*.

> [**Et ascendi et vidi spatium horti immensum**] And I went up, and saw an immense expanse of garden, and in the middle of the garden an old man sitting in the dress of a shepherd, a big man, milking sheep, and standing around were many thousands in white, and he raised his head, and looked at me, and said to me, 'you are well come, child.' And he called me and gave me a bit of the cheese he was milking and I took it in joined hands, and ate, and all those standing around said 'Amen.' And at the sound of the word I woke, still eating something sweet, not knowing what it was, and I told my brother at once, and we knew there would be pain in the future and we began to have no hope in this world.

Later she concludes the report of her vision of fighting the Egyptian:

> [**Et exivit quidam contra me Aegyptius, foedus specie**] And an Egyptian, with a foul look, came out against me with his seconds to fight me. And handsome young men [adolescentes

---

his sentences are often of considerable length and periodic in structure, he is fond of epigram, he is often difficult." Perpetua's writing is "marked by extreme simplicity and a complete absence of literary artifice . . . the sentences . . . are usually connected by 'et' ('and'), Perpetua employs it 152 times in 172 lines . . . , the editor, as he may be called, only 90 times in 170 lines . . . Perpetua and Saturus lay their thoughts simply side by side, the editor subordinates one to another to show their logical connexion." (*Authentic Acts*, 74.

10. See Dronke, *Women Writers*, 6–16. The only model I am aware of for a detailed study of the relationship between stylistic analysis of hagiographic writing and the capacities of the genre is a powerful one centering on a text dating from between the 4th to the 6th century: Leo Spitzer's essay, "The Epic Style of the Pilgrim Aetheria," *Comparative Literature* 1, 225–58, reprinted in his *Romanische Literaturstudien, 1936–1956* (Tübingen: Max Niemeyer Verlag, 1959), 871–912.

decori] came out to me as seconds and supporters. And I was stripped and I was made a man [et facta sum masculus], and my supporters began to rub me down with oil as they do before combat. . . . And I took hold of his head, and he fell on his face, and I put my foot on his head. And people began to shout, and my supporters began to sing for me, and I came forward to my trainer and received the [green] bough [with golden apples], and he kissed me, and said to me, 'Daughter, peace be with you.' And I began to walk in glory to the Gate-of-the-Living [ad portam Sanavivaria]. And I woke, and I knew that I would fight the devil and not the animals and I knew that the coming victory would be mine. Such were the things that happened up to the day before the games; let whoever will write about what was done at the games themselves.

These are extraordinary events told in a laconic manner that mirrors the ways in which such extraordinary events in fact often do seem to occur in dreams: a tall man in white milks cheese out of a sheep; the mother still suckling a child reports she was changed into a man and rubbed down with oil by her good-looking male supporters. These examples of radical telescoping and cross-dressing are all addressed as if they were ordinary events occurring in the prosaic light of day, linked by endless anaphora, an unending string of "ands." The images themselves are startling to begin with, and it is precisely because they are linked by the *same* particle "and," a language particle almost bled of any meaning by such programmatic repetition, that these images begin to glow separately in, of, and for themselves. The "ands" do not link these images in any relationship other than the mere gathering of them together into the same fortuitous inventory of experience suffered in serial time. As the linguistic style appears increasingly and incessantly additive, the images so linked appear more and more separate, to declare themselves in an ever sharper paratactic relation to one another: disconnected, autonomous, they are strikingly present, but not ordered in a way through which we can sense any significant relationship of meaning among them.

Therefore it is not enough to call this an "additive" style. As Perpetua "runs" on and on, she begins to declare for her images a hard autonomy; by means of a grammar that refuses to allow any one image to subordinate any other image (much less allow the group of images to build up into some over-arching whole) each item is deeded an implied equality of value. She has democratized her images, and thereby graced each one with its own virtue and power. The result is death for the habitual exegete: for the lack of the normal hypotaxis of internal relations between and among images sucks the wind out of the sails of the act of interpretation, and allegoresis reveals itself as an act of futility. Of course there is a signifying pattern of a sort.

Consider the way her images dance around the center of her consciousness in her description of the two consecutive visions she had of her dead brother, Dinocrates:

> [**Continuo ipsa nocte ostensum est mihi hoc in oromate**] On this very night this was shown me while praying: I saw Dinocrates coming from a dark place where there were several others, very hot and thirsty, shabby looking and pale, the wound in his face which he had when he died. This Dinocrates had been my brother in the flesh, seven years old, and had suffered the infirmity of cancer of the face, and had died miserably, so that his dying was odious to everybody. . . . There was in the very place where Dinocrates was a basin [piscina] full of water having its rim above the height of the boy, and Dinocrates stretched up as if to drink. I grieved because the basin had water in it and yet it could not be drunk because of the height of the rim. I woke and knew my brother was in agitation [laborare].

And then on the day she was transferred to the garrison prison where she was to be delivered to the beasts:

> [**Die autem quo in nervo mansimus, ostensum est mihi hoc**] During the day, while in the stocks, this was shown me: I saw the same place I saw before that was dark but it was light, and Dinocrates clean in body, well-clothed, and refreshed; where there was a wound I saw a scar; and the basin that I had seen before had lowered its rim to the boy's navel and poured water unceasingly, and above the rim there was a shallow bowl [phiala] full of water. And Dinocrates came forward and began to drink from it and the bowl never failed. And when sated he stopped drinking and he played with the water as happy children do. Then I knew he was released from pain [poena].

One can and should wonder about the resonances the basin of water (piscina) might or might not bear to either the baptismal font—or to the basin of water traditionally withheld from Tantalus in the iconography of pre-Christian Hades. We may wonder if the dream signifies that the boy is suffering infernal pain because he did not enjoy baptism when alive, or that he was baptized but sinned without absolution before he died, and has been released from suffering by the efficacy of Perpetua's acts of prayer. Augustine, among many of her later readers, wonders about all this at some length, but Perpetua herself does not.[11] She never raises the issue of what her images mean. Instead she worries (and thereby forces us to worry with her) about the presence after death of the grotesque lesion of the cancer (a wound that in the Christian dispensation cannot really **mean** anything beyond its own pain and the disfigurement of the face of a child of seven) and about the strenuous, but futile effort the little boy makes as he tries to stretch up to reach the rim of the basin. So it is not that we are led to any implied theological problematic involving sin, innocence, and redemption, or issues regarding the efficacy of prayer, but it is the image of the boy on tiptoe, forever unable to reach the water that lingers with us instead, suggesting to Perpetua, and then to us, that Dinocrates is undergoing some sort of travail (laborare) in the afterlife.

In the second dream, any attempt to "read" the meaning of the bowl-that-does-not-fail in the tradition of either Hellenistic or Latin literature or that of Holy Scripture is short-circuited by the unforgettable image of the laughing boy playing with the water when he has had enough of it to drink. So Perpetua's modes of ordination force us to consider, not so much how the meaning of any of these images radiates outward in any urgent reference to the world beyond the image, but rather how her images signify the intensity of their quiddity inward onto the intelligence of the dreamer—and to us as we witness the dreaming.

The compression of these images inward upon an implied consciousness is analogous to the etymology of *syn + ballein* (to symbolize), in older Greek a throwing together, as we still use the words today in pottery or in the kitchen: to "throw a pot," or to "throw dinner together." This mode or style of selection, concentration, and compression is singled out here in Perpetua's discourse not to elevate it above, or substitute it for, some other mode of meaning, but to help us see again the co-ordinating forces, both inward as well as outward, that always operate in the normal orchestrations of language and discourse. For Bakhtin as well as for Frye, as we move outward in external reference, we mean centrifugally; but as we also and always simultaneously move inward, we mean centripetally, we protect the autonomy of our

---

11. Dronke cites Augustine's *De anima et origine ejus*, 1.10 (*Women Writers*, 224).

words and images even as we weave them into more complex grids of intelligibility.[12]

Finally, it is for conceptual and methodological reasons as well as to achieve even more pointed discussion that I also risk insisting on conflating the gender distinction with all the other issues of signification involved here, and attach, at least tentatively, the sobriquet of "male" to the outward reaching, centrifugal directions of signification and that of "feminine" to the inward pointing, centripetal directions of signification.

This dialectic is not as anachronistically postmodern as one might suppose: there are medieval anticipations, though I grant they come nearly a millennium after the martyrdom of Perpetua. They are most clearly sounded in the schools of Paris. In terms of the twelfth-century Victorine programs of biblical exegesis, Richard of St. Victor pulls more to the "male" mission of seeking the spirit of the letter, whereas Andrew of St. Victor pulls more toward the "feminine" mission of protecting and extending the domain of the literal. Hugh of St. Victor, mentor and spiritual father of both Richard and Andrew, argued for attending to the myriad, delicate adjustments that must always be made in the interests of balance. And for Hugh, especially in the *Didascalicon*, such balanced reading clearly reflects balanced thinking.[13]

Of course linking gender and style has little or nothing to do with biological specificity: a male can use the feminine style as well. In the *Passio*, the vision of Perpetua is followed by that of her colleague Saturus, also "written in his own hand." At first, in its repeated attempt to find equivalents of astral experience in the quotidian world, his style seems male enough:

> [**Et dum gestamur ad ipsis quatuor angelis**] And while we were carried by those four angels, we came upon a great space, **which was like as if it were a** [quod tale fuit quasi] garden, having rose-trees and all sorts of flowers. The height of the trees was **like** [in modum] the height of a cypress whose leaves were falling forever . . . and we came near a place whose walls

---

12. Northrop Frye, *Anatomy of Criticism* (Princeton: Princeton University Press, 1957), 73–74; For a more wide ranging, independently arrived at, yet deeply related use of the same double metaphor from physics, see Mikhail Bakhtin, *The Dialogic Imagination*, Michael Holquist, ed. (Austin: University of Texas Press, 1981), 272–73.

13. See my discussion of Victorine programs of exegesis in "Self as Other: Medieval Commentary and the Domain of the Letter," in *Now through a Glass Darkly: Specular Images of Being and Knowing from Virgil to Chaucer* (Ann Arbor: University of Michigan Press, 1990), 93–98.

were built **like as if they might be of** [tales erant quasi de]
light. . . . And we saw sitting in the middle of this same place
someone **who looked like** [quasi] an old man with hairs white
as snow but with the face of a young man whose feet we could
not see.

But however much Saturus' discourse appears normatively male in its
drive to discover and set down inner connections and larger patterns
of meaning, closer examination shows that in fact he protects the autonomy of his images not only by the frequent use of "ands" and the
avoidance of grammatical subordinators, but even more effectively by
means of the strategy of the simile itself—however prosaically he introduces them. The phrases "like", "such as," "in the mode of," etc. are
not necessarily reflective of a schoolboy refusal to engage in the search
for true and clear relations, which for scholiasts are often best figured
in bright metaphor. In fact simile, often considered a "weak" form
of comparison, can be even tougher, even "stronger" than the fabled
identities of metaphor. Simile, although implying likeness, actually acts
as an iron-hard buffer or separator. It insists as much on difference
and severance as it does on comparability, sometimes even more.

When Dante suggests, in *Inferno* XV.124, that Brunetto Latini runs
the race "like a winner," he reminds us that Brunetto, precisely when
we see him figured **like** a winner, is revealed to be **not** a winner, but a
loser. "Like" is never "is"—that's one of the main points about it. So
Saturus' discourse, although in some ways in accord with the male style
of Tertullian, and perhaps a shade too florid for many tastes, can in
fact also be read as a co-conspirator against the male style along with
the discourse of his "Domina Soror" Vibia Perpetua. His mixed style
speaks in imitation of the cadence of the male style that abets interpretation, but it must finally be read as in deep cahoots with the feminine
style that is in fact subversive of interpretation: all its efforts working
hard to maintain freedom, integrity, and autonomy of the self in resistance to political (and in this case theological) appropriation by the
Other.

Finally, it must be stipulated that the male style of Tertullian also has
its literary triumphs, not least when praising the existential triumphs
of Perpetua: as he narrates the final ecstasies of Perpetua and her
companion Felicitas (who has just given birth on the field of martyrdom) the interpretive impulse of Tertullian begins with simile but then
flares into a concatenation of brilliant metaphor that "literally" trans-
lates their procession into martyrdom into the entry into Paradise:

[**Illuxit dies victoriae illorum**] The day of their victory dawned and they marched in procession from the prison to the amphitheater **as if into heaven** [quasi in coelum]. . . . Perpetua followed with quiet face and sturdy feet **as the wife of Christ and darling of God** [ut matrona Christi Dei dilecta] **throwing back, with her vigorous eyes, the gaze of the onlookers** [vigore oculorum dejiciens ab omnium conspectu]. And Felicitas, rejoicing she had given birth in safety, so that she might fight the beasts, **from blood of midwife to blood of gladiator, to find in her Second Baptism her child-birth washing** [de sanguine ab obstetrice ad retiarium, lotura post partum baptismo secundo] . . .

So far, my revisionist encounter with the syntaxes of word and image in the *Passio* of Vibia Perpetua has generated the following set of working hypotheses for consideration in our study of Hildegard of Bingen and Julian of Norwich:

The "Male" style of meaning moves out and links up with a skein of otherness, a grid of intelligibility that is relational. It is metaphoric, centrifugal, hypotactic, expansive, hegemonistic. It abhors silence, the space between, it will bridge its way to the other even at the cost of obliterating the saving distinctions that obtain between the self and the other. And without the countering presence and pressures of the feminine style, the male style loses control by totalizing its appropriation of the other, ultimately by a kind of metaphysical murder and cannibalism.

The "Feminine" style of meaning folds in, isolates the image in the pressure of the revelation of its Itness, its Isness, its Thereness, its quiddity-in-gnostic-reflexivity. It is metonymic, centripetal, paratactic, condensive: it revels in severance, and remains unabashed at the apparent nullities of the space between. It is hence resistant to the obliterating forces of symmetry forwarded by the male imperative of filling in the vacuums of space and silence with reasons for things. The feminine style uses those spaces and their corresponding silences as an echo-chamber in which to celebrate the Isness of the things that ARE there. And without the countering presence and pressures of the male style, the feminine style threatens to become excessively obscurantist, arcane, and disordered: it can self-destruct.

Of course these are imaginary, heuristic extremes between which lies the continuum of actual rhetorical and syntactical possibility, perhaps best figured in the *Passio* of Perpetua in the discourse of Saturus. In the real world, each mode, along with many others, is alive and simultaneously present in all sane discourse, though in differing mixes of domination and subordination.

As one moves toward a purer domination of one style over another, however, one moves closer and closer to the borders of heaven or hell, to the unintelligible world beyond space and time, to a world of content without form or to a world of form without content. Such a world may be one with the vision of the beatified, or one with the nightmare of the insane.[14]

In the visionary company of love I wish this project to help us better understand, both aspects loom. In third-century Carthage there is, in Huizinga's unforgettable doublet, the mixed odor of blood and roses: both joy and the grotesque figure together in Vibia Perpetua's words as she guides the hand of the gladiator to meet her neck with the sword: "Stand fast in the faith and love one another: be not offended by our sufferings." In the luminous worlds that captured the interior twelfth-century eye of Hildegard of Bingen, horror and beatitude are often inseparable aspects of the same vision. And in plague-ridden fourteenth-century England, although universal terror threatened, beatific vision consistently contended with and finally illuminated the loving, but glittering and unrelenting gaze of Julian of Norwich. In all three voices we hear a coolness and severity of tonal orchestration: their language is nonrhapsodic, nonecstatic.

Often on the pilgrimage to revelation, the irresistible heat of the imperative onrush of divinity holds the victim of divine visitation captive: the seer suffers an ecstasy that is hard for the outsider to distinguish from nightmare; something like that dream-world, for example, that haunts the interior primal scream figured in the incessant and terrible weeping and roaring of Julian's younger follower on the pilgrimage: Marjorie Kempe.

But the works of Perpetua, Hildegard, and Julian, precisely because they form together a body of non-ecstatic visionary synthesis, provide us with a universe of recorded experience that is gratifyingly subject to analysis. An inescapable irony that resides in this happy fact is to be found in my claim that the search for overview by means of analytic modes is a chief characteristic of the male style. And that the female

---

14. See "Two Aspects of Language and Two Types of Aphasic Disturbance," in R. Jakobson and M. Halle, *Fundamentals of Language* (The Hague: Mouton, 1956). Jakobson argues that there are two driving forces that simultaneously impel all sane discourse: the force for metaphor, which is essentially lexical, and the force for metonymy, which is essentially syntactic. The idea of such forces is no doubt of greater heuristic than scientific value, but it is nonetheless useful to think that the domination of one such force over another might begin the constitution of a style; and as a direct result of his examination of actual recordings of aphasic discourse, he posits that the exclusion of one of these forces indicates a radically unbalanced mind.

style, a style chiefly characterized by nonreferential synthesis, so often asserts the freedom of its presence in the world most successfully by acting in subversive resistance to the attempts of the hegemonistic male style to gain and exercise control.

Nonetheless, my hope is that a more systematic analysis of the often doubly-gendered syntax of language and imagery in these medieval women's visionary discourse will help us better see the ways in which the frequent tensions that obtained between the female seer and her male scribes and readers can ultimately be seen as reconciled and trans-figured by a sense of community of men and women walking together into the light.

CHAPTER 3

◇ ◇ ◇

Hildegard of Bingen
and the Via Affirmativa

Hildegard concluded the preface of her first great visionary work, the *Scivias* (a short title for "Scito vias Domini," or "Know the ways of the Lord"), with the report that she heard a voice speaking with implacable urgency: "And again I heard a voice from heaven saying to me: therefore cry out and write this! [Et iterum audivi vocem de caelo mihi dicentem: Clama ergo et scribe sic!]"[1]

Shortly after she heard that sudden voice, Europe heard hers; it was an arresting voice that sounded out of the ether and broke unforgettably into the work of the world. She lived, cried out, and wrote from 1098 to 1179, four score years, a long life in any dispensation. Her energy was electric, percussive, and unflagging, her efforts to move herself and others to right action was insistent and unceasing, and the legacy in word and in deed that she left was huge in scale and reach. There never was, nor has there ever been, anyone quite like her. And because of that, and the fact that her voice was at the same time so new and so old, it was a difficult voice to hear. It is an even more difficult voice to listen to now: for the same reasons, along with many more.

One of them, of course, is the ever-widening gap that has opened up in the course of the near-millennium that intervenes between us and her originating voice. We now live in a world in which the Christian religion has long ceased to provide the deeply consensual, cultural glue that more or less held twelfth-century Europe together. For collective us, the incarnation and virgin birth of Christ, his mission, passion, and universally redemptive resurrection no longer comprise a central fact of life, but rather constitute a set of tenets within a particular given belief system that many share and many do not. Most of us have become accustomed to learning and sharing a mediating discourse re-

---

1. Fuehrkoetter's *Scivias*, 6. Cf. *PL* 197, 386B.

garding history that allows us to speak across the boundaries of belief systems without really having to think very much about them. We have even learned to suspend our disbelief, to make that crucial leap of imaginative sympathy, so we can proceed, in some degree of reasonable approximation, to think and speak "as if" we actually were a partner within another's given belief system, at least for a while. And that all seems sane enough if we are to have any hopes of continuing civility.

But real differences of view do exist, and often the ones that lie quietly are the ones that are also most massive, resistant, and extremely difficult to deal with. Not that we can change real cultural difference, or that we would necessarily wish to do so even if we could. But we do need to find ways to recognize such alterities both for what they are and what they can mean to all of us if we are to deal with them creatively in ways that will enhance our presence and vision. The voice of Hildegard, crying out and writing from the Rupertsberg, that monastic refuge she built on the Rhine in the middle of the twelfth century, provides one of the most intriguing challenges of just such an alterity.

We may well sense, because of its penetrating and haunting tenor, that her voice sounds out of a vast and silent absence. But as we look back nearly a thousand years in an effort to meet the challenge of her voice, we can also see, in our reconstructions of history, the presence, however blurred, of a public context out of which she called to her fellow creatures then and still calls now. Ever since her death at the end of a vivid, famous old age, many people with the widest conceivable range of public interests and private agendas worked to validate and broadcast what they felt was of particular value in her extraordinary production. All that effort has left its mark in the record. And in this century a sometimes uneasy alliance of sacred and secular scholars has approached her textual legacy in an effort to sort out more systematically, and often more neutrally, her texts as well as her contexts. All of this work, but particularly that accomplished since 1945 or so, has begun to coalesce in diverse but supporting ways. This is not the place to trace the rich history of that work, though the bibliography at the back of the book should provide some useful access for those who wish to do so. But here we do need, if only for that "male" sense of linear order, a biographical sketch with a few landmark dates and events, notions and names.

Hildegardis Vita Brevis

1098	Born in Bermersheim bei Alzey in Rhine-Hessen, as the tenth child of the family. Parents dedicated her to God as a tithe.

1106	At age eight, she was given by parents into the care of Jutta von Spanheim in an anchorage attached to the monastery of St. Disibod. Learned to "read the psaltery" (i.e., learned basic Latin).
1112–15	Professed virginity and received the veil from Otto, Bishop of Bamberg. Confided in Jutta, and the learned and trusted monk Volmar, that she had long been visited by visions.
1136	Anchorage had by now developed into a cloister; on Jutta's death, Hildegard was elected abbess.
1141	Received the call to manifest the fact that God had spoken to her in vision, and to begin writing the *Scivias*, which took ten years, assisted by provost and secretary Volmar, and by Richardis von Stade, a young nun for whom she had a special affection.
1146–47	Wrote St. Bernard of Clairvaux her famous letter (see detailed analysis below) in which she described her vision and asked for understanding and support.
1147–8	Synod in Trier. Pope Eugenius III, a disciple of Bernard, heard about Hildegard's visionary work; sent legates to St. Disibod, who returned with draft of *Scivias*. Eugenius read portions to the assembled prelates, and sent her official approval and apostolic license to continue her work (see excerpt of letter below)
1148–50	Hildegard's musical compositions well-known. Letter from Odo of Soissons, master of theology in Paris, asking for assistance in current debate regarding the trinity. Had vision telling her to secede from the monks of St. Disibod and found her own convent on the Rupertsberg near Bingen. Monks resisted secession, Hildegard used family influence, Rupertsberg property acquired, Hildegard and eighteen or twenty nuns moved to new foundation in 1150.
1151–58	Wrote scientific and medical works (*Physica*, *Causae et Curae*).
1151–52	*Scivias* completed. Richardis von Stade elected abbess of Bassum, left the Rupertsberg, despite long and tortuous efforts of Hildegard to prevent her departure and then seek her return. Richardis fell ill and died 29 October, 1152 (see analysis of related correspondence below)
1155	Hildegard secured exclusive property rights to the Rupertsberg. Sometime in mid-50's, she visited Frederick I

(Barbarossa) at the imperial pfalz in Ingelheim by his invitation, substance of meeting unrecorded.

1158　　　　Arnold, Bishop of Mainz, issued protection and regulated matters temporal and spiritual between Rupertsberg and St. Disibod.

1158–1163　Three of four preaching tours. Wrote second visionary book: *Liber Vitae Meritorum* (Book of Life's Merits).

1163–73　　Barbarossa granted her written and perpetual imperial protection for the convent at Rupertsberg in 1163. At first she took a neutral position, followed later (1164 and 1168) by increasingly vociferous denunciation of Barbarossa's role in the German papal schism, siding with Alexander III (1159–77)—see letters below; but his original letter of protection held. In 1163 she began her last great visionary work: *Liber divinorum operum* (Book of God's Works), also known as *De operatione Dei* (On the Activity of God). In 1165 Hildegard founded daughter-house at nearby Eibingen (still standing and active, Rupertsberg was destroyed in Thirty Years War); wrote Henry II of England and his Queen, Eleanore of Aquitaine (see letters below). After a three-year illness, she took her fourth and final preaching tour through Swabia (1170).

1173–76　　Volmar died (1173), and Helenger, abbot of St. Disibod, refused to appoint a replacement. Hildegard appealed to Pope Alexander III, and through mediation of her nephew Wezelin, the monk Gottfried was appointed by Helenger as provost and secretary. Correspondence began with Walloon monk Guibert of Gembloux, Autumn, 1175; Hildegard wrote Guibert detailed letter recalling phenomena of her visions (see below, passim). Gottfried completed volume one of Hildegard's *Vita* before he died in 1176. *Liber Divinorum Operum* not quite finished. Abbot and monks of St. Eucharius in Trier, as well as nephew Wezelin of St. Andrew's in Cologne, provided assistance for completion of work.

1177　　　　Guibert of Gembloux, for several years an epistolary admirer of Hildegard, took Gottfried's place as provost and secretary (and remained at the Rupertsberg for nearly a year after Hildegard's death).

1178　　　　Hildegard faced prelatical interdiction. After refusing to exhume the body of a man who the Church claimed died ex communicate (she was convinced that the man had been reconciled), the see of Mainz forbade Hildegard's community the sacrament of the eucharist as well as the right to use music in the divine service. In her fight to have the interdiction overturned, she wrote what was perhaps her greatest letter: *Ad prelatos Moguntinenses* (To the Prelates of Mainz—see detailed analysis of letter below).

1179   Hildegard died on the Rupertsberg at 81 on September 17.[2]

* * * * *

From the beginning, it has been the plan of this book to encounter these visionary women directly in and through their texts; the obvious question in the case of Hildegard is which texts? Her huge and varied production dictates selectivity. And because her major literary contribution is clearly constituted by the three great visionary works: the *Scivias*, the *Book of Life's Merits*, and the *Book of Divine Works*, it may seem logical to focus on one of them as an exemplar by which we can sense how she mediated her visionary powers to her world. It turns out that these major visionary works, however central they are to her canon, are almost intractable without some historical as well as theoretical preparation.

Perhaps the first thing to keep in mind is that Hildegard's life and career spanned most of the twelfth century, an epoch in European history that was intellectually so volatile and creative that it has been fashionable for some time to call it the first true renaissance of the golden age. But if we feel the surge of a new beginning stirring in the twelfth century, many of its inhabitants felt haunted by the threat of universal ending. An important habit of mind flourished that sought to read any particularly startling events of the moment in terms of patterns of universal history as reported and promised in that privileged world-as-text called the Bible. Of the many who thought in this essentially apocalyptic way, two are important to us here: Hildegard herself, and Rupert of Deutz (died 1130).

Rupert prefaced a history of his monastery by parading forth apocalyptic images figured in the Bible as being useful because they provided both a sense of resonant contrast, as well as an underlying coherent link to current events. For Rupert, the resonance between the pattern of cosmic revelation and the sense of urgency of current event helped maintain one's faith in the notion that reality was a stage on which all could witness, if shown how to see it, the final triumph of the Logos,

---

2. I am particularly indebted for biographical detail to Newman's *Sisters*, 4–15, and to Fuehrkoetter's chronology in *Das Leben*, 129–35.

the voice of God as creator, impeller, and judge of the world.[3] This near compulsion to see the quotidian as nested in divinely ordained pattern is obviously no isolated figure of human desire, but rather a medieval variant of one of the perdurables of human culture, what Wallace Stevens has called our "blessed rage for order."

That very perdurability helps us see more sympathetically into the real alterities, the truly radical differences of world-view, that shaped Hildegard's major visionary works and makes them so seductive, even as they are at the same time so difficult of access. Without some mundane groundwork in the vineyards, the romance of our desire for the embracing overview of her major visionary work helps only rarely in the instances of particularity that finally matter. As we read Hildegard's central books for the first time, her *Scivias, Liber Vitae Meritorum,* and *Liber Divinorum Operum,* few of us feel confident, for any significant stretch, that we are in fact keeping up with her in any adequate way. We may win some sense of possessing that "big picture"—and sometimes we have sudden, particular shocks of recognition, but most of us have to stipulate that a compelling sense of the signification of the true scale and reach of her brilliantly colored canvases of revelation escapes us most of the time.

For this reason it is not advantageous, however helpful the state of current scholarship may be, to begin a study of her work by taking one of her visionary books as the primary exemplar of the reach and power of her visionary modes of engaging the world. It turns out we get farther attending to the minor genres first. Barbara Newman, in addition to her helpful vademecum into the problematics of the feminine divine in the works of Hildegard, has also made extremely useful special contributions to our understanding of Hildegard's musical compositions.[4] Peter Dronke, pathbreaker and dean of twentieth-century Hildegard studies in English, has shown brilliantly how some of her scientific and medical work, the *Causae et Curae* for example, turns out to be of inestimable value as we seek to assess the impact of her visionary energy and intelligence in and upon the world.[5] He was also one of the first to show how useful her letters are, letters written in and against mundane rather than cosmic occasions. We too shall find in several of her letters a rich and illuminating inventory of her modes of using her visionary powers to help mediate conflict, especially when she found herself at its very center.

---

3. See Liebeschuetz, *Das allegorische Weltbild,* 181–82.
4. See her edition of Hildegard's *Symphonia Caelestis.*
5. See his "Hildegard of Bingen," in *Women Writers of the Middle Ages* (Cambridge: Cambridge University Press, 1984), 144–201, and 231–64; also his "Hildegard of Bingen

At the end of this chapter, we shall return to her great visionary books and examine the haunting vision of the Fall of Eve near the beginning of the *Scivias*, as well as the final *visio* of the End of Time concluding her last, and arguably her greatest work, the *Liber Divinorum Operum*. But we prepare best for that encounter by first looking into three existential crises in her personal life: a crucial victory, a major loss, and a final triumph. We shall see, by a close reading of two or three key letters written during each crisis, how she worked, all life long, to develop a way of writing in which she mediated, by and through her own rich and willful voice, what she surely heard as the voice of God. As she affirmed at the age of seventy-seven to Guibert de Gembloux, when people wrote to her asking personal and/or political questions, she often sought to answer them. Before she did, she looked into the "shadowy reflection of the living light [umbra viventis luminis]":

> [**Et in ipso video**] And in it I see those things of which I often speak, and I respond to those who ask questions of me with the fore-tellings I see within the brilliance of the living light [et quae interrogantibus de fulgore praedictae viventis lucis respondeo]. [Dronke, *Women Writers*, 253]

One of the pleasures of reading Hildegard's minor genres is the rich opportunity for browsing, a reading strategy far too fraught with danger when encountering the major visionary works. Her letters, for example, are addressed to the widest conceivable range of correspondents: from popes and emperors, kings and queens, to fellow church administrators and curious, though lesser-ranked nuns and monks, to many nameless folks who sought advice regarding lesser issues as varied as errant husbands and running sores. A natural curiosity arises when perusing her letters to the great; one notices a confidence of tone and a brisk level of energy it is hard to imagine emanating from "me, in the form of a poor little female" [ego paupercula feminea forma]—a favored signature of hers.[6] A glance at just a few of her letters to the mighty shows that part of her energy and confidence comes from her conviction that she speaks with the authority found in the *lux vivens* of which she wrote to Guibert de Gembloux.

For instance, there are two letters on record in which she wrote to the monarchs of England—both of them extremely powerful and

---

as Poetess and Dramatist," and "The Text of the *Ordo Virtutum*," in *Poetic Individuality in the Middle Ages* (Oxford: Clarendon Press, 1970), 150–92.

6. See, for example, the opening of her first letter to Guibert de Gembloux below.

notoriously willful. Here is the letter to Henry II, father of Richard Lionheart and Prince John:

Hildegard to Henry II, King of England

[**Ad quemdam virum quoddam officium habentem**] To a man with great responsibilities the Lord says: Gifts upon gifts are now yours: by ruling, protecting, defending, providing, you will have heaven. But a deeply black bird comes at you out of the North [sed nigerrima avis de Aquilone ad te venit] and says: "You have the power to do what you want. Do this, do that, let this and that go. Keeping an eye on justice brings no profit. If that's all you have your mind on, you'll not be king, but a slave." "But pay no mind to the Robber who gives that advice. He stripped you of great glory in the very beginning, after you were shaped from ashes into beautiful form [quando pulchra forma de cinere factus est] and received the breath of life. Look with greater zeal to your Father who made you. Your mind is benevolent and disposed to good, as long as the filthy passions of humanity do not fall on you and trap you for a while within them. Flee such, beloved son of God, and call on your Father who's disposed to reach out his hand in your aid. Now live in eternity [nunc in aeternum vive], and remain forever happy.[7]

There is an even shorter letter to his wife, Eleanore of Aquitaine, one of the most volatile and exciting women in Europe, who had divorced King Louis of France in order to marry Henry; but who also spent years of her old age in prison as Henry's "political" prisoner.

Hildegard to Eleanore of Aquitaine, Queen of England.

[**Mens tua similis est parieti qui est in vicissitudine nubis**] It is as if your mind is on a wall in the midst of shifting clouds. You look all around but have no rest [circumspicis sed requiem non habes]. Flee this! Stand your ground with God and man [sta in stabilitate cum Deo et hominibus], and in all your trials God will rule in your favor. May God give you his blessing and help in all your works.[8]

---

7. Pitra, *Analecta*, 556. Probably written, according to Pitra, in 1154, when Henry ascended the throne, and long before the murder of Beckett (1170).

8. Pitra, *Analecta*, 556. Pitra had serious doubts that the addressee was in fact Eleanore of Aquitaine, but at least some of the more recent scholarship (cf. *Briefwechsel*, 91) believes

For such a brief letter, the richness of attitude and function is impressive; the image of Eleanore's mind wandering the battlements alone on watch is extremely deft, as is her "moving" the queen from the heights of isolated self-absorption down to the earth of religious and ethical responsibility and the closing legal metaphor of court, not as panoply of power, but as trial, arguments, judge, and rulings. But there is a collegial sympathy and warmth here that expands the function of this letter far beyond that of a nagging intruder; one has the sense, perhaps illusory, that a real connection had been made.

There are three letters extant that she undoubtedly wrote to Frederick Barbarossa. The first is early, lengthy, encouraging, fulsome in praise, and thus of little interest; but the later two are extremely illuminating. As we saw in her short vita above, she was not only invited to the imperial pfalz for an extended and secret consultation with Barbarossa, but he issued her, in 1163, a letter of protection in perpetuity. As usual, he probably knew very well what he was doing. As he manipulated the papacy by rigging elections with increasingly public muscle, Hildegard began to get alarmed, and then very angry, finally supporting Barbarossa's nemesis, the legal incumbent Alexander III. In 1164, a year after Frederick I gave her his letter of protection, he meddled with papal election a second time, and the anti-Pope Paschal III was elected. Hildegard's response to this moved into the form and tone of Jeremiah:

Hildegard to Emperor Frederick I.

[**O rex, valde necesse est in causis tuis**] O King, there is great necessity that you be careful in your dealings. I see you, in mystical Vision [video te in mystica visione], like a child playing insanely before the Living Eyes [velut parvulum et velut insane viventem ante vivos oculos]. You have yet time to get earthly things in control. Be wary, lest the highest King strike you to earth for the blindness of your own eyes which do not see aright [non recte vident], how you should hold that scepter in your hand for right ruling [recte regendi]. So look to it. Be such that the Mercy of God not die out in you [Vide etiam ut talis sis, ne gratia Dei in te deficiat].[9]

---

the letter genuinely addressed to her. Eleanore married Henry in 1153; after 1172, two years after Beckett's martyrdom, she spent years in prison. For a lively if informal biography, see Regine Peroud, *Eleanore of Aquitaine* (London: Collins, 1967).

9. My translation from text as edited in Schrader, *Echtheit*, 128.

In her final letter, written after Barbarossa "elects" yet a third anti-pope, Calixtus III, in 1168, Hildegard pulls out all the stops: she rants at Barbarossa in the very voice of God:

Hildegard to Emperor Frederick I.

> [**Qui est dicit: Contumacium deleo**] He-who-is speaks: "I shall destroy the insolent along with the contradiction of those who despise me, I shall crush them by myself. Pain, Pain to this evil of the evils spurning me [ve, ve huic malo iniquorum me spernentium]. Hear this, King, if you wish to live. Or I run you through with my sword! [Hoc audi, rex, si vivere vis, alioquin gladius meus percutiet te]"[10]

Whatever Barbarossa may have felt upon receipt of this missive, his letter of protection held firm; never, through the long years of schism, did Hildegard have any serious political trouble with the emperor.

So as we undertake to read a few more key passages drawn from the epistolary collection of over 300 of her extant letters, we shall find a kind of writing more accessible than that of her three great books, a kind of writing to cut our teeth on, in which she also systematically uses her visionary resources, not so much to voice apocalyptic prophecy about first and last things, but as a way of helping us all, including on more than one occasion herself, to better understand the daily world of the middle.

LEGITIMACY OF VOICE

As we have seen in the short vita sketched above, Hildegard managed to convince both Pope and Emperor to provide her with written legitimation of her calling and her work. But it is behind this political maneuvering that the issues of real interest for us are to be found. Ultimately what must have convinced both Pope Eugenius and Emperor Barbarossa must convince us as well, though we must perforce put our questions in modern rather than medieval terms. These questions are not only important singly, they are also interlinked, and the evidence we can draw on from her correspondence comes with the differing perspectives of letters written in her prime (1147–52) and in her old age (1175–78).

---

10. Schrader, *Echtheit*, 129.

We shall see that the relatively cool control that old age brought with temporal distance by no means cancels out for us the telling and forceful heat generated by proximity to the event embodied in the perspective of her middle years. Within the framework of alternating temporal perspectives, we shall address the following questions:

1. The feminist issues reflected in the dual presence of self-abasement and self-assertion figured in her reports of physical suffering during the illuminations.

2. The issue she raises repeatedly herself: how she was taught to "understand" the holy texts of the Bible, not through institutional training, but through the direct "instruction" of her visions. This issue links intimately to the vexed issues surrounding medieval biblical exegesis, literacy in general, and women's access to education in the middle ages.

3. We shall need to deal with the phenomenology of the modalities of her visionary experience itself: of the simultaneity of her double sight. There are some very important implications concerning her poetics of revelation that are embedded in the fact that she saw holy vision within her soul even as she saw normal daily event proceeding around her.

Finally, examining these three interrelated sets of issues together should bring us to a first articulation in our search for a working hypothesis regarding Hildegard's major contribution to a fully integrative, feminine poetics of revelation. We shall begin to see that Hildegard's poetics of revelation involved, at least for her, the stereoscopic as well as polyphonic simultaneity of double perception and double voicing. As we see the implications of that more fully, we shall be able to suggest ways by which her visionary discourse can be read as functioning for her and her contemporaries, and perhaps for us, as a living figure of the hypostatic union of the Verbum-qua-Caro of Christ.

Let us take these questions separately, and as far as possible, before trying to put them together. Four documents should provide all we need in terms of primary evidence; two from the middle years: the letter to St. Bernard of Clairvaux and the "Protestificatio" that opens the *Scivias*; and two from old age: the autobiographical passages of the *Vita*, and her famous first letter to Guibert de Gembloux. As all of the issues are explicitly present or at least nascent in the crucial letter that she wrote to St. Bernard, we begin with that.

Question 1. The Letter to St. Bernard, the "Protestificatio," and feminist pathology: suffering and self-assertion.

We have some extremely valuable testimonies in which Hildegard reports the experience of revelatory vision with intriguing, near clinical candor. One of the earliest she included in her crucial letter to St. Bernard of Clairvaux, written some years after she experienced a particularly traumatic vision at the age of forty-two, whose painful pressure [pressura magna dolorum] forced her to reveal to all that she had had visionary experiences ever since she could remember. She was close to fifty when she wrote the Bernard letter, and had been for at least five, and perhaps nearer to ten years, hard at work on the *Scivias*, for which she sought, as a woman, wider legitimation within the male dominated establishment through the solicitation of Bernard's understanding and support. She must have felt that she was poised on the crest of a wave; and the terms in which she depicts herself as a woman are of as much interest to us as the detail with which she depicts the nature of her visionary experience.

Hildegard to Bernard, Abbot of Clairvaux. 1146–47. Excerpt.

> [**O venerabilis pater B<ernarde>**] O Venerable father B(ernard) how wonderful you are in the honor of God's power, how terrible to the vaunting fools of this world. With the banner of the holy cross you capture the ardent love of man for the Son of God to wage holy war with great zeal against the evil of the pagans. I beg you by the living God that you hear me questioning you [audias me interrogantem te].
>
> Father I am much disturbed by a kind of vision [valde sollicita de hac visione] that appears to me through the mysteries of the spirit [apparuit mihi in spiritu mysterii] which I never see with the outer eyes of the flesh. I, wretched and more than wretched in the name of woman [ego misera et plus quam misera in nomine femineo], have looked since childhood on great wonders which my tongue could not speak about did not God's Spirit teach me to believe.
>
> Most assured and gentlest father [certissime et mitissime pater] respond in your goodness to me your lowly handmaid [indigne famule tue] who has never lived since my infancy a single hour in certainty [que numquam vixi ab infantia mea unam horam secura] and as you search in your soul with affection [pietate] and wisdom in whatever ways you are led to by the Holy Ghost, bring some comfort to your servant from your heart [adhibe consolationem ancille tue de tuo corde]. . . .
>
> I know and understand a kind of inner knowledge of the exposition of the text [in textu interiorem intelligentiam expo-

sitionis] of the Psalms and the Gospels and other books which
have been shown to me by that vision that touches my heart
and soul like a burning flame, teaching me such depths of
meaning [docens me hec profunda expositionis]. But it
teaches me no writings unknown to me in the German language [non docet me litteras in Teutonica lingua quas nescio].
I know how to read directly [scio in simplicitatem legere], but
not by means of textual analysis [non in abscisione textus]. So
tell me what you think. I have never been taught by external
means [cum exteriori materia], but only within, in my soul
[sed intus in animea mea sum docta]. And so I speak as if in
doubt [unde loquor quasi dubitando]. . . . I beg you father for
the love of God to encourage me [me consoleris]: then I will
be sure [et certo ero] . . .[11]

First, there appears to be a real degree of felt truth as well as rhetorical
panache as she expresses her sensed condition of female inferiority in
the phrase: *"misera, plus quam misera in nomine femineo."* Yet that signal
of anxiety and vulnerability is nested within a strong sense of inner
conviction of self-integrity, and that mixed sense of things is in full
accord with the rest of the letter. Even as she pays the politically shrewd
dues of self-abasement to the most powerful representative of the
Church in the theater of Europe, she declares the integrity of her own
voice. Precisely by appropriating a typically male, anti-feminist cliché
back into her own particular situation and personal history, she reviv-
ifies it into fresh meaning. She plays what in a male mouth would be
a tired tag as a startling trump card of her very own, making of the
male *langue* that she inherited, a particular *parole* through which she,
as a woman, can forcefully speak. And yet the claim of self-assertiveness
here should by no means obscure our sense that her experiences of
divine vision were accompanied by enormous emotional stress and
physical suffering.

In the "Protestificatio" to the *Scivias*, she not only tells us what wasn't
there, she tells us what was.

[Et ecce quaddragesimo tertio temporalis cursus mei anno]
And Behold! In the forty third year in my course of time,

---

11. All translations of Latin texts are mine. The text translated here is the letter
as edited by Van Acker, *Hildegardis Bingensis Epistolarium*, 3–6. See also Schrader and
Fuehrkoetter, *Echtheit*, 104–7; and *PL* 29, 189C-190D. In all these translations I first
quote the Latin incipit, or at least the opening phrase of the passage quoted, and interlace
other key phrases from the original text as I go; my hope is that both the accuracy and
the registers of my "imitation" of Hildegard's voice in English can thus be tested against
the phonic mirror of what is at least the textual echo of her originating voice in Latin.

while gazing at a heavenly vision with much fear and trembling, I saw great splendor from which a voice was formed [in quo facta est vox] that said to me from heaven: O fragile human, dust of dust, filth of filth [O homo fragilis, et cinis cineris, et putredo putredinis], say and write what you hear and see. But as you are fearful in speaking, and simple in explaining, and ignorant in writing, say and speak not according to a human mouth [os hominis], nor according to the mind of human invention, nor according to the conventions of human writing, but according to that which you see and hear among the wonders of God in high heaven . . .[12]

Hildegard skirts the gender issue only at first (and only briefly) by locating the energy and authority of the discourse in the voice of God, and positioning herself as the object of address, making her "lowliness" less gender-specific and more the general human problem—but this is only for generic starters. It does not really avoid, but rather contextualizes the gender issue, because she then quickly shifts to her own voice:

[**Facta sunt**] It happened when I was forty two and seven months old, a fiery light of greatest brilliance coming from above transfused my whole brain and heart and breast with a flame that did not burn so much as warmed, as the sun warms all it touches with its rays. And I suddenly knew the meaning of the books [et repente intellectum expositionis librorum], such as the psalter and the gospels and I understood other catholic volumes from both Old and New Testaments but not by way of interpreting the words of their texts, nor dividing the syllables, nor did I have knowledge of the cases and tenses [non autem interpretationem verborum textus eorum nec divisionem syllabarum nec cognitionem casuum aut temporum habebam]. [*Scivias*, 4]

As we gloss *divisionem* in this passage, perhaps we can ask whether de-visioning a vision is something like post-modernist deconstructions of a construct. In any case, the technique of division was a favorite glossing method of the scholiasts. Over a hundred years later, Dante was still fond of it (cf. his mode of self-interpreting his own poetry in the *Vita Nuova*). Part of the attraction of that method, even down to dividing the syllables and distinguishing the cases and tenses, lay in this: to know

---

12. Fuehrkoetter's *Scivias*, 4.

how a thing falls into parts is to know something about how it works together, which is the logos of its ordination—and to know how something works together which would otherwise be apart is to know something crucial about what it means. The fact that Hildegard says she didn't use this method takes not one whit away from the even more important fact, which is made obvious here in the discourse itself, that she knew exactly what that method was. Such knowledge is seldom in the purview of the truly uneducated illiterate.

But to return to the text. At this juncture of the *protestificatio* it is important to realize that Hildegard continues to complicate matters by shifting the voice once again to a voice *in persona Dei*. Her strategy here, after allowing us to see how it felt from her point of view, is to render the report of her own suffering as justified by the voice of God:

> [**audivi vocem de coelo dicentem: Ego lux vivens**] I heard a voice from on high saying: I am the living light . . . I have laid her low on the earth, so that no elation may rise in her mind [quod se non erigeret in ulla elatione mentis suae] . . . she lives in fear and is timid in her work . . . she feels pain in her marrow and in the veins of her flesh [in medullis et in venis carnis suae doluit] . . . she is allowed no sense of security, but feels guilt in all she does . . . the fissures in her heart I have closed, that her mind not feel elevated by pride or by glory [nam rimas cordis eius circumsaepsi, ne mens ipsius per superbiam aut per gloriam se elevaret], but feel fear and sorrow rather than joy and delight. [*Scivias*, 4–5]

The real as well as rhetorical self-abasement in the letter to Bernard of her *miser in nomine femineo* rings true because there is a real self-asserting passion that sounds that ringing. But I believe we can read and hear the presence of that passion far more clearly here in the *protestificatio* to the *Scivias*, that great text that surrounds Bernard's letter in time. Something about the *protestificatio* as title alone can strike us as piquantly, if mildly aggressive in approach and tone, tinged with a tonality that a modern, up-to-date anti-feminist might well call willful or uppity.

But it is really the shift of speaker from her own voice to the voice of God and back that problematizes the issue most effectively for us. One could easily call that shift a transparent strategy of self-protection as well as one of self-legitimization as she has him tell us what he did to her in order to make her good and credible to us: surely both positions make a kind of sense. One might even feel as if she were thereby trying to remove herself from the calculus of divine interaction; but that would surely go too far. Behind the pain she surely felt as she suffered divine degradation, there is a fierce joy emanating from the rhetoric of that God-voice that makes it very clear that she celebrates the fact that she feels she is the first person since the Old Testament prophets whom God has CHOSEN for such privileged humiliation. The equation that emerges for Hildegard is full of Christian irony: the voice of God, as she herself hears it sounding through her own voice, *misera in nomine femineo*, sounds all the more brilliantly and lucidly by the very discrepancy of contrast between source and vehicle of mediation: in her self-perceived role as handmaiden [*famule, ancille*]. She indirectly asserts herself as an analog of Mary, mediating the divine logos not through her womb but through her mouth. It strikes this reader, in any case, that we should easily be able to stipulate that as far as she was concerned, Hildegard felt deeply and completely God-driven, and that her situating the catalogue of her personal sufferings within the voice of God, however much it served her interior vulnerabilities, was also an ironic, perhaps even paradoxical declaration of self-worth, as well as being "honest to God." For though it is clear that for her it was surely God's will that she suffered, her way of incorporating that suffering in her own discourse in what she felt was the voice of God shows it was a will she willed as well. As she appropriates the divine will as her own, she declares herself as a free, full, willing, even interdependent collaborator with God.

Question 2. The *Vita*, and the First Letter to Guibert de Gembloux: how Hildegard's visions taught her to "read" holy texts, and the institutional problematics relating her vision to the medieval arts of biblical exegesis, to the issue of literacy, and to the question of Hildegard's access to formal education.

If we return to the letter to Bernard, another important, and not unrelated set of problems surfaces in the final paragraph quoted and needs addressing. We start with Hildegard's report to Bernard that her vision taught her to read the meaning, not only of her own privileged revelations, but also the universal revelations accessible to all as embodied in the form of biblical texts: "I know and understand a kind of inner exposition of the text of the Psalms and the Gospels and other books which have been shown to me by that vision. . . . I know how to read directly [scio in simplicitatem legere], but not by means of textual analysis [non in abscisione textus]."

In the twelfth century, modes of biblical interpretation were not only matters of vital interest to the medieval community of discourse in general, but for Hildegard, access to and credibility within that community was vital for her if she, *misera in nomine femineo,* was to validate her role and mission as the vehicle of the will of God to mankind in general, and more specifically to her contemporary male power structure. And none of these issues surrounding biblical exegesis can be discussed adequately without attending to the thorny cultural issues of literacy itself, as well as the system of education that enabled and constituted literacy in her time.

To begin with, as we saw in Chapter 1, it is very difficult to assess what she meant by writing Bernard that in vision she was privileged to "a kind of inner knowledge of the exposition of the text [in textu interiorem intelligentiam expositionis]," as opposed to getting the meaning "by means of textual analysis [in abscisione textus]." But whatever such difficulties her discourse may pose for us, they are not those posed by an illiterate woman, but rather by someone who is in fact fully literate, but insufficiently trained as an exegete in the full range of canonical texts and available interpretive methodologies. We get a little more help concerning this, though not very much, from her recollections inscribed over two decades later in the *Vita*:

> . . . [In eadem visione scripta prophetarum] In that same vision I suddenly had knowledge [intellexi] of the writings of the prophets, the evangelists, and other saints, and some philosophers, but without any human teaching [sine ulla humana doctrina] and I explicated some of them [et quodam ex illis exposui] though I hardly had much knowledge of letters [cum vix notitiam litterarum haberem] since an unlearned woman taught me [sicut indocta mulier me docuerat]. But I also produced the melodies of songs in praise of God and the saints without any human instruction, and I sang them too, without being able to dictate or notate modes of singing.[13]

In this passage, as well as for a few key phrases in the *protestificatio* and the letter to Bernard, we do best by first turning to the dictionaries.[14] Let us begin with a more detailed gloss of two phrases from the Bernardian letter. When she says *in textu interiorem expositionis* she reveals

---

13. Translation drawn from text edited by Peter Dronke, *Women Writers of the Middle Ages* (Cambridge: Cambridge University Press, 1984), 231–32.

14. Latin is relatively poor (in comparison to, say, Greek or English) in terms of the actual number of lexical items that comprise it. But perhaps just because the number of words are fewer, many of them have to fulfill a wider range of denotational and connotational functions than in lexically richer languages. In addition to the *Oxford Latin Dictionary* (Oxford, 1968–82) I have also used the classic 1879 edition of Lewis and Short's *A New Latin Dictionary.*

that she views the text as having inner and outer aspects of meaning. This would correspond to images then fairly popular among medieval exegetes, such as that of the text itself as an *integumentum* or "cloak" protecting (by obscuring) the real meaning within.[15] So it seems clear enough that she is asserting to Bernard that her visions have taught her ways of reaching within a text and pulling out hidden meaning. But by denying that she uses any modes of interpretation involving *in abscisione textus*, "by means of cutting up the text," she rejects the more analytic modes of exegesis associated with the male dominated institutional establishments of the scholiast.

As for the more telling phrases from the *Vita*, we need to get some sense of the range of meanings that she might have chosen for *scripta intellexi, ex illis exposui*, and *cum vix notitiam litterarum haberem*. The primary sense of the verb *intellego* is "to see into" [inter + lego], and then by extension to "perceive" or "understand." As she "sees into" the writings [scripta] of the prophets and saints, we see again that for her the meaning of a phrase or image is to be found by moving inward, from the exteriority of the text as already constituting a signified language to be read, back into the interiority of the text as a voice in the act of signifying. And again, popular images of her time come to mind which view the search for meaning, not as reaching out beyond the words to some abstract referent, but rather moving inward in exactly this way: such as the image of cracking the nutshell to get at the meat, or that of removing the chaff to get at the kernel of wheat. Similarly in the phrase *ex illis exposui*, she envisions herself as having been taught to expound the meaning of a text by getting inside of it and thereby finding herself positioned to "expose" the hidden meaning.

Some of my students have been tempted to read *cum vix notitiam litterarum haberem sicut indocta mulier me docuerat* as meaning that she "had difficulty in reading and writing because she had been taught by a woman who was herself illiterate [*indocta*]." But I would argue that is far too reductive. It is true that the singular form of "letter": i.e., *littera,-as* was generally and traditionally used to indicate the radical presence or absence of literacy: *scire/nescire litteras* has always referred to the ability, or not, to read and write. But Hildegard uses the plural: *litterae,-arum*, which usually refers to texts, documents, and literature in general, and sometimes even to a wide-ranging liberal education. So somewhat softer, but still very legitimate equivalents of the Latin are far more likely to capture what it is that Hildegard means here. A more just translation would read: "I would have had great difficulty in being

---

15. See the chapter on medieval modes of exegesis in my *Now through a Glass Darkly*, 83–113.

acquainted with the full range of the literature [without this divine help], having been taught to read by a woman who was herself uninstructed in it." So whatever the degree to which women in general were kept from the fruits of the male-dominated educational establishment in the middle ages, in the case of Hildegard's own growth, she seems to have had access to a fairly rich tradition of literacy as she grew up in St. Disibod. Part of the evidence for that is the fact that she has reached an important aspect of the Socratic goal of knowledge: she knows what it is she doesn't know.

My sense of things is that current discussions of the literacy problems in the middle ages are generally far too strict in construing a socially realistic set of meanings for the term. Surely not everyone in a community of discourse must be equally capable of reading and writing texts at an expert level of proficiency; the whole point of a community is that members can specialize in many different tasks, and yet benefit from the combined expertise of everyone taken together. We know that in the latinate as well as vernacular tradition of sharing texts, the normative mode within the family and community was to read aloud (this was also the common practice in extended American families, for example, right up to the end of the nineteenth century).

It is difficult for me to see any necessity of imposing particularly harsh strictures on members of Hildegard's community in order to certify their capacity for engaging in literate discourse: as I have already said, not everyone needs to be a professional lector in order to be literate. And the evidence in Hildegard's work alone should be convincing enough to allow us to allow her the kind of literacy she required to produce her richly allusive texts.

As we turn now to Hildegard's first letter to Guibert de Gembloux, written in old age, we become even more impressed with the sophistication of her range of control over important areas of literary tradition, ranging from the epistolary tradition of the evangelists—to the more philosophic investigations I believe she refers to regarding the exciting developments currently underway in light metaphysics. Let us begin our examination of her letter to Guibert:

Hildegard to Guibert de Gembloux.

> [**O serve fidelis, ego paupercula feminea forma, in vera visione haec verba iterum dico tibi**] O faithful servant, I, poor thing in feminine form say to you again these words [heard] in true vision. . . . It is like what happened to Paul who preceded the other disciples in preaching yet held himself to be worth nearly nothing, and John the Evangelist who was full

of gentle humility because he drank so much divinity [quapropter de Divinitate multa hauriebat]. And how is it that I, poor thing, cannot know myself [si ego paupercula me non **cognoscerem**]? God works as he will for the glory of his name and not for earthly humanity. I am always full of shaking fear, and I know not the slightest possibility of security within, and I stretch my hands out to God, so that I am sustained and carried without weight like a feather by the power of the wind. I cannot know perfectly what it is I see, for I am still in a functioning body with an invisible soul which in this double state is imperfect [quandiu in corporali officio sum et in anima invisibili quoniam in his duobus homini defectus est].[16]

It is not just a general reference to Paul as exemplary preacher that she is making here. With the verb *cognoscere* and with her gentle, but firm insistence that self-knowledge on this side of death is always partial, she is making clear, if indirect allusion to the famous pauline passage in 1 Corinthians 13.12:

> "Now we see through a glass darkly, then face to face; now we know only in part, then we shall know as we are known [Nunc videmus per speculum in aenigmate, tunc facies ad faciem; nunc **cognosco** ex parte, tunc autem **cognoscam** sicut et cognitus sum]."

Her discourse here begins to act as a kind of informal, running gloss on the passage from Paul: a passage not directly sounded, but present nonetheless by means of her artful allusion to it. She adds to the pauline inventory one of her favorite images from nature, that of the weightless feather (eagles have been on her mind lately) carried by the wind, and then returns to meditate on the ramifications of the Pauline "now-then" [nunc = tunc] axis of concern. "Now" is this side of death, where we are invisible souls inhabiting the all-too visible body, that double state of imperfection of continuance in time [in his duobus homini defectus est]. "Then" is on the other side of death: where we shall blaze in the resurrected glory of the body in the final perfection of time, in its overness and completion, fully at rest in the eternity of the mind of God: knowing then as we are always already known now.

The point of course is not to aver that Hildegard intended that this particular skein of meditation should arise in the mind of Guibert as

---

16. Pitra, *Epistolae*, 332 (Pitra dates the letter as 1171; both Newman and *Briefwechsel* as 1175).

he read her letter, but that her discourse is so tightly organized in its allusive range across the world of received texts that such a coherent meditation can in fact arise from it. This is the kind of literacy that matters, way beyond the naked question of whether someone has the brute capacity to read and write the letters of the alphabet.

Question 3. The visionary phenomenology of double sight: simultaneity of the revelatory and the quotidian, Hildegard's metaphysics of light, and the words of a woman as an imago of the Logos of Fire.

An extremely important aspect of her visionary experience is the cool, non-ecstatic quality she reports she felt while having it. Part of that sense of a relatively cool control that she exudes seems to have derived from the multiple points of view from which she could see herself seeing two realities at once, the phenomenon of double sight. We need to backtrack a bit.

In her letter to Bernard she says "I never see [the inner vision] with the outer eye of the flesh." But it appears that she also saw the daily doings of the exterior world with waking eyes even as she saw interior revelations with the "eye of the soul."

In the *protestificatio* to the *Scivias*, she expands a bit more than in her letter to Bernard on what this felt like:

> [**Visiones vero quas vidi**] These visions I truly saw not in dream, nor in sleep, nor in ecstasy [nec in phrenesi], nor through the eyes nor the ears of the human body; I saw them while awake [sed eas vigilans vidi], I received them through the eyes and ears of our pure mind [in pura mente hominis], in open places, according to the will of God [in apertis locis secundum voluntatem Dei]. [*Scivias*, 4]

For those who have come into contact with what one might call the ecstatic tradition (in the sensuous visions of Hildegard's contemporary and correspondent Elizabeth of Schoenau, say, or in the roarings and groanings of Julian's visitor at Norwich, Margery Kempe), the presence of such a relatively cool degree of "non-frenetic" calculation in Hildegard's inventory of her visionary experiences is, at least by contrast, arresting. More important, her multiple points of view bring both her and us closer to points of middle distance: close enough to feel the heat and rush of the vision as experienced, yet also distant enough to be aware of other realities occurring simultaneously—a vantage point that maximizes the benefits of both breathtaking proximity and self-control.

It is relatively easy to assess her personal and political agenda as voiced in her prime during the heat of her effort to achieve official legitimation of her charismatic gift, both in the personal agenda embodied in her letter to Bernard, as well as in her larger missionary agenda as she prepared to encounter the world in the *Scivias*'s *protestificatio* (both completed prior to 1150). She scored, of course, a huge victory: Pope Eugenius III sent Hildegard his official commendation to continue her work of prophetic dissemination of the Word.

But it is a bit more difficult to sort from those earlier reports the actual phenomenology of her visionary experience, as she saw it **qua** experience, absent the urgencies of politics and apologia. This difficulty fades considerably when we witness her return to the memory of that experience in her 70s, when all question of her legitimacy and credentialing had been long since answered.

We have two extremely useful testimonies on the phenomenology of double sight that she saw from the perspective of old age. The first comes from the letter, from which we have already drawn, that she wrote between 1171 and 1175 in answer to questions put by her distant admirer, the Walloon monk Guibert of Gembloux:

> [**Ab infantia autem mea**] From infancy, before my bones and veins and nerves were strong, I have always seen visions [visionem video] right up to the present time, and I am over seventy years old now, and my soul, if God wills, ascends in this vision up to the heights of the firmament into the shifting air . . . and I see things by means of my soul [et quoniam haec tali modo in anima mea video] . . . for I do not hear with my outer ears, nor by the reasonings of my heart [cogitationibus cordis mei], nor do I perceive by any collation of my five senses, but directly into my soul, with my exterior eyes wide open, I never fall into weakness of ecstasy, but have visions while awake, both day and night [ita ut nunquam in eis defectum extasis passa sim, sed vigilanter die ac nocte illa video] . . . [Dronke, *Women Writers*, 252]

For the second testimony, we return to the *Vita*. She wrote (or at least dictated to Gottfried for notes used by Theodoric) that as a growing child she came to a kind of consciousness that she had been visited by divine vision even prior to birth:

> [**In prima formatione mea**] In my early formation, as God breathed sustaining life into me in the uterus of my mother, he implanted this capacity-for-vision into my soul [visionem

istam infixit animae meae]. . . . In the third year of my life I
saw such light as shook my soul [tantum lumen vidi quod
anima mea contremuit], but because of my infancy I could
not speak to anyone about it . . . and from then until I was
fifteen I saw many things of which I spoke most simply, but
those who heard me wondered where it all came from. . . .
And I wondered at myself that as I saw all this within my soul,
I also had exterior sight [quod cum infra in anima mea hec
vidi, exteriorem etiam visum habui], which I never heard
about anyone else. . . . And for the fear I had of others, I
never told anyone how I heard and saw things [quomode vid-
erem nulli dicere audebam]. . . . And I kept seeing like this
until I was forty. Then in a vision I felt forced by great pressure of pain [magna pressura dolorum] to reveal what I had
heard and seen . . .[17]

In these two passages she focuses on the way the interior visionary eye
sees with radical independence from the usual exterior modes of sensual reception. It is important to note that she does not see her holy
visions with any of the five senses, but rather "from within," or "by
means of" the soul [in anima video]. But it is perhaps just as important
to understand that this kind of inner vision occurs when she is awake
[vigilanter] and that she simultaneously sees with exterior vision [exte-
riorem visum habui] as well. My sense is that it was precisely her co-
awareness of two realities that directly derived from the simultaneity
of her double vision, the co-presence in her being of the revelatory
and the quotidian, which kept her from passing into what she called
the "failure" or "weakness" of ecstasy [defectum extasis]. The negative
spin that she put on that diction clearly indicates her antipathy to
the more ecstatic, and perhaps more fashionable modes of mystical
transport. And her double sight of things inheres in the breathtaking
image she painted of the ascent of her soul into the shimmering, shifting airs of the celestial heights, even as she tells us she saw exclusively
from within the confines of her soul. This double-sight of her mode
of perception, then, is thus mirrored in her juxtaposed image of the
co-presence in her text of the vastness of cosmic space and the seques-
tration of psychic interiority.

   As we shall see, much of crucial importance stems from this sense,
both in her as seer and in us as readers, of this simultaneity of apper-
ceptive modalities. There is a passage in the letter to Guibert that cap-

---

17. See *PL* 197, 102D-103C.

tures something of this rushed intensity which I am seeking to
picture forth:

> [**Quicquid autem in hac visione videre seu didicero**] Every-
> thing I see and learn in these visions, I have long in memory;
> for when I see and hear it, I record it, and **I simultaneously
> see, hear, know and almost in that very moment that I know
> it, I teach it [et simul video, audio, scio, et quasi in momento
> hoc quod scio, disco].**[18]

She always spoke in a double voice, and her texts are double-voiced as
well: God's and hers. Sometimes, as in the great visionary works, we
read and hear them in strict alteration. But more often, especially in
the *Vita* and in the letters, we encounter more informal modes. Only
rarely is one of the voices suppressed, but usually not for long. She
tells us over and over again that she saw simultaneously with inner and
outer eyes. More important, she re-creates for us, over and over again
in her discourse, that sense of dual presence. We recall that she said to
Bernard that she only "knows how to read the texts [scio in simplicitatem legere]," which is to read them as uncompounded, as unified
wholes of the spirit: not as divisible entities of the flesh [non textus in
abcisione]. So in terms of a series of double texts: the "words" in her
visions and the words in the Bible; and by extension the human words
she writes "out" of the vision and the Word that she "sees" in her
vision, we have double senses. The privately seen words of God (which
Pope Eugenius, as Christ's vicar, legitimized as authentic) and the cor-
porately relayed words of the Bible. She sees and hears both at once,
and weaves them together in a double discourse for us. Of course,
being subject to the exigencies of being alive this side of death, she
must say one word at a time. But rather than merely moving alternately
from vision to gloss, back to vision and then back to gloss (which she
often does do, thereby imitating the male mode of biblical exegesis)
there is also something different here, and more. We do better to think
of it as two discourses hitting us simultaneously, stereoscopically and
stereophonically, (the twelfth century invented polyphony, after all). As
we shall see in her soaring finish to the Letter to the Prelates of Mainz,
she believed deeply in the musical implications of the *symphonia* of the
incarnation: of the word of God made flesh in the words of humanity,
and she figured that sense of the incarnation forth in her written
discourse: the public and private avenues of the logos channeled into

---

18. Pitra, 332, emphasis mine.

her head and out of her mouth, onto wax tablets, and then, through the added mediation of her provost Volmar, onto parchment.

Of course we hear the two voices informing her discourse in our "outer ears" antiphonally; but if we listen for them with the eyes as well as the ear of the soul, as she bids us to do, we can imagine them as sounding simultaneously. We have to "see" the ineluctable modality of the visual (nebeneinander) **even as** we "hear" the ineluctable modality of the audible (nacheinander).[19] We hear and see, cry out and write *pictura et verbum*, the many and one, nunc and tunc: all now.

Perhaps the best demonstration of the impossible challenges offered by such synthesizing discourse can be seen in her meditations on how, on the one hand, she strives to achieve absolute accuracy of translation between the words she "saw" in the vision of God, and her human words. We begin to see more deeply when we listen to her meditate, on the other hand, on the undeniable fact that her human words are radically unlike any of the words she "saw" in the vision. Both like and unlike at once: we are in Augustine's Land of Unlikeness [regione dissimilitudinis, *Confessions* 7.10]. It is instructive to watch how she meditates on the words she hears and the words she writes as she is drawn irrevocably toward the Logos as Light. We can see here how deeply she has intuited the convergence of the physics and metaphysics of the dionysian theology of *lux nova*. I'd say this is her final, most illuminating form of literacy. To see it, we return to the letter to Guibert:

> [**Lumen igitur quod video, locale non est**] And the light that I see is not spatial, but is much, much brighter than clouds that carry the sun: I know no values of height, nor length, nor breadth and I call it the Shadowy Reflection of the Living Light [umbra viventis lucis mihi nominatur]. And just as the sun, the moon and the stars are reflected in water, so scriptures, sermons, virtues and other forms of the work of humans are mirrored in it. I have no way of knowing about the form of this light, any more than I can see clearly into the sun. Yet there is a light within this light, which it occurs to me to call the Living Light [Lux Vivens] that I can see sometimes but not often. And when, and how I see it, I have no way of telling forth, but for the time that I see it, all sadness and all

---

19. See Stephen Dedalus's soliloquy on the "German" ineluctables of "afteroneanother" and "nexttooneanother" in his walk on Sandymount Strand in the third chapter of Joyce's *Ulysses*.

anxiety is lifted from me, and I feel like a simple young girl, and not like an old woman. [Dronke, 252–53]

Hildegard's anticipation of Dante here is astonishing. The light she sees is not the natural light of the natural sun that we awake to in the morning: if we look into that sun we go blind. We can, however, with proper prayer and training, look into this new light (lux nova) and live. This light Dante calls the Light of the Pure Mind (luce intellettuale). And his version of Hildegard's reflection of that light, her *umbra viventis lucis*, is promised a century later by Manfred in the purgatorial Valley of the Kings as "umbriferi prefazi," or "shadowy prefaces" of the living light that will shine from our bodies after resurrection. As she continues her letter to Guibert, she becomes suddenly almost defensive. She insists that she forms her own words in the closest possible *imitatio* of the words she receives from God:

> [**Quod autem non video, illud nescio**] And what I do not see, I do not know, for I am not educated; but have been instructed only to read directly [sed tantum litteras in simplicitate legere instructa sum]. And I write what I see and hear in the vision, I put down no other words, and that which I hear I bring forth in unpolished Latin words just the way I hear them in the vision [quam illa quae audio et latinis verbis non limatis ea profero, quemadmodum illa in visione audio] [for] I am not taught in vision how to write as philosophers write.

One feels here the price she always pays in her effort to reach the highest degree possible of verbal accuracy in her process of translating vision into words; and the clear discomfort reflected in her diction shows how fundamentally impossible the task is in any naturalistic sense of achieving veridical match. It is therefore quite wonderful to come across her complete candor in the next passage. After insisting on the need for extreme conservatism regarding transmission of the words she sees in her vision, she turns quite around and insists to Guibert that the original words she saw in vision are not like our human words at all:

> [**Et verba in visione ista non sunt sicut verba quae ab ore hominis sonant**] But the words in the vision are not like the words that are sounded in the human mouth, rather they are like shaking flames, and like the pure moving of clouds in the air [sed sicut flamma coruscans, et ut nubis in aere pura mota].

Is this Dionysian? or proto-Dantesque? It is all that if we see it there. But far more importantly, we move toward an image of the words she sees as shimmering fire and flame: the Logos, which she tries, in full knowledge of the inevitable discrepancy, to mirror in her unpolished Latin. As she proceeds with the project both with and in spite of that nicer knowledge, we see that her text can be fruitfully read as a very figure of the incarnation itself: her words form an *imago Dei*, an *obumbratio viventis lucis*, or in Dante's confirmations, they become *umbriferi prefazi*, shadowy prefaces of the unimaginable, longed-for fire of the Logos. It is in this sense that I argue her light metaphysic constitutes her final, sovereign, and ultimate literacy.

Near the end of this extraordinary letter, she writes Guibert that the Light has brought her to some sort of peace in her final years: more than that, she admits to a fulfilling joy that she sees in it, a joy that has begun, finally, to still her deeply unquiet, Augustinian heart:

> **[Sed et prae assidua infirmitate]** For it is hard work, in constant sickness, to bring forth the words and the visions that are shown to me. But then when my soul can taste and see them, all is changed, and as I said above, all sorrow and tribulation vanish into oblivion. And what I see and hear in these visions my soul drinks in as from a fountain that is always full and never empty. There is no hour that my soul is denied the light, which I have called the shadowy reflection of the living light [umbra viventis luminis] and I see it as if I were looking at a cloud lit up in the sky when no stars shine. In it I see those things of which I often speak, and I respond to those who ask questions of me with the foretellings that I see within the brilliance of this living light [et quae interrogantibus de fulgore praedictae viventis lucis respondeo]. [Pitra, 333]

* * * * *

There should be no doubt now as to the kinds of power that surged behind her quest for the legitimization of her voice. Frederick Barbarossa wrote her a letter of perpetual protection. And Pope Eugenius III sent her his official apostolic approval, license, and blessing [apostolicam benedictionem], affirming his conviction of the truth of her voice by weaving the voices of Paul and the singer of the Song of Songs into his own:

Pope Eugenius III to Hildegard. 1152.

> **[Gaudeamus, filia, et exsultamus in Domino]** Let us rejoice, my daughter, and exult in the Lord, that your honored fame

has spread into the length and the breadth so that for many you are a "the savour of life unto life" [odor vitae in vitam], and a crowd of believing people full of your praise cries out, "Who is this that cometh out of the wilderness like pillars of smoke, perfumed with myrrh and frankincense [que est ista, que ascendit per desertum tamquam virgula fumi et aromatibus]?" We are convinced that your soul so burns with the love of God that you require no urging toward righteousness. That's why we find it superfluous to send either words of warning or encouragement to you, who are so completely supported by the power of God.[20]

All these answers to the three listed questions also form a base for proceeding further in our examination of Hildegard's poetics of revelation. At the end of the entire chapter, as we directly encounter some central images from her great visionary books, we will more fully address the ways in which all of Hildegard's epistolary strategies can be seen as integrative, as working together to comprise Hildegard's contribution to a feminine poetics of revelation, one of the great contributions of the high middle ages.

But first we shall examine how she used the form of the letter to mediate holy vision in the more earthly cases of a major personal loss and a final public triumph.

THE AFFAIR OF RICHARDIS VON STADE

Hildegard moved to the Rupertsberg in 1150 and finished the *Scivias* by 1151. For the years it took to complete both the book and the foundation, she depended on support from many friends and colleagues, among them Richardis von Stade, a young nun from a brilliant aristocratic family. Richardis had been dedicated to Hildegard's cloister by her mother, also named Richardis, the Marchioness von Stade, much as Hildegard had been dedicated at the age of eight by her own parents years earlier to the anchorage of Jutta von Spanheim, a cousin of the Marchioness. It may be that the very fundamental mirroring relationship between them enhanced the affection and co-dependence that grew between Hildegard and her younger protégée through the years. It is surely true that the love she had for the younger woman, a love which Hildegard called being *in plena charitatem*, was sorely tested by

---

20. Van Acker, *Epistolarium*, 10.

the sudden departure of the younger woman to take up duties elsewhere as abbess of her own convent. The rupture evoked a powerful passion in Hildegard, and her means of coming to some sort of peace with it became an important part of the record, primarily because she wrote so movingly and candidly about it in her letters. But before turning to those letters written in her prime, we gain a useful ground and context for them by seeing how she viewed her loss of Richardis from the distance of old age. In the *Vita* we find the following:

> [**Nam cum librum** *Scivias* **scriberem**] During the time when I was writing the *Scivias*, I had a great affection [in plena charitatem habebam], just as Paul had for Timothy, for a noble girl, the daughter of the above-mentioned Marchioness, who in loving friendship bound herself to me in all things and consoled me in my distractions [in passionibus meis] until I finished the book. But after that, because of her family's elevated position, she wished for a title of greater dignity, to be nominated as the mother of a splendid church; she sought this not according to God, but for her honor in the world. There, in that region remote from us, after she left me, she presently lost her life, along with her title and office.[1]

Perhaps the first thing to notice here is her allusion to the scriptural filiation between Paul and Timothy of Lystra, against which she situates her relationship to Richardis. The structural similarity is fielded primarily to illuminate the many differences. If Timothy was a surrogate son to Paul who proved true in loyalty to the end, Richardis was a surrogate daughter whose worldly ambition, fed by her earthly mother the Marchioness, led her to betray Hildegard, her spiritual mother. This reference to Paul as an anticipatory mirror of herself is no casual bit of biblical name-dropping. We shall find that each textual reference in her letter calls up particular relationships of others that richly and deeply complicate and thicken our sense of her own. She consistently uses the textures of biblical event to capture a paradigm in human interaction that provides a ground for greater understanding of what otherwise appears gratuitous and arbitrary in our lives.

As to her attitude in old age to the defection of Richardis, she speaks with a clear sense won from that distance, that whatever pain the severance cost Hildegard (and it obviously caused significant pain), that the difficulty that led to it was unwarranted ambition on the part of the younger nun, and no sudden change in their mutual affection. There

---

1. *PL* 107C-D.

is a hint of contempt for weakness here as well as the possible echo of a kind of jealousy. There is no reason to doubt the cool sincerity of her view. But as we move back nearly a quarter of a century to the time of Richardis's departure from the Rupertsberg, we sense a richer heat in her discourse, and, as we might well expect, a more textured sense of the situation that reveals the complexities of an extremely difficult love.

For years it had been assumed that Richardis had been elected abbess of the foundation at Hildesheim; and difficulties had long plagued historians because there was no independent record in Hildesheim corroborating that assumption. It has recently been discovered, however, that Richardis had in fact been elected Abbess of the convent Brisum, now Bassum, located near Bremen.[2] Richardis's brother Hartwig happened to have been Archbishop of Bremen at the time, and had therefore certainly something to do with her elevation, if only because he would, by virtue of his office, have had to ratify it. It is already clear from Hildegard's own letter that Richardis's mother, the Marchioness, had also been active behind the scenes.

And the record also shows that Hildegard managed, at least for some time, to keep Richardis with her on the Rupertsberg in spite of her election. This is clear from the first relevant letter in the record. It came to Hildegard from her own master Henry, Archbishop of Mainz. Henry was the very same official who, with the outside help and insistence of the very same Marchioness von Stade, had only recently paved the way for Hildegard's secession from St. Disibod in order that she might found her own new cloister on the Rupertsberg. The tone of Henry's letter seems rather cold and harsh, but could well be accounted for by frustration arising from such resistance from a woman to whom he had so recently given such significant aid. Nearer as well as more distant historical parallels reverberated within the increasingly uncomfortable situation. They must to some extent have been clear to those nearby; Hildegard's care in finding suitable parallels in biblical texts indicate, at least to this reader, that they had not quite escaped her either. Here is the relevant portion of Henry's letter. After much elaborate and polite hemming and hawing, he shifts to a tonality anticipatory of what one often hears today in the memos of certain CEOs to middle management:

Henry, Archbishop of Mainz, to Hildegard. 1151 Excerpt.

[**veniamus ad quod intendimus**] we arrive at our intention: we make known to you that religious emissaries have arrived

---

2. See Schrader, *Echtheit*, 133–34.

from a noble church well-known to us. They request that the sister who resides with you in religious habit, and who has been duly elected as their abbess, be sent to them. Thus by the authority vested in our office and our priesthood we bid you, in the form of a command, that you give her over to said petitioners for installation in that office. Should you do this, you will sense the presence of our grace in even greater degree than heretofore. If not, then I shall order you yet again more forcefully, nor will I cease doing so until you have obeyed my command by performing the deed.[3]

Hildegard lost no time in replying. Her tone reveals she also lost no time in raising the stakes. Any modern reader at all sympathetic with the feminist cause will feel a tickle of glee when encountering the sovereignty of her response, but also, perhaps, some compassion for Henry as well, as she replies to her recently very supportive Archbishop directly in the voice of God:

Hildegard to Henry, Archbishop of Mainz. 1151

[**Perspicuus fons qui non est fallax, sed iustus, dicit**] The transparent spring which is never false but just, says this: The reasons which have been brought forward as grounds for the girl's elevation have no weight with God because I, the Height, the Depth, the Circling, who am the Light breaking through, have neither chosen nor elected her, rather she comes forward out of the untamed audacity of ignorant hearts. All of the faithful will hear with the capacious ears of the heart [capacibus auribus cordis], and not the ears that hear only from outside, like the herd of cattle that takes in the sound but not the word [pecus quod sonum capit et non verbum]. The Spirit of God speaks in its zeal: O Shepherds, weep and mourn at this time, for you know not what you do, when, in offices founded by God, you play their desire for gold against the foolishness of crooked men who have no fear of God. That is why no one may listen to your evil, damning, threatening words. The up-raised whips of your arrogance are poised ready in the name of God not for me, but rather to punish the flagrance of your own presumptuous will.[4]

---

3. See Van Acker, *Epistolarium*, 34.
4. Van Acker, *Epistolarium*, 54.

Halfway through the letter, the Voice of God transforms into her own. And one notes the scrupulous care underlying the apparent ease with which she makes the switch. Speaking first in the voice of God, she reminds us as well as Henry of the necessity of listening simultaneously to the double-voiced call of reality: to the Logos that speaks to the ears of the heart [auribus cordis], as well as to the words the world speaks to the outer ears of the beasts that we also are [pecus quod sonum capit]. The switch to her own voice is no accidental slip, but a maneuver shrewdly mediated, carefully stitched by the phrase "the Spirit of God Speaks." This single phrase points in two directions: backward, in order to clarify the force behind the previous locution as indeed spoken by the mouth of God, and forward in order to legitimize and validate the implied assertion that the same spirit will now speak through her own mouth. By rhetorical implication we then assume that in between the two voices, in the phrase beginning "O Shepherds weep and mourn," her voice speaks in unison with, and overlaps that of God. Then she continues, and speaks in her own voice, no everyday voice, but a prophetic one now impelled and pre-validated by the Holy Spirit. As she turns on Henry with only slightly veiled accusations of simony, she curls her epistolary lip with an anger and contempt now privileged by divine justice, and warns him that the whips of his arrogance will land on his own back, and not on hers.

The situation on the Rupertsberg was even more complicated by the fact that there was another favorite in her community, a nun named Adelheid, who had also been elected abbess, in this case *magistra* of the prestigious foundation of Gandersheim. This occurred even in the midst of the swirl of activity surrounding Richardis von Stade. Adelheid was not only another favorite of Hildegard's, but also a granddaughter of the Marchioness of Stade who had brought her up after the sudden death of her son-in-law, Friedrich von Sommerschenburg, Adelheid's father. The densely profuse proximities in time and blood between the two abbatial elections no doubt increased the intensity of Hildegard's reactions to all this. In any case both women eventually departed (or were liberated from) the Rupertsberg. But that departure did not seal the matter as far as Hildegard was concerned: she had a few more epistolary cards to play. The first was to write directly to the Marchioness:

Hildegard to the Marchioness Richardis von Stade, mother of the nun Richardis. 1151

> [**Obsecro te et admoneo**] I implore and beseech you not to confound my soul [non ita animam meam conturbes] so as to

draw out bitter tears from my eyes [lacrimas de oculis meis educas] and pierce my heart with terrible wounds [et cor meum diris vulneribus saucies] on account of my most dearly-loved daughters Richardis and Adelheid whom I now see in the ruby aurora of morning adorned with the pearls of virtue [quas modo in aurora rubentes et margaritis virtutum ornatas video]. Keep from deflecting their sense and their souls from this great beauty by your acts of will, advice, and support. For the newly-won rank that you desired for her of Abbess surely, surely, surely, did not come from God [quia hec potestas, ut desideras in abbatissis, certe, certe, certe, non est cum Deo], nor does it work to the health of their souls. If you are indeed the mother of these daughters, keep them from losing their souls, or you shall later suffer the sighs and tears of enormous pain simply because you chose to forego any pain at all earlier on. May God illuminate and strengthen your mind and your spirit in the short time left for triumph [in hoc brevi tempore, quo victura est].[5]

She speaks to the Marchioness in complex intimacy as mother to mother sharing two daughters. Within this triangle of filial allegiance and bondage, Hildegard proceeds smoothly and irrevocably in a trajectory that moves from a double-focus on Hildegard and the Marchioness as mutual mirrors of each other now as she writes, to a kind of elegiac hovering over the figures of Richardis and Adelheid as they shine in the suspension of holy vision, to a prefiguration of the Marchioness in near future, already isolated in what Hildegard foresees as an almost inevitable desolation.

And for each point in that trajectory, she indicates, by clear verbal echo, a paradigmatic parallel from scripture whose similarities ultimately illuminate a breathtaking difference. Again this is no automatic bible-thumping; this is a thoughtful and delicate art of allusive conversation, which calls up related situations not only to shed light, but also to further complicate and enrich our sense of the situation to which they are called up to bear witness. We need to proceed in detail and with some care.

Because she uses none of the tricks that she appropriates with such pyrotechnic skill in the letter above to Henry of Mainz, it may seem at first that she is speaking to the Marchioness entirely in her own voice. But in fact the letter is a symphony of other voices speaking in full accord with her own. They speak from two sources that are, for Hilde-

---

5. Schrader, *Echtheit*, 135.

gard, ultimately the same source: the Logos, or Holy Spirit. One voice is the voice of the *umbra viventis lucis*, the reflection of the living light, by which Hildegard synaesthetically hears that the physically missing daughters are alive in "ruby morning light" of her inner eye. The other speaks from the same Spirit, but now through the revelatory texts of scripture, and these voices show the painful situation of both women, the Marchioness and herself, as always already prefigured in the Old Testament. Let's look at how this second kind of voicing works.

We hear the textual voices of Jeremiah and 2 Maccabees echoing with absolute clarity through the diction with which she begins her letter. First, there is a textual echo of Jeremiah's sad compassion as he foreknows that Jerusalem once again will not listen, a compassion that figures forth and is fulfilled in that compassion which Hildegard feels for the inevitable misery she knows is coming to the Marchioness. There follows another echo, this one from 2 Maccabees that reflects her own sense of anger at herself, her frustration, and helplessness in the face of event.

In charity she begins with the first. In a verbal allusion to Jeremiah she encodes her primary concern for the Marchioness—whom she figures to herself as so closely co-mother in this matter that the act of either woman is equivalent to an act of the other. The Latin of Hildegard's pleas to the Marchioness "do not confound my soul and draw bitter tears from my eyes" reads: *non ita* **animam meam** *conturbes et* **lacrimas** *de* **oculis meis educas.** This phrasing echoes the haunting verse in which Jeremiah speaks to Jerusalem, begging her to listen while there is still time, however short it is, and knowing she will not:

> Hear ye, and give ear; be not proud . . . Give glory to the Lord your God, before he cause darkness and before your feet stumble upon the dark mountains, and while ye look for light, he turn it into the shadow of death, and make it gross darkness. But if ye will not hear it, my soul shall weep [plorabit **anima mea**] in secret places, and mine eye shall weep sore [et **deducet oculus meus lacrymam**], and run down with tears fleet, because the Lord's flock [Richardis and Adelheid] is carried away captive. Say unto the king and to the mother-queen [regi et dominatrice] "Humble yourselves, sit down: for your principalities shall come down, even the crown of your glory." [Jer. 13, 17–18, my emphasis]

Hildegard's knowledge of Jeremiah is deep; we see that by the way the extended passage to which she alludes embodies the paradigm of the Marchioness in the figura of the "dominatrix." And this richly allusive passage from scripture converges with her private and privileged knowledge from the *umbra viventis lucis,* and all coalesces for us in a new sense of the perdurable in the relationship that she, as mother, bears to the Marchioness, as mother, and that the time is always short.[6] It is in the literary power of that compressed simultaneity of her understandings that Hildegard's charism is so powerfully demonstrated. But she does not remove herself from the ethical calculus she is observing by means of compassion for the Marchioness. She remains, because she too shares and bears responsibility.

When she begs the Marchioness to desist in her efforts at the beginning, her original Latin of her phrase, "do not pierce my heart with terrible wounds, is *et cor meum diris* **vulneribus saucies.** This diction echoes and thus calls to mind the terrible, ultimately self-inflicted anguish of Razis in 2 Maccabees 14, 37–46, who also suffered **vulneribus saucies,** and in his rage and frustration at having bungled his suicide, he pulled out his intestines and threw them at the attacking crowd and died, even as he called out to the Lord to give them back to him again. Surely Hildegard did not for a moment suspect that the Marchioness would catch this terrible reference, much less ever think of it as possibly illuminating her own situation. But just as surely (why else would she allude to it) it did occur to Hildegard as an event so charged with passion for the other, and so filled with inflaming anger at the self as to figure her own share of involvement and responsibility for a now unavoidable catastrophe.

After painting the haunting, pastel image of the two girls in the aurora of holy vision, Hildegard's rhetorical heat peaks in the marvelous triplet, that Richardis's election "surely surely surely [certe certe certe]" did not come from God. And then comes the valedictory hope, "may God illuminate and strengthen your mind" to which is added the ice of *memento mori,* "in the short time left," and the letter breaks off.

As she foresaw, the Marchioness did not give in. So Hildegard wrote to the girl's brother, Hartwig:

Hildegard to Hartwig, Archbishop of Bremen, brother of the nun Richardis von Stade. 1151–52. Excerpt. [Van Acker, 27–28]

[**Et esto lucida stella lucens in tenebris**] And be a brilliant star, shining in the dark of night for wayward man, and be a rapid stag running to the spring of living waters. Observe that

---

6. In actual historical fact, their common daughter, Richardis, will be dead in less than a year.

in these days many a pastor is blind and lame, robbing the poor unto death, and stifling the justice of God.

O beloved, how dear your soul is to me, dearer than your engendering [pre genere tuo]. Now listen to me, who lies before your feet in sobs and tears, because my soul is so desolated by a certain dreadful man who in the matter of our dearly beloved daughter Richardis has defied the counsel and will of myself, my other sisters and friends, and has, by his own reckless will, seduced the girl out of our cloister. The almighty God knows well where a shepherd is needed, and a man of belief has no need to go sniffing around for an office. When an unquiet spirit longs to be master, he looks out more for power than for the will of God, and becomes in his office a ravening wolf [lupus rapax est in persona sua]. Such a soul never, believingly, seeks for the Spirit. This is simony [Sed ibi est simonia].

It was not necessary for our abbot to lead this soul, destined for glory, but still unlit and unready, into this act, so blind in mind, and with such great recklessness. If our daughter had remained quiet, God had prepared her well enough for the glory he had willed.

So I implore you, who sit on the episcopal throne according to the order of Melchizedek, begging you by him who gave his life for you, and for the sake of his most noble mother, send my most beloved daughter back to me. A true election of God I will never contest or hinder, wherever it happens. May God bless you with the blessing that Isaac gave his son Jacob; may he bless you with the blessing he gave Abraham for his obedience to the angel.

Now listen to me, do not throw away my words as your mother and your sister and Count Herman threw them away. I do you no injury; this is all without the will of God, or consideration of the health of your sister's soul. I beg you for help so I can console her, and she me. But as I say, I will not contest whatever God orders [quod Deus ordinavit, non contradico].

May God give you the blessing of the dew of heaven, and may the chorus of angels bless you, if you listen to me, the handmaid of God, and fulfill his will in this business [si audieris me famulam Dei et si perfeceris voluntatem Dei in hac causa].

This letter is complicated by the real affection Hildegard obviously felt for Richardis's brother; "your soul is much dearer to me than your engendering" is a poor translation of *multum est mihi amabilis anima tua pre genere tuo*. Hildegard is not talking here only in theological abstractions about the transience of the generated body as opposed to the eternality of the soul. Her term *genere tuo* is also indicative of Hartwig's actual family, his genus, his people: the von Stades. This family had long been close to her; her beloved teacher and sister-anchorite Jutta von Spanheim was a daughter of the Marchioness's uncle, Stephan von Spanheim-Freckleben. The Marchioness herself had helped Hildegard immensely in her own secession from the resistant monks of St. Disibod (who knew a good thing when they saw it) by successfully intervening with Henry, Archbishop of Mainz. In fact, without the Marchioness it is difficult to imagine how she could have been successful in the much more important and much more difficult struggle she waged for her own foundation on the Rupertsberg. The love was difficult all around. Shortly, as we shall see below, Hartwig will answer this letter of Hildegard's with a letter filled with his own bittersweet affection for this older woman, whose only fault had been that she lavished too much love upon his sister. And later, in her final answer to Hartwig, Hildegard will reveal to him that she herself finally saw what must have been all too plain to her friends, as we can deduce by their refusal to acquiesce to her pleas. Dante divided all of our capacity for sin into three kinds of love: misdirected, defective, and excessive. The intensity of Hildegard's excessive love was crushing these girls; it seems very clear that their relatives, who were also close friends of Hildegard, did what they had to do to release them from her power.

There was still one more arrow to shoot: one she had shot before and would shoot again: she wrote to the Pope:

Hildegard to Pope Eugenius III. 1151. [Van Acker, 8–9]

> [**Qui non silet, hec dicit**] He who is not silent speaks this in the face of the weakness of those who are blind while they see and deaf while they hear and mute while they speak in the insidious deathbringing robber's snares of the night. What does he say? The sword flashes and circles and kills them who are crooked in mind.
>
> You in your role are a glittering corselet, first root in the new nuptial of Christ, you are split into two, in the one part the soul is renewed in a mystical flowering, a lady in virginal service, in the other you are root of the Church. Listen to him who is piercing in name and flows in the torrent and who says to you: Turn not the eye from the Eye, deflect not the light from the Light, but stand in the open road; do not be accused

on account of those souls who have been put in your care [in sinum tuum] nor allow them to sink by the power of conniving prelates into the lake of perdition.

A jewel lies in the road; but a bear comes and sees the delicate gem and raises his paw, wishing to lift it and hide it in his breast [in sinum suum]. But an eagle flies down and snatches the jewel into his wings of protection and carries it through the windows into the palace of the king. And now the gem gives off brilliant light before the face of the king, and the king delights in it greatly. And the king, for his love of the gem, gives golden shoes to the eagle, and praises him much for his probity.

Now you who sit in the chair of Christ in his stead, choose for yourself the better part, be the eagle who outwits the bear, adorn the windows of the church with the souls committed to your care, so you will steal away from the enemy and ascend, in golden shoes, to the heights.

Except for the final short paragraph, this entire letter is an elaborate figure spoken in the voice of God that seeks and offers no meaning beyond its own articulation, and certainly there is no pointing outward in external reference. Only at the end does she shift into her own voice in order to provide a kind of gloss; and even here she avoids any search for exterior equivalents, a mode of the characteristically male route of exegesis. Instead she glosses the centripetal compression of the figure of the jewel contended for by the eagle and the bear by bringing forward variants of the same image: she pleads with Eugenius to be an eagle, not a bear. She treats the figure AS a literary, if not actually literal figure: an important characteristic of the feminine style of exegesis. But in whatever style, feminine or male, that Pope Eugenius III read her letter, he read it correctly. For even if he decided to be the bear rather than the eagle, he surely understood about the jewel.

Pope Eugenius III to Hildegard. 1151. Excerpt. [Van Acker, 11]

[... **De cetero super hoc quod a nobis requirere voluisti**] ... By the way, regarding the request you addressed to us, we have given our worthy brother, the Archbishop Henry of Mainz, the following directive: either the Rule will be strictly followed by the sister whom you have transferred to his care in her new institution, or he is to return her to your jurisdiction. This you will read in greater detail from your copy of our letter sent by my chancellery.

His assurance to Hildegard that Richardis would be returned to her if Bassum did not follow the Benedictine Rule rings so resoundingly because it is so hollow.

With no allies in the establishment, Hildegard now wrote Richardis directly. She seems to have begun to come to grips with the ethical ambiguity inherent in the enormous degree of her own personal investment in her love. The severance is now "perfected" in her eyes, there is no further plea for return: now she sees face to face what must be faced.

Hildegard to Richardis, Abbess of Bassum, 1151–52. [Schrader, 137]

[Audi me, *filia*, matrem tuam, in Spiritu tibi dicentem: Dolor meus ascendit.] Hear me daughter. Your mother, within the Spirit, says to you: Pain rises within me. Pain destroys the great trust and comfort I once had in mankind [magnam fiduciam et consolationem quam habui in homine]. From now on I say: "It is better to put trust in the Lord than to put confidence in princes [bonum est sperare in Domino, quam sperare in principibus]. That is, we should look to the one alive on high without any darkenings of earthly love [sine obumbratione amoris] or confidence in the weak, which love possesses the airy humor of earth for such a short time [quam aerius humor terre per breve tempus habet]. Who looks to God aims, like the eagle, his eye into the sun. And that's why we should not place hope in great people, who fall "as the flower falls [sicut flos cadit]." And so I transgressed in loving a noble human being [Hoc transgressa sum, propter amorem nobilis hominis].

Now I say to you: every time I sinned this way, God showed me my sin through some strain or some pain [aut in aliquibus angustiis aut in aliquibus doloribus], as you well know.

Now I say again: Ai me, mother, Ai me, daughter [Heu me mater, heu me filia], "why hast thou forsaken me?" [quare me dereliquisti"] like an orphan? I loved the nobility of your ways, and the wisdom, and the chastity, and your soul, and all of your life; so much that many said to me, What are you doing?

Now all should mourn with me, all those "who have any sorrow, like unto my sorrow [omnes qui habent dolorem similem dolori meo]," who have in their love of God such charity in their hearts and in their minds toward mankind, like that which I had in you, which in an instant is ravished away from me, even as you have been taken from me. But may God's angel stride always the path before you, and may the Son of God protect you, and his mother keep you. Remember your wretched mother Hildegard, and may your felicity not fade.

Before examining this letter sequentially, it is important to capture a vivid sense of its central, cohering theme: which is the way in which time, in a lapsed world, reveals its passage most tellingly in those entropic transformations that figure the process of dissolution. The letter closes with the hope that Richardis's "felicity may not fade away." But this sense of metamorphic process is sounded in this letter earlier, and most authoritatively by the voice of the Psalmist as he warns about placing hope in people rather than the Lord, and that is most cohesively captured in the concentrated image: *flos cadit* (the flower falls, fails, fades).

Yet even as Hildegard figures this dissolving sense of time's flow in the flow of her own discourse, she also shores up particular moments, by recapturing for us images in which this hemorrhaging of time seems to stop, and is reconfigured, for a moment, into a sense of space and perdurability. To help create two such "spatial moments" she chooses two successive tableaux from the collective memory of the crucifixion: Christ *in extremis*, and the pietà, the image of Mary holding the body of her dead son on her lap after he has been taken down from the cross. By inserting allusions to these tableaux, she engages her arts of suspension, which is at the heart of the feminine poetics of revelation. And she manages, in this letter that seems and is so personal, so directly mediating her uniquely personal anguish to her lost daughter, to reveal, at the same time, its ultimate validation as an imperfect fulfillment of that filial relation figured in the history of Jerusalem, and "perfectly" figured in the final events of the life of Christ.

To proceed in more detail. In Psalm 117 from which Hildegard quotes, the Psalmist teaches, from the particularity of his own experience, that:

> it is better to trust in the Lord
> than to put confidence in man;
> it is better to trust in the Lord
> than to put confidence in princes.

Hildegard chooses the second half of this verse, with its reference to princes, rather than the first, with its more democratic, generic "man," because it is precisely the aristocratic position of the von Stades that she sees has seduced Richardis away from her. Just as important, however, is that Hildegard's attitude is deeply ambivalent: in fact she made it no secret that she felt that part of the true value of Richardis lay precisely in her aristocratic generation: that she WAS a descendant of princes, and thus embodied all the promise and value of that heritage. This real admiration Hildegard felt for the aristocracy may also help prepare us for the stunning move she makes later on, as she identifies Richardis with Christ, who also carried the promise of his human heritage within him, as the son of David.

But the point of the Psalmist is still a general lesson learned out of the particularity of experience: because the flesh fails, we pass the words along. And that sense of deterioration in a lapsed world is concentrated in the classic image that Hildegard also brings forward from the Psalmist: *sicut flos cadit*, as the flower falls, fails, fades. The phrase occurs at least three times in scripture, twice in another double verse of the Old Testament (Isaiah 40. 7 and 8), and once in New Testament James, in a moment when he is recalling specifically the same forefiguring moment in Isaiah. By using a phrase by which the New Testament itself recalls the Old Testament to establish the truth of its own experience, Hildegard doubles the effect by using both testaments to validate the truth of her own. We do well to hear a bit more of the contextual resonance that the phrase *sicut flos cadit* brings to the ear of one versed in the text, as we hear Hildegard both use and quote the image:

First Isaiah:

> All flesh is grass, and all the goodliness therof is as the flower of the field: The grass withereth, the flower fadeth; Because the spirit of the Lord bloweth upon it: Surely the people is grass. The grass withereth, the flower fadeth: But the word of our God shall stand forever.

And then James, who emphasized how especially bitter it is when the rich and powerful (one thinks of such as the von Stades) reveal the same weakness as the poor:

> For the sun is no sooner risen with a burning heat, but it withereth the grass, and the flower therof falleth, and the grace of the fashion of it perisheth: so also shall the rich man fade away in his ways.

For the biblically "literate" Richardis, long a student of Hildegard, all these images must have resonated in her memory when she read Hildegard saying:

And that's why we should not place hope in great people, who fail as the flower falls [quo deficit *sicut flos cadit*].

This extraordinarily personal letter to Richardis actually begins with quotation: ***Audi** me filia*, two tiny fragments of the voice of the Psalmist surrounding Hildegard's reference to her self in the first person pronoun: "**Hearken** to me **O Daughter.**" We have seen how powerful such tiny fragments can be: they call up entire vistas embedded in the more extended discourse from which they are snatched, and these vistas linger before the eyes of the reader as a kind of enabling context for reading the passage in which they are quoted. Here, *Audi* and *filia* represent the corporate wisdom of revelation as embodied in the Latin of the Psalmist. That authority of the ages frames and thereby validates as universally significant the vernacular of her own private self-referencing. And it is not just the general resonance of these two words; but the fact that the situation they call up in Psalm 44/45 is paradigmatic for the situation of Richardis, as seen by that avatar of the Old Testament, Hildegard herself as prophet and psalmist rediviva:

> Hearken O daughter, and consider, and incline thine ear;
> Forget also thine own people, and thy father's house;
> So shall the king greatly desire thy beauty:
> For he is thy Lord; and worship thou him.

Hildegard pleads with Richardis as the Psalmist pleaded to Jerusalem: leave the sphere of influence of your family and cleave to God as Father and King. We should probably also listen to the delicate, but insistent way that the Old Testament verse mingles echoes of the erotic tradition of the epithalamion here: "leave thy father's house and cleave to thy husband." It slightly tickles the ear as one hears in Hildegard's quotation the merest whisper of a suppressed erotics at work, raising even further our sense of the temperature of the discourse written on the Rupertsberg.

Hildegard moves to closure in this letter with what may appear a wildly extravagant gesture: she addresses Richardis in a double identification of both mother and daughter: "heu me mater, heu me filia," even as she identifies herself as Christ by speaking, in Vulgate translation, his last words: *Eli, Eli, lamma sabbacthani*: "God, my God: Why hast thou forsaken me [quare dereliquisti]?"[7] In the echo chamber of

---

7. Cf. Matthew 27.46. "Eli, Eli, lamma sabbacthani? hoc est: Deus meus, Deus meus, utquid dereliquisti me?" And Mark 15.34 "Et hora nona exclamavit Jesus voce magna, dicens: Eloi, Eloi, lamma sabbacthani? quod est interpretatum: Deus meus, Deus meus,

this phonic ricochet, Richardis appears to Hildegard as a sudden trinity of Mother–Daughter–God, while Hildegard projects herself to Richardis as the Christ-God hanging *in extremis* on the cross in front of Richardis as his/her observing mother Mary. By means of her feminine weave of quotation, we see in our mind's eye Hildegard and Richardis in both places (on the cross and on the ground), in both genders, in both natures (God and humanity) and in both roles (as mother and daughter), all at once.

If such a thing seems possible, she then intensifies the maternity of her parental imagery even further as she adds to Christ's last question, "why hast thou forsaken me," this tag from John's report of the Last Supper: "like an orphan [sicut orphanam]." But it is really a mirror-echo of John. As we hear Mother Hildegard as Christ say "**quare me dereliquisti sicut orphanum**" we hear the voice of Christ at once speaking to the Father in isolation on the cross, and also speaking to his disciples around the Passover table, when he spoke to them at length about joining the Father:

> I am the way . . . No one comes to the Father except through me. . . . Do you not believe that I am in the Father and the Father is in me? . . . I do not speak on my own. . . . I will not leave you orphans [**non relinquam vos orphanos**]: I am coming to you . . . In a little while the world will no longer see me, but you will see me because I live. On that day you will know that I am in my Father, and you in me, and I in you. [John 14, my emphasis]

As the promise of filial linkage resounds in Christ's promise not to forsake his disciples as if they were orphans, so Hildegard says, in his voice, surely with the sense of John's Christ and the Father speaking in and through her: "I [your mother/father] will not abandon you [my daughter] like an orphan [as you, my mother, have abandoned me, your daughter]: I will come to you on that latter day and you and I will know that we are in the Father and in one another."

The coalescing figure that finally reconciles all this difference-present-in-simultaneity is, appropriately, the Blessed Virgin herself. As Hildegard crafts her discourse so as to figure the simultaneity of Richardis and herself as both mother and daughter to and for each other, she

---

utquid dereliquisti me?" Christ's words here are of course a fulfilling echo of the voice of the Psalmist in 21/22.2: "Deus, Deus meus, quare me dereliquisti?" As the Psalmist to God "in his incessant roaring day and night," so Christ to God in the agony of his extremity, and so Hildegard to Richardis in her abandonment.

also, by quoting to Richardis several key words from the Lamentations of Jeremiah, figures forth the paradigmatic, reconciling image of Mary in the posture of the pietà: Mary who is herself both the mother and the daughter of her own son; so Dante's St. Bernard in later confirmation prays to her: "O Virgin, daughter of thy son [O virgine, figlia del tuo figlio]."

Hildegard sounds this marian resonance by writing: "now all should mourn with me, all those who have any sorrow like unto my sorrow [omnes qui habent dolorem similem dolori meo]. In Lamentations, Jeremiah cries out in the voice of a lamenting woman: "All ye that pass by, behold and see if there be any sorrow like unto my sorrow [O vos omnes, qui transistis per viam, attendite, et videte, si est dolor sicut dolor meus]." Hildegard's diction is very close, but not identical with that of Jeremiah. The closeness nails down the parallel, the slight difference in words reminds one of the difference in situation: "How does the City sit solitary that was full of people [Quomodo sedet sola civitas plena populo]?" Hildegard signals to Richardis that she speaks as the City/Mother who has lost her People/children. But traditional iconography of the pietà also appropriates this verse of Jeremiah and assigns it in a New Testament fulfillment to the lips of mourning Mary holding and beholding her dead son. So in quoting Jeremiah, and speaking in the voice of the *cività dolente,* she echoes down from the prophet to the Mary who has lost her Christ, and ends up speaking in her own voice as the Hildegard who has lost her Richardis.

In her last letter to Richardis, she takes even further the doubling that she figured so powerfully in her letter to Richardis's mother, the Marchioness. As she sees both Richardis and herself as Mother to each other she reveals the way in which, for her, woman is always already mother to all otherness. And the maternal promise of both Richardis and Hildegard as potential biological mothers of real children will of course, by necessity of abbatial office and profession of virginity, be lost to actual history. But as Hildegard places their situation firmly within the paradigms of biblical revelation, she reveals how their common motherhood nonetheless lives in the greater reality of the Mind of God as an inherent, feminine, and eternal latency for both women; this cosmic fact of the religious life is also celebrated here *in figura.*

Hildegard's letter to Richardis closes with a prayer: "May God's angel stride always the path before you [Sed **precedat te angelus** Dei]. We must hear behind the voice of Hildegard, as Richardis surely did, the more extended voice of the God of Exodus full of warning as well as promise, as he freed his people from bondage and sent them off on the pilgrimage to the promised land:

[Behold I send an angel of mine to stride before thee [Ecce ego mittam **angelum** meum, qui **precedat te**], to keep thee in the way, and to bring thee into the place which I have prepared. Beware of him, and obey his voice, provoke him not; for he will not pardon your transgressions: for my name is in him. but if thou shalt indeed obey his voice, and do all that I speak: then I will be an enemy unto thine enemies, and an adversary unto thine adversaries. [Exodus, 23, 20–23, emphasis mine]

In the echo of this passage from Exodus sounds the true note of valedictory in her letter to Richardis. The struggle is over; Hildegard is really letting her go, just as God let the Hebrews go out of bondage. It is illuminating, even moving, to imagine Hildegard calculating the full implication of this allusion: also figuring herself as a possible Egypt. Perhaps just as moving is our hindsight knowledge that the promised land for Richardis was not, after all, a *renovatio* of the cloister of Bassum near Bremen, but the Jerusalem Celestial on the other side of death.

It is not on record that Richardis answered this letter; yet in a way she did, but through the voice of her brother Hartwig. Richardis fell ill and died, on October 29, 1152—the year her brother joined Barbarossa in Würzburg. Hartwig sent Hildegard this news:

Hartwig, Archbishop of Bremen, to Hildegard, 1152. [Van Acker, 29]

[**Hildegardi, magistre sororum sancti Ruperti in Christo**] To Hildegard, mistress of sisters in Christ of Saint Rupert, from Hartwig, Archbishop of Bremen, and brother of abbess Richardis, in place of his sister, and more than his sister, obedient.

I tell you that she, our sister, mine, no yours, mine in the body, yours in the soul, [sororem nostram illam, meam, immo tuam, meam corpore, tuam anima] has gone the way of all flesh. She learned to hold as little the honor I secured for her, and as I must go to the King of the earth, she submitted to her Lord the King of heaven, and confessed in piety and sanctity, and was anointed with holy oil after confession, she had lived fully to the end a Christian [et habita plena christianitate] and in tears, desired, with all her heart, to return to your cloister, and she committed herself to the Lord through his mother and John. She confessed the trinity by three times crossing herself, and, we are certain of it, she died in perfect faith in God, and in hope, and in love, in the fourth calends of November.

Therefore I beg you, if I be worthy, and as forcefully as I can, that you love her as she loved you, and if it appears to you that she failed your love, it came not from her, but from me; there are many witnesses to the tears that she shed as she left your cloister. And if death had not stopped her, she would have come, by the permission just arrived, back to you. And since death has kept her, know this, that I shall come, if God wills, in her stead.

But God, who repays all goodness [qui remunerator omnium bonorum est], for that goodness that you, among and above all her relatives and friends, showed to her, for which she thanked God—and even me, may he now and in future repay you according to your every desire [et in futuro ad omnem voluntatem tuam te remuneret]. And pass on to your sisters as well her thanks for all their beneficence [referas sororibus tuis de omnibus beneficiis suis gratias].

This is a deeply moving and highly rhetorical letter; and Hartwig's scrupulous care for rhetorical craft has much to do with its affective power.

Hartwig's central theme that threads through this letter is the fundamental substitutability between Richardis and himself that he hopes will lead to parity in Hildegard's eyes. Hartwig obviously sees this as a prerequisite for reaching some sort of balance between justice and grace; this concern culminates in his emphasis on the interlock between divine and human repayment [*remunere*] and gratitude [*gratias*] at the close of his letter.

The letter opens as if it were somehow being sent by both the sister and the brother, as he addresses Hildegard as a *magistra* of sisters, and himself as "brother of abbess Richardis, in place of his sister, and more than his sister, obedient [loco sororis et plus quam sororis, obedientiam]."

But as so often, the similarity that makes the notion of substitutability possible also insists on an often illuminating difference. And the opening difference for Hartwig is that at least now, Hartwig, more than his sister Richardis, will be obedient. As he then informs Hildegard, in scriptural formula, that Richardis has departed this life, we wonder perhaps what Hartwig really means by "obedientiam." In any primary sense, of course, he is referring to Richardis's refusal to remain on the Rupertsberg with Hildegard. But are we to hear a subtext here that also hints that Richardis's dying was an act of disobedience to Hartwig? Or that her apparent decision to return to the Rupertsberg, would have involved disobedience to him even as it would be a renewal of her original vow of obedience to Hildegard? Hartwig clearly shows real affection for Hildegard in this letter; is there a hint of suppressed rivalry as well?

Then, in accord with the theme of substitutability, Hartwig claims a deep familial relationship with Hildegard by means of the lovely and brilliant *confusio* by which he identifies the dead Richardis not by name now, but rather in terms of the sibling relationship that she bore to each of them: "she our sister, mine, no thine, mine in the body, thine in the spirit [sororem nostram illam, meam, immo tuam, meam corpore, tuam anima].

Hartwig continues to balance the theme of substitutability and parity again in another trope: each has been called to their king. "I must go to the earthly king[8], and she obeyed the summons of the Lord, King of heaven [Regi celorum Domino obedisse suo]." We hear the word obedient yet again in the discourse.

Then he says Richardis committed herself to God through his mother and John. This bears some consideration. He can only be referring to the *stabat mater* as uniquely dramatized in the gospel of John:

> When Jesus saw his mother and the disciple whom he loved standing beside her, he said to his mother, "Woman, here is your son." Then he said to the disciple, "Here is your mother."

Who, for Hartwig, is figuring forth whom as he calls up this image of Richardis committing her spirit into the hands of the Lord? Surely he is signalling iconographically to Hildegard that in this trinity of love, the dying Richardis figured for him Christ dying on the Cross, while he himself is "represented" by Christ's "brother" John, the disciple whom he loved standing beside the mother: and the final implication is that the mother(s) attending this act of dying, is a composite of the Marchioness and Hildegard, who, like all women, in some deep blend of body and spirit, were always already prefigured, as well as ultimately to be fulfilled, by Mary the mother of Jesus.

In the penultimate paragraph comes his confession, his intention to make sufficient satisfaction, and his request for absolution. And again his imaging includes the reciprocal substitutability of himself for and by his dead sister. We hear that Richardis had already decided to give up her abbatial rank and return to Hildegard on the Rupertsberg, and that official permission for her to do so had only recently arrived. But as God kept her back, Hartwig offers himself in substitution, and he

---

8. Hartwig has been summoned to the imperial parliament in Würzburg, that was held in the last half of October in 1152. That fact allows us to date Richardis's death.

shall, if God wills, come in her stead. What to make of all this substitution: including the figural substitution of Richardis for the dying Christ?

We know from her own letters to Richardis and the Marchioness that precisely this kind of figuration is part of Hildegard's own profound intuition concerning human relationships in this world. But if Hartwig reflects what is essentially a "male" understanding of the figural relation, which involves keeping the entities separate so as to allow for such substitution, Hildegard figures the entities as co-present, as joined and integrated in the new feminine synthesis of her holy vision, as simultaneously there. For Hartwig, things are either/or, hence this **for** that: for Hildegard, things are both/and, hence this **as** that. Both the male and feminine modes of such figural intuition are in full accord with the medieval doctrine that each of us has the power to mirror forth the possibility inherent in the other. This doctrine also reconciles gender difference into a holistic vision of the plurality of man and woman joined and read as a single, unified image of God. It ultimately derives from the double guarantee of Genesis: "In the image of God created he him; man and woman created he them [ad imaginem Dei creavit illum, masculum et feminam creavit eos]." This is the theological linchpin that enables and validates both Hartwig's and Hildegard's modes of mutual figuration.

Hartwig closes his letter hoping for the "remuneration" of God in the heart of Hildegard and, since the flesh of Richardis failed, requesting Hildegard to pass her "gratias" on to her sisters in "remuneration" for their many beneficent works.

We close this brief study of Hildegard's epistolary record of the affair of Richardis von Stade with her reply to Archbishop Hartwig. Perhaps the most striking aspects of her last letter in the record regarding the now double loss of Richardis is the haunting image of a mystic love affair between God and her daughter. It is also important for her to say, and for Hartwig and for us to know, that she was taught to love Richardis by God himself, as he impelled her from the living light of her inner vision:

Hildegard to Hartwig, Archbishop of Bremen, 1152. [Van Acker, 30–31]

[O quam magnum miraculum est in salvatione animarum]
How great is the wonder of the soul's salvation of those God looked on, so that his glory does not darken within them. For God works in them as a fierce warrior, who strives not to be overcome by anyone, so that victory will last.

Now listen, beloved. So it was with my daughter Richardis, whom I name both daughter and mother. My heart was full of love for her, for the living light, in a most powerful vision [vivens lux fortissima visione], taught me to love her.

Listen. God took her with zeal, so that mortal desire [voluptas seculi] would have no power to embrace her; and she always fought it, even though she herself appeared as a flower in the beauty and adornment and in the symphony of this world. But as she remained in the body, I heard, in true revelation [in vera visione], this said of her: "O Virginity standing in the royal bridal chamber [O Virginitas, in regali thalamo stas]." For she ranks as a virginal branch in the most holy orders, and the daughters of Zion delight in her. But the ancient of serpents desired to pull her away from the sacred honor of her high human birthright. So the high judge drew her, my daughter, to him, and cut her off from all human praise and desire. And now my soul has great trust in her, though they loved her beautiful form and her prudence when she lived in the world. But God loved her more. For God would not accede to her lover, would not abandon to his rival, the world, his beloved [noluit Deus amicam suam dare inimoco amatori, id est mundo].

And now to you, dearest Hartwig, as you sit in the chair of Christ, perfect the will of the soul of your sister, just as necessity requires obedience. As she always looked after you, look after her soul; do good works as she herself studied to do [fac bona opera secundum studium ipsius]. And I shall ban from my heart the pain that you brought through my daughter. May God grant you dew of his grace through the voice of his saints, and blessed repayment in life's future [et beatam remunerationem in futuro seculo].

We jump now nearly a quarter of a century, to watch Hildegard in old age answer what she seems to have agreed was the most difficult challenge of her life.

LETTER TO THE
PRELATES OF MAINZ

We turn to one of Hildegard's greatest epistles, her Letter to the Prelates of Mainz. In the last year of her life, a local citizen was buried on the Rupertsberg in accordance with custom. Several days after the burial, Hildegard received notice from the chapter house in Mainz that she must exhume the man and remove the corpse from the sacred precinct because he had died ex communicate. She refused to do so, for she was convinced by everything she knew that the man had fully reconciled himself to the church before he died, and the entire service had been conducted in "the presence of all Bingen" without anyone's having made any objection. To exhume him now, she argued, would be to violate the holy sacrament of burial. Her masters in Mainz then laid on Hildegard and her community the penalty of interdiction: in particular, they forbade the sacrament of the Eucharist and the performance of music in the orders of worship. Such interdiction, as the prelates in Mainz well knew, would work as extremely harsh punishment for the "disobedience" of Hildegard and her sisters.

After having "obeyed" the interdict for some time, Hildegard "looked into the true light, as was my custom," and was told that she should communicate with the cathedral in Mainz and argue for a reversal of the interdict. She then, at the age of eighty, composed her Letter to the Prelates of Mainz and went in person to read it to them. Whatever their personal response, in terms of providing any official relief, they remained unmoved. She then wrote to the Archbishop of Mainz, Christian von Buch, a brilliant field marshall and chancellor of the empire, who was currently in Rome, negotiating an end to schism between Barbarossa and Pope Alexander III. He answered her request to lift the interdiction with a face-saving set of conditions: that a special investigation must show that the man in question had in fact been reconciled to the church before he died. Such an investigation was duly made, the findings were as Hildegard had maintained all along, and the interdict was lifted six months before her death.

The entire letter is well worth careful reading and detailed commentary. Because of its length relative to other letters examined here, I will identify each paragraph of the letter with the Van Acker line numbers of the *Continuatio Medievalis* edition for easier cross reference, and, rather than leaving discussion of particulars to the end of the letter, I will interrupt at major thematic shifts and interleave commentary between sections.

Hildegard to the Prelates of Mainz. 1178–79.[9]

[1–12]
> **[In visione que anime mee antequam nata procederem]** In that vision imprinted in my soul already prior to birth by the

---

9. Van Acker, *Epistolarium*, 61–66. The letter as published in *PL* 197(218C-43B) is in fact a mixed string of letters and for our purposes unreliable. See also *PL* 46(218C-21D).

God of Creation, I saw myself impelled to write the following regarding the interdict laid upon us by our spiritual superiors on account of the dead man, carried, without any objections, by his priests and by us, to his grave [conductu sacerdotis sui apud nos sine calumnia sepultum]. When a few days after the burial our masters ordered his ejection from the cemetery, I felt no little horror, and looked, as is my custom, into the true light [ad verum lumen ut soleo aspexi] and with vigilant eyes I saw within my soul that, if the body of the dead man were in fact exhumed according to their order, the removal would cause the threat of great danger, like a black cloud announcing bad weather and storms.

[13–26]

So we did not presume to remove the body of the dead man who had confessed, received communion and extreme unction, and been buried without disputation. And we did not agree with those who had advised or ordered this counsel or command. Not that we gave little weight to the advice of wise men, nor the orders of prelates, but wished to forestall the hue and cry of outraged women by removing the sacrament of Christ that had strengthened the man when alive. But that we not appear disobedient in all things, we have, according to the interdict, stopped singing the songs of the praise of the Lord, and abstained from partaking of our Lord's body, as we by custom have done every month—for which my sisters and I were afflicted with great bitterness and fell into deep sorrow. Then finally, nearly crushed by that heavy burden, I heard, in my vision, the following words [verba ista in visione audivi]:

[26–36]

"Because of the words of men [propter verba humana], it is forbidden to send you the sacrament, which is for your health, and dressed in the Words of God [indumenti Verbi Dei], who was born in virginal nature of Mary the Virgin [in virginea natura ex Maria Virgine]; therefore you must seek permission from the prelates who have forbidden it. For ever since Adam was expelled from the bright region of paradise into the exile of this world, the conceiving of all people has been corrupted by the power of that primal transgression. Thus it was found necessary, within the impenetrable counsels of God, that a man be born of human nature, but without the blemish of any wound [homo ex humana natura sine contagio totius lesionis]; by whom all those predestined to life will be cleansed of filth.

[36–46]

"And in order that they will remain joined forever in him, and he in them, they shall, in partaking of his body, become one with him, and thus sanctified. And whoever like Adam are disobedient to the prescriptions of God and completely forget Him, they must be kept from receiving his body—even as they have themselves turned away from him in their disobedience—until cleansed through contrition, they receive again their superior's license to unite themselves to the body of Christ through communion. But those who know truly that they are not bound by such interdiction, neither in conscience nor will [nec conscientia nec voluntate], they may in full confidence partake of this vivifying sacrament [vivifici sacramenti], so as to cleanse themselves with the blood of the unspotted Lamb [mundandus sanguine Agni immaculati] which, itself in obedience to the Father, permitted for all our sakes its own immolation on the altar of the cross [in ara crucis immolari]."

[47–55]

In this same vision I heard I am guilty in this: that I did not come in all humility and devotion to the presence of my masters, in order to beg license from them for communion, especially since we had done no sin by accepting the corpse of a man for whom all Christian rites had been performed, who was brought by his priests, with all of Bingen in procession, and without disputation, laid to rest in a grave in our precinct [sine contradictione apud nos sepultus esset]. And this was laid upon me by our Lord to announce [nuntianda mihi divinitus imposita sunt] to you, our lords and bishops.

[1–26] She begins with the story, told from her perspective, of the burial of the man in question. Her web of reasons for refusing to exhume him captures a number of arresting images: avoiding black clouds announcing bad weather, and forestalling the bacchantic cries of outraged women. These women, presumably of the family of the deceased, would be outraged because she would have removed from them the solace of the sacrament of Christ, in this case the sacrament of holy burial, a sacrament which had provided balm for the soul of the man while living, and the incentive to reconcile himself to the church in the first place. Such solace, of course, is precisely what the prelates have removed from her and her sisters: the solace of Christ; but for them it was the sacrament of the new life brought by the Eucharist. True to her revelatory style, Hildegard establishes contrastive, yet co-present (not alternative) pairs of images to set up and help establish her meaning.

Her obedience to Christ in burying the man has been read by her masters as disobedience to them, and brought interdiction. "And that we not appear disobedient in all things, we have, according to the interdict, stopped singing the songs in praise of the Lord, and abstained from partaking of his body." And so she sounds the main theme of her letter, the complicated calculus of obedience, and begins to weave its rich linking to the benefits of sacred communion and the practice of music within and across the shared, and often colliding domains of God and humanity.

Even as she signals her decision to humble herself as a suppliant in obedience to the prelates, she asserts her moral and theological superiority over them. She uses the plural form, which in the humility of supplication would include her sisters, but on the high ground from which she feels herself speaking, can be attributed to her as the grammatical and rhetorical right of her own singular and particular person, due to the elevation and power of her rank and office: "We did not agree with those who advised or ordered this counsel or command." The ambiguity that she assumes can be read into the situation, that the order to exhume could be read as advice and counsel rather than order or command, buys considerable space for her at this "negotiation" table, even as one is sure that the prelates themselves read no such ambiguity into the situation. It is, after all, a rhetorical and not a legal space that she appropriates for herself here. She also floats the gender issue in terms that the male prelates might be likely to swallow, at least at first, because it seems so appropriately antifeminist: "Not that we gave little weight to the advice of wise men, nor the orders of prelates." But the trained ear hears that in this apparent sop to their male superiority she has in fact rhetorically vitiated any possibility that prelates could also be wise men; or that their orders could really be construed as collegial advice. She refused to exhume because she wished to "forestall the hue and cry of outraged women." But even as she seems to privilege the words of wise men, and feed male vanity by marginalizing the noise of outraged women, the more perceptive of the prelates she is addressing would soon realize that such female outrage would have been justified, just as her sisters' sorrow justifies their request for a lifting of the interdiction by these unwise, order-giving men. The rhetorical risks she runs here are high, but so are the stakes; and God, she is sure, is on her side. And one shouldn't forget, after all, that she ultimately triumphed.

In any case, she reports that the abstinence from the soul-healing harmonies of communion and music brought so much sorrow and pain to her community that she turned to the living light of inner vision and heard a voice command her to seek from the prelates a reversal of interdiction.

[26–55] It is the voice of God (vox Dei) that now speaks and gives her this command, a voice that then delivers a sermon on the theology of the Eucharist as grounded in the linked need for, and role played by, the Incarnation in universal history.

Her vox Dei opens with word play on the word "word." The interdict forbidding God's "sending" the Eucharist is made up of human words [*verba humana*] while the sacrament which is being denied the community is imaged as a holy parody of the Incarnation: the sacrament is figured as the very body of Christ "dressed in the words of God [*indumenti Verbi Dei*]. This verbal cloak of ritual sanctification that dresses the presence of Christ in the form of the Eucharist is, in the living sign of the sacrament, the manna of our daily bread, but it is also the flesh that dresses the Word that is the historical Christ which one partakes in the bread as transubstantiated. This elaborate incarnational "word/Word" play spoken by the vox Dei leads immediately into a meditation on the original need for the Incarnation in the first place. And the ludic extension of paronomasia in the double use of the word virgin is extended back in history to Mary and her nature [in virginea natura ex Maria Virgine]. Among its other functions here, the word play itself comprises a ludic figure of the mutual reciprocities in which we see the capacity of human language to incarnate the Word of God.

According to Hildegard's vox Dei, it was because of the need to purge the filth caused by the lesions of the fall that Christ was sent to us, and in order that the original link of union between Christ and humanity that was present in Eden may be restored, the sacrament of the Eucharist was instantiated. Hildegard then has the vox Dei completely collapse any sense of historical time between then and now, as she moves from the image of the fall in Eden as the originating reason for the instantiation of the Eucharist, directly to the act of prelatical interdiction in Bingen that is now preventing her from partaking of it. And with the recall of the fact of interdiction comes the recall of the issue of obedience that is supposed to have led to it.

The vox Dei directly stipulates that all who disobey the prescriptions of God **should** be kept from receiving his body, "even as they have turned away from it in their disobedience." Such interdiction, says her Vox, should hold firm until there is a "cleansing through contrition and they receive once again license from their superiors to receive holy communion." Her divine voice may at first seem to be acquiescing to the prelatical reading of the situation; but this is only a trap for the prelates. We find at the end of the letter, as they must have done, that the "cleansing of contrition" on which renewed license is contingent will be required not of Hildegard and her sisters, but of the prelates themselves (see her later reference to Paul, Romans 12.8). But we do not have to wait that long for a reversal. Her vox Dei takes away with the other hand what it seems to have just granted with this one. It goes on to say that those who "know truly that they are not bound by such interdiction, neither in conscience nor in will, may in full confidence partake of this vivifying sacrament." The "they" obviously refers to herself and her community, and constitutes, at least rhetorically, a divinely sanctioned threat to disobey interdiction. It is a threat only slightly veiled; her community may at any time, in full theological justification, violate the interdict in order to "cleanse themselves" not by contrition, which in their case is unnecessary, but by the primary sacrament itself, of partaking, in an Antigone-like higher obedience to God, of the cleansing blood of the Lamb: "which itself, in obedience to the Father [qui **seipsum obediens** Patri], permitted its own immolation on the altar of the cross [in ara crucis immolari permisit]. The Latin through which Hildegard's vox Dei here speaks is also the translated Latin of the Greek written by Paul to the Phillipians (2.6–8): "but he emptied himself [sed semetipsum exinanivit] . . . and became obedient to death, even death upon the cross [humiliavit **semetipsum** factus **obediens** usque ad mortem, mortem autem crucis]." These "mots sous les mots," these "words under the words" reveal the larger matrix of theological authority that she dramatically demonstrates, rather than explicitly claims, stands behind her: i.e., in speaking Paul's word as it speaks to and for Hildegard, the vox Dei reveals that the authority with which Paul wrote his epistles is also hers. She needs no greater parity with any man than this.

This opening section of the letter concludes with a shift back to her own voice, in which Hildegard herself repeats the divine command to seek a reversal of the interdict. She uses this intermediate rhetorical peroration to state, once again, the evidence that had convinced her that the man had died fully reconciled with the church. And she bypasses any need to make a public spectacle of her own reversal in the matter simply by announcing that her supplication to the prelates was laid upon her by divine imposition [nuntianda mihi divinitus imposita sunt]

The Letter continues, and moves into the realm of music:

[51–61] [**Aspexi etiam aliquid super hoc quod vobis obediendo**]
I also saw something about the fact that we, up to now, in

obedience to you, ceased singing the songs of divine office, which we celebrate only by quietly reading [illud tantum legentes remisse celebramus]. And I heard a voice proceeding from the living light speaking about the diverse kinds of instruments used for praise as spoken by David in the psalm: "Praise him with the sound of the trumpet, praise him with psaltery and the harp," (etc. until): "Let every thing that hath breath praise the Lord [Omnis spiritus laudet Dominum]!"

[61–71]

In such words by which the interior is instructed by the exterior [In quibus verbis per exteriora de interioribus instruimur], how we should convert and give new form to our interior humanity [interioris hominis nostri debeamus] according to the material, composition and quality of the instruments [secundam materialem compositionem vel qualitatem instrumentorum] of holy office used in praising God. And when we set ourselves to it in love, we can rework anew the way in which mankind, seeking the voice of the living Spirit, awoke to the calling [recolimus qualiter homo vocem viventis Spiritus requisivit], which Adam lost through disobedience. Adam's voice before the fall, in his innocence, had no little resonance with the voices of angels singing in praise [non minimam societatem cum angelicarum laudum vocibus], which voice, because of the spirit of his nature, was called to join the spirit by that Spirit which is God [quas ipsi ex spiritali natura sua possident, qui a Spiritu qui Deus est spiritus vocantur].

[71–77]

But that resonance which Adam's voice had with the angel's [similitudinem vocis angelice] in paradise, he lost it, and that kind of knowing [scientia], deeded to him before sinning, died in his sleep [obdormivit], like people awaking grow slowly unsure about what they saw in their dreams. When he gave in to the devil's suggestive deceptions, repugnant to the will of his Creator, he became entangled in the dark of inner unknowing [tenebris interioris ignorantie involutus] by virtue of evil [ex merito iniquitatis].

[78–94]

The True God, who ever pervades the souls of the elect with the light of truth, thus reserving for them their early beatitude, decided in counsel [ex hoc adinvenit consilio], to renew many hearts by the infusion of the prophetic spirit [corda quamplurium infusione prophetici Spiritus innovaret]; through such inner illumination such souls can somewhat recapture the Light that Adam possessed before falling under the sentence of darkness. And to live in that divine sweetness and praise which Adam prior to falling rejoiced in with angels in heaven, and not in the memory of this his exile, the holy prophets, called and led by the same spirit, sang not only psalms and canticles to fire their hearers to devotion, but also invented diverse instruments for the arts and crafts of music [instrumenta musice artis diversa], capable of making many differing sounds, so that with respect to their composition, both in the form as well as in the quality of sound made by those instruments, along with the sense of the words which were sung to them, the audience, as I've said, would be moved and excited by exterior means to interior instruction [audientes, ut predictum est, per exteriora admoniti et exercitati de interioribus erudirentur].

[95–103]

And it is easy to see that eager and wise ones, in imitation of the holy prophets, invented, by their own human arts, many kinds of instruments so they could sing according to the delight in their souls [humana ipsi arte nonnulla organorum genera invenerunt, ut secundum delectationem anime cantare possent]. And a system of finger-like notes was adopted to inscribe the melody which is to be sung, recollecting Adam and the Finger of God, who in the Holy Spirit, formed him, in whose voice could be heard the full and sweet harmonious sound of all the musical arts. And if he had remained in the state he was formed in, the weakness of mortal humanity could never have borne the fullness and power of his voice [infirmitas mortalis hominis virtutem et sonoritatem vocis illius nullatenus ferre posset]

This section of the letter contains one of the most illuminating essays on the theological justification of music in the literature of the middle ages. Hildegard uses her image of the inherent harmonics of musica mundana to illustrate a richly conceived, theologically based psychology that bridges and reconciles the normally tensive domains of divine and human, Old and New Testament, knowing and doing, speculative and practical, all of which dance together in her images of how the interior soul is taught to adjust itself according to love and will by means of its resonant nature, how it can reform its interior in harmonic response to the exterior sounds of instrumental and vocal music. For Hildegard, the human voice, like the humanity that speaks with it, was made in the image of God's logos. And the instruments of music, invented for the purpose of the soul's reformation by the prophets, are a condensed and efficacious imago of the instrumentality of the things of this world which accompany, and thus contextualise and give greater meaning to, the words of praise by which the vox humana images forth its own foundational capacity to mirror, and thus praise, the logos of God.

[56–61] But true to her feminine style of revelation, she begins with a powerful visual image, not an abstract theory. Our mind's eye is called upon to envision Hildegard and her sisters reading the offices quietly behind locked doors, in obedience to the prelatical interdiction, surrounded by conspicuous silence. In the echo chamber of the silence of obedience to the prelates, we hear them disobey the command of the Psalmist, a command that is full of unheard music: "Praise him with the sound of the trumpet . . . , with the psaltery and the harp . . . , with tambourine . . . with strings and pipe . . . with clanging cymbals . . . with loud clashing cymbals . . . Let everything that hath breath praise the Lord [omnis spiritus laudet Dominum].

The breath [spiritus] of all the world's creatures on which the Psalmist calls is the imago of the Holy Ghost [spiritus] which at the point of Genesis thus quickened the world. Hildegard's poetic daring anticipates and matches that of Dante a century later, as she moves ever more deeply into the reciprocities that she envisions at play between God and Creation.

[61–77] She then articulates the core relationship, or *ratio*, by which the soul can reform its own interior by "tuning" itself to the harmonic structures it "hears" ordinating the music of the liturgy. By the ways in which exterior reality can "instruct" interior reality, we can learn "how we should convert and give new form to our interior humanity [interioris hominis nostri debeamus] according to the material, composition and quality of the instruments [secundam materialem compositionem vel qualitatem instrumentorum] of holy office used in praising God."

If we perform this work with appropriate love, we can, in a sense, reverse the process that led to the fall, i.e., "rework anew the way that mankind, at the voice of that calling of the living Spirit, awoke." As she opens this period of her argument with the image of her sisters reading in silence, she closes it with the image of the voice of Adam singing in perfect harmony with the angelic voices in praise of God. And this image slips into the more psychological imagery of dream: Adam lost his voice-as-knowledge, his prelapsarian gift at Creation: it died in his sleep, even as when we awaken, the bright and revelatory dreams we had during the night inevitably fade and disappear. The linking of the singing voice to a kind of prelapsarian mode of knowing, is not only a brilliant and moving image, it is an image of identity and not metaphor. Such linking helps us see how for Hildegard, as well as for the middle ages generally, music was not only an "*ars*" (*musica instrumentalis*), a way of doing and making, but also a true "*scientia,*" (*musica speculativa*), a way of knowing. So when he "lost" his paradisal voice, Adam became entangled in the dark of inner unknowing [tenebris interioris igno-rantie involutus]. Hildegard emphasizes the cosmic dislocation of the fall by the use of a marvelously clashing oxymoron: Lucifer was able to accomplish this undoing by "virtue of his iniquity" [ex merito iniquitatis].

[78–103] Hildegard's next move is to take us back into the time of Old Testamental prophecy and help us imagine the invention of the Psalmist's instruments as part of the program of redemption: to pro-vide a way of countering the enervating memory of our fall, by imagin-ing us as possessing a kind of interior "symphony hall" in which we can "somewhat recapture the light that Adam possessed before falling under the sentence of darkness"—hear an analog of that divine sweet-ness and praise of Adam singing with the angels, and not only the memory of his exile. She anticipates the modernist "new critical" insist-ence on the integrative function in poetry of sound and sense, of form and content, when she repeats (78–94) that the audience would be moved by exterior means to interior instruction as they heard "both the form and quality of the sound made by those instruments, along with the sense of the words which were sung to them."

We note the insistent repetition of how the outer world can be used by the inner life to reshape itself, an implied pedagogics as well as an explicit psychology. Even more illuminating is the sounding of a new theme in the letter, the deeper, Neo-Platonist theme of the role of memory as an urger and instructor of the will in this matter. The theme of recollection comes to the fore in Hildegard's image of how the "fingerlike" notation system for medieval music, she says, makes us "recollect" the finger of God at the point of our creation. Again an image of Genesis is juxtaposed to an image from the contemporary world, and the momentary evacuation of all intervening history makes the two images of then and now extraordinarily vivid in their juxtaposi-tion: the female style here does not assert identity, but rather similitude in which both difference and severance are seen and celebrated even as the similitude provides the ground of comparability required to illuminate that difference. She closes this section with another kind of oxymoron: this is an oxymoron of thought rather than one of words. If Adam had not fallen, his voice would have been so piercingly beautiful that it could not have been borne by we who fell. This apparently "feminine illogicality" is no illogicality at all: the juxtaposition of the world fallen with the world as if still innocent combines both the nostalgia for the might-have-been with the hard reality of what actually occurred: a hauntingly tensive mixture of memory and desire. The letter moves on to link once again, and now in a firmer, more textured manner, the Incarnation to the role of music in holy office, in order to combine the two aspects of the interdict which she sees as complementary mirrors of one another:

[104–115]

[Cum autem deceptor eius, diabolus, audisset quod homo ex inspiratione Dei cantare cepisset] And then his deceiver, the devil, hearing how mankind could sing when inspired by God, was put in mind of the sweet canticles he once heard sung in his celestial fatherland. Seeing his cunning machinations rendered vain and powerless, he became frightened. He used his powerful and multifarious iniquities to bring the comforts, beauty and sweetness of the Songs of Praise to God into discord and dispersion within the hearts of men, not only by means of evil suggestions and unclean thoughts and countless distractions, but also, wherever he could, even in the mouth of the church, by means of disputes, scandal, and unjust sanctions.

[116–125]

Therefore you and all great prelates must proceed with the greatest care, before you stop up the mouth of the church from singing the praise of God through interdiction, or suspend either performance or participation in divine sacrament; you must prove to the utmost whether the case warrants the action, and be moved only by desire for God's justice, and not by perturbation of spirit, or desire for revenge. You must in such cases of judgment remain vigilant, so as not to be deceived by Satan, who desires nothing more but to remove and withhold from humanity the harmony of heaven and pleasure of paradise.

[126–137]

Consider then, as the Body of Jesus Christ was born, through the agency of the Holy Spirit, from the chastity of the Virgin Mary [ex integritatis Virginis Marie natum est], just so is the canticle of praise, which accords with the harmony of the spheres, rooted, by the power of that same Holy Spirit, in the church [sic etiam canticum laudum secundum celestem harmoniam per Spiritum Sanctum in Ecclesia radicatum est]. In truth, the body is the cloak of the soul [Corpus vero indumentum est anime] which speaks its life through the voice; that is why body must sing the praise of God with the soul in one voice. And so the prophetic spirit rejoices in the sound and the joy of the cymbals, and God is praised by the sounding of the other instruments of music which the wise and the fervent invented, because all of the arts which are useful and necessary to humanity have been quickened by the breath which God blew into the human body; and thus it is just that God be praised in and by all things.

[138–145]
Often in hearing the canticles, man breathes and sighs, and thus by his nature recollecting celestial harmony, the prophets, most subtly sounding the natural depth of the spirit, and knowing something of the symphony of the soul, exhort us in the psalm to praise God with the zither, and sing psalms to him in the accompaniment of the ten-stringed psaltery. The deeper tone of the zither figures the body's energy, the harp with its higher tones the will of the spirit, and the ten strings the sum of the commandments.

[104–125] Hildegard again collapses history as she begins this penultimate section of her letter with a recollection of the role of the serpent in the fall. As she completes her inventory of his strategies for disrupting the harmony in Eden, she includes the interdict of the prelates of Mainz: "Not only by means of evil suggestions, etc., but also . . . even in the mouth of the church, by means of disputes, scandal, and unjust sanctions." She warns the prelates, in the light of the lesson of Eden, not to be deceived by Satan, who, like the prelates, likes nothing better than to "withhold from humanity the harmony of heaven."

[126–137] She recalls again the Incarnation in the womb of the Virgin by the means of the logos, the musical breath of God, and she repeats the parallel of the body-as-cloak to the soul and the Verbum-qua-Caro of Christ even as she repeats the exterior/interior relationship that obtains between the sound of music and the state of the soul. The set-up for the final articulation of exactly HOW this relationship between exteriority and interiority works is complete, and we move once again into the domain of memory.

[138–145] She situates her enabling, and ultimately Platonic theory of memory firmly within the theory of the capacity of the psyche to "adjust" itself, to harmonize with the unheard Pythagorean structures that ordinate the heard music of liturgical performance. This implied theory of the informing power of psychological resonance with phenomenal structures also provides a way of understanding our response to truth and beauty as one of overwhelming delight, even, and especially perhaps, when it happens the first time. When we see something true and beautiful we react with the delight of recognition, a kind of déjà vu, even if we have never experienced the phenomenon that triggers it in our lives before. How does this happen?

The answer lies implicit in Hildegard's unforgettable image of our breathing and sighing as we remember heaven upon hearing the canticles. "Often in hearing the canticles, man breathes and sighs, thus by his nature recollecting celestial harmony [in auditu alicuius cantionis homo sepe suspirat et gemit, naturam celestis harmonie recolens]." The path to Hildegard leads a significant distance from what Dronke calls the "neo-Platonist koinê" (the commonplaces at the heart of the neo-platonist tradition) and it continues on from her and is fulfilled and confirmed by Dante. In the first lines of the *Paradiso*, Dante admits that he cannot remember pictorially what he actually saw in revelation: "for when the intellect approaches its desire, it goes so deep that memory cannot follow it" (Paradiso 1.7–8). What is then his procedure for mediating his vision to us, if he cannot remember what it was he saw? He crafts an image; and he knows that he is approaching truth when inner joy increases as he looks at it. This must be a kind of memory of harmonic resonance that is different from the usual pictorial memory by which we remember images.

In the *Phaedrus*, Plato has Socrates suggest that although the soul has passed through the Lethe of forgetfulness in order to be able to bear the sorrow of separation from the One occasioned by reincarnation, some kind of mnemonic charge remains resident in his soul. When the soul sees something beautiful, it reacts with delight and desire because it **remembers**: it remembers not what it saw when it was one with the guests at the banquet of the gods in heaven, but it does remember a bit of what it felt like to be there. So the beautiful here-and-now object of desire evokes a memory of the **feeling** of delight we had and lost in heaven, but not, the particular **image** that evoked the delight.

Dante at the end of the Paradiso, seems to conform to this underground, post-Lethean tradition of reverberatory memory. He reports seeing the universe-in-love as the volume of a book, in which what in the universe normally seems separate and scattered, appears now in the image as completely unified. "I think I saw the universal form of this nexus, because just saying this makes me feel more joy" (Paradiso 33, 91–3).

As Dante is eager to relive an image, a *pictura*, Hildegard allies with the word, the *verbum*, the voice and sounds by which the logos-bearing music triggers in our hearts, by a shock of recognition, our taste for the pleasures of paradise [deliciis paradisi]. This predilection of Hildegard for the undergirding ratios of music bespeaks her predilection for the way the exteriors of things teach us by the informing power of their interior ordinating structures. The justifying text for this sense of the presence of the logos in the mathematical ratios that obtain in and among things comes from the Book of Wisdom (11.21): "Thou hast disposed the world in number, weight and measure [Sed omnis in mensura, et numero, et pondere disposuisti]." She then relates directly particular instruments as being most effective with the duality of domains in which we find ourselves: "The deeper tone of the zither figures the body's energy, the harp with its higher tones, the will of the spirit." And then peroration and closure:

[142–153]

So those who, without weighing the matter with clear minds, impose silence upon singing God's praise in the church, they rob God of due honor and tribute, if they do so without true contrition and humble satisfaction. Those who hold the keys of heaven must be extremely careful lest they close what should be open, and open what should be closed. As the Apostle says, the harshest of punishments will come to the bishops who fail to perform their office with adequate care.

[154–161]

And I heard a Voice which said: Who created heaven? God. Who opened heaven for his faithful? God. Who is like Him? Nobody. And so, faithful ones, let none of you resist him, or oppose him, lest he fall upon you in his strength, and you have no advocate who can defend you before his justice. These times are womanish times [Istus tempus tempus muliebre est] when the justice of God seems to wane. But the strength of God's justice still works, and she proves herself a warrior heroine against injustice [bellatrix contra iniustitiam existit], until it falls down, beaten to the ground.

[142–161] Her final word to the prelates is to suggest when they rob her community of the sustenance of the now deeply and mutually implicated activities of the sacrament of the Eucharist and the practice of music, they rob God. She urges upon them obedience to the Psalmist by lifting the interdiction. And she closes with a final, magnificent oxymoron in attributing the word womanish, on the one hand, to the flaccidity and vapid sense of the epoch caused by the sort of men these prelates are. But on the other, she takes great rhetorical advantage of the fact that the Latin word justice is "feminine" in gender: and as the times may be womanish, they shall nonetheless be redeemed by a woman: Justitia Bellatrix (Justice the Warrior-woman) will beat these womanish men down into the ground. Just as Hildegard, a *paupercula forma femina*, speaking *in nomine femineo*, is the Bellatrix of Bingen who can speak to men in the voice of God.

The prelates, as usual, did nothing. Hildegard then wrote directly to Christian von Buch, Archbishop of Mainz, whose direction of his episcopal see he had more or less delegated to his prelates in Mainz while negotiating between pope and emperor in Rome. Hildegard reiterated the case and the reasons offered by his prelates for the interdiction, and assured Christian that she would have exhumed the body at once had she believed for a moment that the man had been excommunicate at the point of death. She reports that she wrote what she saw in her vision to the prelates of Mainz, so they would understand what they had done, but "as their eyes had been so darkened that they had not one glance of mercy for me, I walked away from them in tears [sed cum oculi eorum ita caligassent, ut nullo respectu misericordie me respicere potuissent, plena lacrimis ab eis discessi]. Her good friend Phillip, Archbishop of Cologne, came to Mainz with a knight who had, with the man in question, also been excommunicated and witnessed that they both, before the same priest, had reconciled themselves to the church and been restored to community. The prelates then told Hildegard that it was finally in the hands of Archbishop Christian. And so she wrote to Christian in Rome:

Hildegard to Christian, Archbishop of Mainz. 1179. Excerpt. [Van Acker, 68]

> **[Unde in visione anime mee, in qua numquam me aliquo verbo turbasti]** I received in the Vision of my soul, and a voice, whose Word has never deceived me, issued from the heart and said: "better to fall into the hands of mankind, than to abandon the Law of God." And so gentlest father, I swear to you by the Love of the Holy Ghost, and the Goodness of the Will of the eternal Father, who sent, for the redemption of mankind, in the most gentle of quickening power, his Word into the Womb of the Virgin, do not despise the tears of your

saddened, weeping daughters, we who bear, even in the Fear
of God, the sorrow and weight of unjust interdiction. May the
Holy Ghost seize you with mercy for us, and may you receive,
after the run of your days, his mercy as well.

In his response to Hildegard's letter, Christian von Buch addressed
extravagantly the consensus he said all deeply felt concerning the
power and authority of Hildegard's visionary powers, but he followed
his effusion with a clearly stated legalistic condition for the restoration
of her rights to the sacraments and the use of music in the liturgy.

Christian, Archbishop of Mainz, to Hildegard. 1179. Excerpt. [Van
Acker, 69]

> **[Proinde vestre . . . afflictioni ex intimo corde compatientes]**
> Of course, we have deepest sympathy for your unhappiness
> and have directed a letter to the Church in Mainz with the
> following conditions: "We agree that, if and when the truth
> of the absolution of the deceased, as testified by those men, is
> made manifest to our court, you may once again celebrate the
> sacrament of the Eucharist."
> At the same time we beg your Holiness, with the utmost
> sense of inner urgency: if we have caused you increased bur-
> dens in this business through our guilt or our unknowing, do
> not remove your mercy from him who begs your forgiveness.
> Pray also to the Father of Mercy, that He bring us back to
> your Holiness and to the Cathedral of Mainz in soundness
> and health: to the honor of God and the health of our souls.
> May God preserve you in health and sanctity.

Six months before her death, on 17 September, 1179, the ban was
lifted, the Eucharist was once again celebrated, and the music of divine
praise returned to the Rupertsberg.

*   *   *   *   *

Having surveyed Hildegard's epistolary strategies for coping with the
normal events of life that inevitably crop up in a world of winning and
wasting, gaining and losing, birthing, thriving and dying, it comes clear,
to no one's real surprise, that she is essentially like all of us: there is
something about her we have cherished in anyone we have ever known
and loved, and there is something about her we have never seen before
at all. With no intention whatsoever of limiting her powers or our sense
of them, there seem to be some practical strategies that she used, as

she focused her enormous energies on daily cares and joys, to reconcile in her interior as well as exterior realities a devotion to the tic and toc of reality as she encountered it, all the while driven by an insatiable desire for transfiguration into the divine logos that she believed created that reality, and would eventually subsume it once its providential plan was perfected in time.

The revelations she suffered became the lodestone of her life, the primal source of agony and strength. Her mission was to create a web of discourse that would weave new linkage between her God and her world through the mediation of all her mind, all her heart, and all her soul. And as she crafted her major visionary works over thirty years of writing, she crafted a style of dealing with what appeared to be irreconcilable realities in modes that allowed for a grand synthesis, without betraying the great and God-instantiated values of the auton-omy of all the parts. As we survey those modes, we begin to assemble her extraordinary and indispensable contributions to that feminine poetics of revelation that constitutes one of the great collective under-takings of the European middle ages.

IN VERA VISIONE:
BEGINNING, MIDDLE, AND END

We conclude this study of Hildegard's contribution to the feminine poetics of revelation by a kind of testing of the waters, an examination of a few crucial revelatory images drawn from her three great visionary works: the *Scivias* (written in her forties), the *Liber Vitae Meritorum*, "The Book of Life's Merits," or *LVM* (written in her fifties) and the *Liber Divinorum Operum*, "The Book of God's Works" or *LDO* (written in her late sixties and early seventies.

Each book appears from the outside like an impregnable fortress: God presides, the scale of reach is unabashedly cosmic. The images are so gorgeous, but at the same time so outlandish as to appear almost alien. The apparent structure is so ordered-looking, but with a syntax of argument so vermicular and labyrinthine—that few first readers fail to be severely daunted at the point of entry. It is as if each book stood alone like some prefiguration of the Grail Castle, awaiting a foolish Parzival who feels doomed from the start to ask the wrong question and fears, worst of all, that when it most matters, he will fail to see that a question needs to be asked at all. Each master volume appears, as Book, to stand alone, capable of substituting for an entire world.

And as one enters in, all three of these great visionary books report urgently, intricately, and often bafflingly, the complex detail of divine revelation that Hildegard culled alone from what were exquisitely personal and almost unimaginably powerful visitations of divinity. Yet not one of these books, in spite of all appearances to the contrary, stands alone. As one learns to see, each seems to have been designed on a different premise; not to substitute for the world we know, but rather to enhance and enrich the corporate revelations concerning it that are already present in holy scriptures and thus are available, at least in theory, to everyone.

In fact, the vox Dei in Vision One of the *Scivias* makes it clear to us readers standing next to Hildegard and listening with her in our readerly imaginations, that Hildegard herself has been sent to us precisely as a kind of ironic, secret agent of God. She is a flowing female source of power sent by the Father to shake up and irrigate all the heavy-witted men who know the scripture but either can not, will not, or dare not preach its message:

> [**Et ecce idem qui super montem illum sedebat fortissima et acutissima voce clamabat dicens**] And look, he who sat on the mountain called out with a strong, penetrating voice saying:
>
> O fragile human, muck of the earth, ash out of ashes, cry out and speak of the incorruptible way of redemption, so they may know it, even they who already know the inner heart of the scriptures, but dare not or cannot speak it out. For they are tepid and weak-headed in maintaining the justice of God. Open and show them the secrets that in fear they have buried, without fruit, in desolate fields. Flow out like a bubbling fountain, pour secret teachings out on them, so they are shaken loose by your irrigating waters, all those who condemn you for the sliding of Eve. Tell them you are not receiving this sharpness and depth from a man, but from the tremendous celestial judge from on high where the brilliant serenity and power of the light showers light among the lights [ubi praeclara luce haec serenitas inter lucentes fortiter lucebit].[1]

What are we to make of these images as we are carried from the masculine shout of the Man in the Mountain, into the weaving of liquid waterings, irrigations, and flowings, which both figure forth and culminate in the radiantly intellectual sun of divine light that in turn ordi-

---

1. *Fuehrkoetter's Scivias*, 7–8.

nates and illuminates all those "merely" celestial lights in the sky that are visible to the human eye?[2]

As we seek a way into her visionary books, it is tempting, but proves extremely difficult, to take refuge in the old divisions between "content" and "form," and then seek meaning in the constructions of paraphrastic revisions and summaries of content. In fact, that perfectly satisfactory medieval mode of male scribal commentary clearly will not do for Hildegard. On the other hand, the old truisms of the now moribund New Criticism, that content and form are one and indivisible begin to revive in our minds with new possibility as we scan the major visions of Hildegard. And yet, though such a hypothetical interdependency comes a bit closer to the sort of thing we feel we need, it too can finally serve only as a springboard to a more adequate, but, by a kind of inherent necessity, never quite satisfactory descriptive and critical mode of dealing with her texts. Nevertheless, just as Hildegard is daring, often even reckless, in her willingness to take risks to achieve a new synthesis of word and image in her revelatory discourse, so must we be as well as we attempt to find more satisfactory ways of coming to grips with her style of crafting it.

The very syntax of Hildegard's language in the opening salvos of the *Scivias* comprises a formal mirror reflecting the integration of her great, interweaving themes: the inflection of the Latin guarantees grammatical intelligibility, but the disposition of the various adjectives and adverbs across the canvas of the warp and woof of noun and verb becomes a vivid and varying linguistic mirror, with syntax in a dance with semantics, of Women and water, God and light: "Let your love flow as God's logos to shake up the tepid and heavy-headed, and irrigate them, so that their roots will take new hold and flourish." Her liquid lingerings in the middle of the passage give way to a lucid, crystalline serenity. And so we move in syntactic orders and patterns of phonic sounds as well as through visual images: from the sudden violence of "Cry out, Muck of the Earth," through the hummings of a metamorphic liquid discourse, into the edge of silence at an imagined momentary point of lucid rest. We have in fact passed through Hildegard's portal of entry and into her feminine strategies of evocation as she attempts to awaken humanity's attention to the logos of God.

Scivias

Each of the great visionary books scintillates with spectacle: there are mountains, valleys, clouds, towers, cities, wheels, geometric shapes,

---

2. An interesting anachronistic irony resides in some of the latest findings regarding the capacity of the human eye: it sees only the tiniest fraction of the light that is actually flowing around and through the universe.

metamorphic, even amorphic figures of women, men, and beasts, some beautiful, some horrific, all in brilliant ranges of color, odor, texture, scale, and sound.[3] In addition, each of the three books is also driven by a set of extremely stringent formal procedures, one of whose effects, whether by her own design or not, is to hold in check the almost overwhelming electric charge of Hildegard's visionary energy. Another obvious function of her strategy of clearly and candidly signaling her formal design, is to help readers keep some track of where they are. Another is the iconic value that our awareness of the signifying power of the forwarding procedures themselves have as an icon of order in the very book that they in turn ordinate. All the formal displays of numbers and rubrics signal themselves as an analog, among the brilliant and often baffling images of the visions, of the providential presence of an ordering plan, which, of course, acts as an analog of the ordering plan in the cosmos of the Mind of God. So the plan of the *Scivias*, crafted by the mind of Hildegard supposedly with God's help, is like the imago Dei that is its maker, a mirror of the plan of the world at the point of genesis, crafted according to Christian orthodoxy, by the mind of God alone. This essentially specular vision of relationship, this sense of the Creation as mirror of the Created, is the great linchpin of Hildegard's vision of reality, and it is what ultimately renders her work coherent—no matter how startling and baffling individual pyrotechnical displays of her power can be.

The *Scivias* moves in grand and stately fashion. A series of twenty-six master-images of received visions has been carefully set down for the mind's perusal and meditation. Interleaved between them are capacious sections of commentary, often spoken by a "voice" emanating from the vision itself. It is a curious, but effective mode of self-indexing: the image comes to us (in a way analogous to the way it originally came to Hildegard) and then "speaks" to us about itself, tells us what it "means." There is the welcome feel of reliability about this procedure on the one hand, a sense that gives excitement and an almost tactile pleasure; yet there is also an odd sense of being hermetically sealed up within an elaborate, but ultimately only self-referential system on the other—a sense that awakens our critical awareness and makes us ask, however fascinating and compelling we feel the given moment in the work to be, "What has this to do with me?" This question never really goes away; and part of what I hope to accomplish in this concluding discussion of Hildegard, is to show that the tenacity with

---

3. The *LVM* is much subdued in terms of pictorial splendor relative to the framing *Scivias* and *LDO*. But for good reasons as we shall shortly see.

which this question remains in our ears is central to Hildegard's artistic and theological program.

In the original Rupertsberger Codex, these verbal master-images were often accompanied by brilliantly painted illuminations, whose images followed, to a degree of exactitude uncharacteristic of the time, the images as deployed in the text.[4] One tradition has it that Hildegard painted the manuscript illuminations herself. This, for various historical reasons, seems highly unlikely. Another tradition suggests that Hildegard sketched outlines of what she wanted on wax tablets, and directed the artists in the scriptorium as they painted these extraordinary illuminations. Perhaps she even etched her version of the images on the same wax tablets on which she incised her rough text for Volmar's transmission of her words to parchment. There seems no real reason to deny the strong possibility that this may have indeed occurred, though there is also no way to prove it. Let us take it that the original design of the accompanying illuminations, however intimately or distantly dictated by Hildegard, presented, at least according to her general wishes, the central master-image of the vision doubly, in both visual as well as verbal form, as *pictura* and as *verbum*, so that the inner mind of readers would have been bombarded by at least four of the five sense modes as they touched and smelt the book they were holding: they saw the pictures and words, and heard their own voices reading aloud the visually available words of Hildegard. The effect of her images entering the mind through so many channels of sensual input must have been ravishing.

The twenty-six master-images are followed, as I said, by a series of very official-looking glosses, or bits of interpretive commentary, of varying lengths, but each with its own separate rubric, or heading. The glosses offer partial "readings" of either the master-image as a whole, or, much more frequently, of one or some of its parts, and always from an oblique slant of view. The net effect is an ever-growing aggregate of available exposition on the varied kinds, directions, and ranges of significance that Hildegard wishes us to see embodied in her master-images.

Now as to mode. These glosses treat the master-image as the traditional scholiast treated standard biblical passages that sat on the other-

---

4. *The Rupertsberger Scivias* was photocopied in 1927, and the thirty-five miniatures were meticulously copied by the benedictine nuns of Eibingen between 1927–33, shortly before being shipped to Dresden for protection during World War II. They vanished during the fire-bombing in 1945, and have not been seen or heard of since. See B. Newman's very helpful introduction to the Paulist Press translation of the *Scivias* by Columba Hart and Jane Bishop, with a preface by Caroline Walker Bynum (New York, 1989).

wise virginal page as a target for enabling commentary. As I hope I've made clear, the entire *Scivias* proceeds by a grand oscillation between master-image and commentary, and this stately alternation constitutes the base processional rhythm of the book.

But though the separate commentaries have the form and general function of most medieval manuscript glosses, we find, upon closer examination, that they do not work in quite the same way. A favorite strategy of "male" biblical commentary, for example, is to illuminate the text in question by referring it outward to other biblical texts in conjunction with which we see, by both structural and verbal resonance, the outline of a greater plan of which the passage under consideration is only a part. Hildegard also delights in linking her own visionary imagery to biblical texts; but, in opposition to her male counter-scholiasts, she reaches out to the relevant biblical text and returns with it to gloss the image or phrase in question in her "private" vision. The net effect of her "feminine" mode of self-glossing, as opposed to the "male" norm, is that we sense Hildegard's commentary moving inward into the image as if that image were, for the moment, the whole of all there is. The effect is not so much a soaring upward and outward, but rather a kind of diving downward and inward. It is reminiscent of a kingfisher returning to the nest with food, as she glosses her master-image with bootlegged bits of scripture, shared experiences from every day life, and even various bits and pieces of the accompanying imagery that makes up the master-image itself. Let us take an example from early in Book One, Vision Two:

[Deinde vidi velut maximam multitudinem viventium lampadarum] Then I saw what appeared as a great many living lamps burning with brilliance, refulgent fire, and serenest splendor. And behold, a lake of great width and depth appeared, with what appeared to be a mouth emitting, with smoke and flames, a great stink, from which an ugly cloud reached out to touch a deceptive and veiny-looking thing [se extendens quasi venam visum deceptibilem habentem tetigit], and, in a land of clarity, it breathed on a white cloud that came from a lovely human form filled with many and more than many stars [et in quadam clara regione candidam nubem quae de quadam pulchra forma hominis plurimas plurimasque stellas in se continens] and thus cast it out from that land. When that happened a most brilliant splendor surrounded that country, and all the elements of the world, which had up to then rested in great calm, were turned into greatest turbulence and revealed horrible terrors. And again I heard him who had spoken to me before saying. . .

Even before we have a chance to think about our own response to this radiant set of images, we hear Hildegard's vox Dei speaking out of the vision itself, providing us with its own separate, varied, and often quite substantial glosses. What we have just now experienced as a sensually complex **image**, we are now asked to read and interpret as a **text**. We are challenged to participate quite actively, to bring the whole range of our personal experience in life to bear on it, but we also feel we are on an interpretive leash that is in fact rather tightly held and short. Here is the 10th gloss (of 33 separate glosses) on the master-image quoted from *Scivias* Vision Two above: regarding "the veiny thing breathing on the cloud full of stars":

10. QUID DIABOLUS NESCIVIT ARBOREM ILLAM INTERDICTAM ESSE NISI EX RESPONSIONE EVAE

[WHY THE DEVIL DID NOT KNOW THAT THE TREE WAS FORBIDDEN EXCEPT FROM THE RESPONSE OF EVE][5]

[**Nesciebat enim eis arborem illam interdictam**] For he would not have known it was the forbidden tree except by probing them with clever questions and answers. And so, standing "in a land of clarity," he "breathed on a white cloud that came from a lovely human form filled with many and more than many stars," because [quoniam], in that garden of delights, Eve—she whose soul was innocent, raised up as she was from innocent Adam—she in whom the whole human race, brilliant with divine preordination, teemed in her gestating body, she was invaded by the serpent and seduced into downfall. Why? Because . . . [cur hoc? Quia . . .][6]

---

5. The rubrics in the *PL* have been removed from the running text and listed in a summarium preceding each of the 26 visions. Fuehrkoetter is following the photocopy of the earliest Rupertsberger Codex in distributing the rubrics with the relevant glosses they in fact head.

6. Just to provide a sense of the rich variety of angles from which the glosses come, here are several of the thirty-three glosses given for the image of the "veiny thing" as numbered in the *CCCM* edition: 1. That the blessed angels are not moved by injustice to absent themselves from the love and praise of God; 2. That Lucifer was cast from heaven for pride in beauty and power; 3. That God would have been unjust not to cast them down; 4. Words of Job on the same issue; 11. What things are to be kept to and what avoided in marriage; 12. Words of the Apostle on this; 13. Why before the Incarnation men had many wives; 16. Why the consanguineous must not copulate in marriage; 17. The example of milk. . . .

Given this gloss, we see that the point of our own interpretive effort cannot be merely to see that the image of the veiny thing "stands" for Lucifer's serpent and that the star-filled cloud "stands" for Eve. We are told by the exegetical vox Dei to think this way. But the syntax which we read leads us much further in. The discourse is riddled with *quia*'s and *quoniam*'s: we have seen the veiny thing blow on the star-filled cloud **because** Satan blew on Eve **because** of her innocence. "Why that? **Because** . . ." The language of the *visio* tells us that what we are to understand as news, is not so much an allegorical identification freely offered by the gloss between a veiny thing and a snake, but that there is a causal relationship that obtains between this vision revealed by Hildegard in her twelfth-century "now" and that earlier Edenic event revealed by scriptural text as occurring at the beginning of the world.

Further, this causal relationship is not a "male" chain of linear causes and effects linked and stationed in the schemes of historical time. Rather it is a matter of a "feminine" network of intellectual and ethical energies residing at the center of will which when activated, transform the shape of the exterior world.

With that recognition, we enter a third dimension of time. The recollected time of Eve in Eden and the remembering time of Hildegard on the Rupertsberg are coalesced, through the mediation of her text, into the order of time operating in our readerly minds right now, here and as we are. Hildegard's capacity of stereoscoping two moments of time (that of the recollector and that of the recollected), and projecting that double-vision, by means of her text, into a third and for her distant "present"—a present contingent on the reading presence of an attending intelligence such as ourselves—reveals the true nature of her gift of prophecy. Her capacity for weaving separate zones of time also gives us a new sense of the solid dimensionality of interplay between and among the domains of universal, collective, and personal history. We find ourselves as readers at least momentarily in that domain of intellection, mixing memory and desire, that combines what Bonaventure will shortly come to call the "outside ourselves" [*extra nos*] of human history, lit by the "from above ourselves" [*supra nos*] of divine revelation, into the new and redemptive "within ourselves" [*intra-nos*] of our questing minds, always already driven by our divine desiring.

So the main question for us about how to interpret her master-images in the *Scivias* is not so much to see that one side of her head is "explicating" the other: but to see that she provides us with fresh access, through her multiple visions, to a double vision of our own. As we see the veiny-thing blow on the white cloud full of stars (private news from Hildegard), we **also** read how Satan-in-the-worm tempted Eve (corporate news from the Bible). To see and hear this doubly as then and now is itself a figure of our capacity to receive in communion the verbum-qua-caro of the Incarnation. Later, in her great gloss of John's actual phrase *Et Verbum Caro factum est*, which is the centerpiece of the *LDO*, we shall hear her say this all herself. For the moment we must remember that we in the twentieth century see best, (*pace* Vaihinger and Wittgenstein), in the mode of AS IF. We see AS IF the cloud were Eve, at the same time we see Eve AS IF she were a white star-filled cloud. This recuperates old images by means of a new way of seeing reality that Hildegard brings us: it is a prophetic mode of **annunciation** more than of **prediction**, of synthesis more than of exegesis. It is in fact, a feminine style of revelation. Here, for a moment, the Outer and Inner are dancing in consort together. The haunting image of the vile "breathing" of the veiny thing reverses and parodies the originally generative breathing of God into Adam. As we see that parodic reversal of the good, we extrapolate a vision of evil not as a thing, but as a direction of the will, as a grotesque, inverse parody of true being, which is, after all, its orthodox nature. This is the result of attending in a creative, participatory fashion to Hildegard's feminine style of weaving together the *pictura* and the *verbum* in her work. She is the mediating stylus incising the wax, scrivening the image as Word, the word as the Imago. In the scenario we envisage as we read of her seeing and hearing, her voice is the double of Christ's: Christ is in her and the logos speaks through her, but the feminine voice we hear is the voice of a human: just as Christ's was.

Liber Vitae Meritorum

The middle book of the great trilogy is the *Book of Life's Merits*, which we shall tag as *LVM*, the initials of the original Latin title. It figures forth not so much the macrocosm of God's great plan; rather it figures forth the microcosm of the humanity of our daily life lived within that plan. And in the *LVM* that life is presented intensely, both on its and our own terms.

All of the images and voices that make up the book derive from the basic image of the eye of a huge figure of a man that Hildegard sees with feet in the ocean and head in the clouds. This man slowly turns and looks in all directions of creation. He sees various clouds out of which voices speak, and he hears variation after variation of self-description sounding from the mouths of the sins of the world, and then answered in strict alternation by voices spoken by their corresponding and countering virtue. The sins in this book are often hard to formulate in terms of the conventional taxonomy of the "seven deadlies": on the contrary, as in lived reality, they appear inexhaustibly metamorphic, and hard to classify with any confidence apart from their existential occasioning. In Part III of the *LVM*, however, the sins of humanity are given their conventional names:

Liber Vitae Meritorum III.3.21–23.
[The seventh image]

21. [**Sed septima imago quasi formam mulieris habebat**] The seventh appearance had the form of a woman who lay on her right side. She had bent and drawn up her legs like people do who make themselves comfortable. Her hair was flame-fire, and her eyes were like chalk. She had white shoes on her feet that were so slippery that she could neither stand nor walk. A foul-smelling breath came out of her mouth, as well as poisonous dribble. On one breast she nursed a young dog, on the other a serpent. With one hand she playfully combed the blooms among the trees and the grass with her hand, while she took in their odor with her nose. She had not dressed in anything special, on the contrary she was naked but for the cloak of fire, and whoever came near her, dried out like hay from her heat. And she said:

The Voice of Luxury [Verba Luxuriae]

22. [**Ego formam imaginis Dei in spurcitia implicabo**] "This figure made in God's image I'll quietly drag through the muck, even if that bothers the Lord. I can ruin everyone this way. After all I have my own magnificence and stand in my own heights. I allow them all to be drawn to me, for that's my nature: I'm born with it. . . . It's all well and good that heaven has its desire for justice, but earth has its responsibilities too. If the nature of flesh were really such a burden to God, then he would have seen to it that it didn't wear so comfortably well."

Response of Chastity [Responsum Castitatis]

23. [**Et iterum audivi vocem de praefata turbida nube**] And again I heard a voice out of the storm-cloud: the same one from the diadem of the king that gave this form an answer: "I'm not just sitting around with nothing to do here in the midst of your outrageous self-flaunting; I'll not lie with you on that bed, where you toss yourself around, provoking rape. Out of my mouth come no such poisonous words that make a theory out of every dirty gesture . . . I'm not fond of the tail

of that snake that befouls you with its filth. . . . I have joy in the harmony of the happy life of civil discourse and restraint. You, most sordid creature, are the ravening belly of the snake, you were in the hearing of Adam and Eve when their obedience slipped away from them. I spring out of the high Verbum of the Father. Heaven and earth will send you to hell when they see your filthy naked wrangling.

Perhaps most telling here is the absence already noted of what we find so fully present in the *Scivias* and the *LDO:* radiantly colored, formally spectacular images depicting realms of other worlds and altered states. The image we see here of Luxury writhing naked on the couch in postures of attempted seduction is vivid enough, but also familiar enough as part of the hand-me-down iconography of the seven deadly sins. The fiery hair, the nakedness, the suckling of dog and snake, the tossing and turning on the couch, all are drawn from the property box located in the sacristy of any medieval chapel, never far from the pulpit.

Much more intriguing, though much more tricky to deal with, is the female gendering of both the problem figured in the sin, and the solution figured in the virtue. Again inherited cultural forces sway things mightily: the feminization of the sins is "naturally" (and grammatically) forced by the hard linguistic (and not ethical) fact that such abstract nouns happen, in Latin, to belong to the feminine gender: e.g. luxuria, castitas, etc. So grammar in fact plays a small but crucially catalytic role here. But Hildegard makes more capital on this gendering than pure grammaticality would already ensure.

Chastity's verbal bashing of Luxury's appearance on the couch has a strong, almost classical satiric energy. And at the high moment that Hildegard suggests the impossible image of the union of the two on the couch, a female wrestling match looms in the mind that would occur should Chastity in fact join Luxury on the couch—anticipating the realm of soft pornography.

But there is more. We see in the shift of mode in which the imagery is given to us that the power of Hildegard's plasticity of imagination turns here from a focus on the rendering of pictorial to that of verbal imagery. There is an enhanced reliance on narrative images, carried to the imagination by flowing verbal discourse, rather than on static images as imagined before the mind's eye. This fits very well Hildegard's emphasis in this middle book of revelation on the processes of everyday life, on the values and horrors that manifest themselves to us most often by their anchoring in narrative, in words that come at us one at a time, rather than in a description of things as they appear to us clustered in space. Our sense of things is more urgent though not less meditative.

What we see here is consistent throughout the *LVM*. It is a sober, sobering book; it exfoliates out of one basic narrative situation, i.e. a review of the entire inventory of sins of the world and the powers we have been provided with to resist their seduction. The *LVM* has real, quotidian energy, but in spite of the emphasis on narrative imagery, there is a sense at the end that the book is more a tally than a narrative. But that of course is itself a standard and, at least for contemporaneous medieval sensibilities, persuasive and efficient convention of accounting for the richness and vagaries of the world.

The *LVM* also has its own, only slightly hidden, numerological macro-structures, what Hildegard would surely agree to call "musical" or Pythagorean grids of ordination. The book "divides" into six parts, each concerned with two compass directions, all numbers themselves divisible by the trinitarian 3 into 4 and 2. 4 associates with the Old Testamental quadernity of justice, directions, qualities, elements, etc. and the number 2 figures multiplicity, alternity, tension, the many, movement itself. But the essential duality in which we hear the strict alternation of the voices of vices countered by virtues, implies an underlying rhythm of incarnational unity: the colloquy of the Vices and Virtues figure, in Hildegard's special formal setting, the Verbum itself as always already speaking in redemptive correction to, with, and ultimately within, the Flesh.

In sum, we have a palpable sense of on-going process in the *LVM*, but a process that completes a circle rather than reaches a new destination. There is, after all, nowhere to go but to complete the circle of the Central Man's eye as it rotates around the radius of its own center in the course of its review of the inventory of the world of here and now. But as one senses the inevitability of returning to the place where one started, and if not knowing it for the first time, at least knowing it better for the go-around, one also has a sense of roundness and completion of the circle as a perfect figure for the reconciliation of the patterns of history into the unity of eternity. And we feel the aesthetics of a satisfaction concerning the very problematic nature of the middle, as Hildegard presents it to us in the vernacular of everyday experience. To make fuller, and more adequate sense of that middle, however, both in the trilogy of Hildegard's great visionary texts as well as in the more personally intimate texts of our own lives, we require the image-constructs of beginning and ending. We have observed a key image of Hildegard's strategies of beginning in our glance at the temptation of

Eve in the *Scivias*. We now move to her last great book, the *LDO*, in order to assess her strategies of ending.

LIBER DIVINORUM OPERUM: THE END OF TIME

The *LDO* spans the whole of creation as outlined in scripture: from Genesis to Last Judgement and the return to the paradisal rose of divine infinity. But rather than depend on a running antiphonal counterpoint of biblical quotation and reference for steady reinforcement, Hildegard chooses this time to place an emphasis on two massive biblical commentaries of her own, presenting these commentaries as themselves a part of divine revelation. So in this last work, public scripture and private access fully coalesce at the end of her life.

She reports in her *Vita* that she actually had a direct vision of the centrality of the micro-macro link in the incarnation present in John's *in principio erat Verbum*. The *verbum* at the beginning of John insists on Christ's presence in the *principium* of Genesis as well. Love for Hildegard is one with God, and hence present at the beginning and end: Love is fully figured as such in the framing imagery of the *LDO*.

The ten visions of the *LDO* are brilliantly and breathtakingly otherworldly in their imagery, texture and movement: but always at their center is figured, as the central work of God, an image of Humanity Itself, an image we can call the Figura Humana.

The *LDO* is a structural and operational mirror of the *Scivias*. There are ten master-visions (presented in a stately manner over the course of three parts of the book) followed by numerous, carefully ordered sections of commentary, each with their own number and rubric. Again the iconic function of the underlying order is clearly manifest: to order the work, and to be perceived iconically as a figure of order itself. Here a map may be helpful, even if we cannot, within the confines of this study, in fact trace the full terrain.

Incipit: consists of a preface in which the origin of the work is situated within personal and recent political history

Book I. Visions of the World in Time.

1. Vision of Life. The Figura-Humana: a winged figure of splendor that speaks of its power as the life-force, the quickening of the Holy Spirit in which all genesis has its roots.

2. Vision of the World. A circle appears within the breast of the

Figura-Humana; it is revealed to enclose a male figure of both the structuring principle of the world and the image of the world's Creator. At the center of the circle appears the image of yet another human figure, now a female in form.

3. Vision of the Body: its nature and sources of energy. The figure appearing in the circle begins to be anatomized.

4. Vision of the Human Body as Anatomy of the World. Every body part is named, described and related to all others, to the whole, and is underpinned by a moral function and its location in the divine plan of Creation, Fall, and Redemption. The Fourth Vision concludes with two extraordinary "set" pieces: The Calendar and the Gloss of Chapter One of the Johannine Gospel (both to be discussed below).

Book II. Vision of the World Beyond

5: Vision of the World Beyond the Body. Includes a full and elaborate allegorical gloss of the seven days of Genesis.

Book III. Five Visions of Salvation

6. Vision of the Meaning of History. A city with strong walls: architectural embodiment of allegorical principles of structure.

7. Vision of the Preparation for Christ: the city at work

8. Vision of the Work of Love: The source of strength above the city; a Fountain that irrigates the city with living waters, guarded, validated and adorned by a trinity of women.

9. Vision of the Cosmos Perfected: The interlaced "operatio" of two of the allegorical women: Divine Wisdom and Divine Power.

10. Vision of the End of Time (ending as more teleologically than closurally sensed: Time will not so much cease as be fulfilled and perfected in eternity.) The third woman in the originating circle we discover here is Divine Love.

Perhaps one of the reasons that Hildegard's work is so seldom read systematically is that one expects the value of her work to lie in its theological powers of revelation. But I would have to argue that such an expectation, though extremely reasonable at first blush, will most likely be disappointed. I would be among the first to agree that her work is revelatory, but I would have to argue that the power that for most of us brings that revelation to bear is ultimately an artistic, perhaps even a literary power. That is not to deny that the logos may well speak through her, though that issue has been from the start strictly off-limits in a profane essay in comparative literature such as this. But even in the relatively secular realms of literary theory I see no problem about granting the idea that the logos can, may, or does in fact speak through her. After all, *poesis* is *faber* is "making": the word in the work can always figure the word in the body, all figures of the spirit charging and quickening matter. The Johannine doctrine of *verbum caro factum est* is a profoundly intuited truth to Hildegard and as such it is a truth pervading and giving integrity to her work. All I am suggesting is that it is at least as much an artistic as a theological principle of composition that ordinates her work and lends it great power over a sympathetic reader. The Johannine intuition of the Incarnation is unarguably at the heart of the Christian religion. But it is also, albeit debatably, at the heart of the secret calculus of all Christian art as well. We can demonstrate that most efficiently, and perhaps most persuasively, in Hildegard's poetics of revelation by attending to the roles she creates for the human body to play in her images of both the perdurables as well as the irreconcilables: in the role her images of the middle play as she images forth first and last things. Let's take three central images from the *LDO*: the Calendar, the Commentary of John from the Fourth Vision, and the final and Tenth Vision, of the figura feminea of Caritas in the Wheel of God at the End of Time.

In the Fourth Vision of Book One, after elaborately fleshing out Ezekiel's dry bones vision by means of her own fully fleshed anatomy of the body, Hildegard suggests that the principle of quickening of the body by the chemistry of its organic structural principles is every-where—even in the twelve winds that blow through the cosmos. And as we think of the great world as figured forth by the small, she gives us, as a kind of Christmas gift, an unforgettable calendar of the twelve months of the year. That sense of a carefully wrapped and extremely valuable gift is neither unduly personal nor overstated, rather it is simply unavoidable on reading this extraordinary diversion: a diversion one suspects is as much at the center as at the margin of the book. Each month of the year has a member of the human body as part of its Hildegardian signature. I will attempt to convey an accurate, if impressionistic sense of how the whole "works" by means of a collage of quotation of a few of the parts:

> [**Sed et sicut creaturas Deus in homine signavit, sic etiam tempora anni in illo ordinavit**] As God figured creation in mankind, so he ordered the seasons of the year in humanity as well.
>
> In the first month the sun flares up again, but it is cold and wet, full of contradiction, and sweats in transformations of snow. It's qualities are linked to those of the brain, which is also cold and wet, and rids itself of excess liquid through the eyes and ears and nose. And the soul works in joy through

childhood, the season that knows no cunning or fleshly lust against its nature. . . .

The fourth month is greening and odoriferous; even when thundering terribly, it's a time for the nose, through which the breathing soul inhales and exhales the aromas of diversity from which in awe it selects for its pleasure . . .

The fifth month is delicious and light and glorious in all the things of the earth. Tastes are sweet and fill the mouth, make it felt and known for the wonder it is for us, fills us with joy. Reason is backbone and marrow of all five senses and puts them to work; just as the earth, when turned by the plow, shows itself fruitful in seed. Sight, that touch of the eyes, by which we see and know everything, holds principal place among all of the senses . . .

The eighth month comes up in full strength, like a great prince in all his virility, ruling his realm in the fullness of power: his joy beams out of him. As he burns in the singeing Sun, he already draws, because of a certain humidity, the dew behind him, and his tempests are terrible, for the sun begins its decline toward the south. The qualities of this month show in our hands that do the work, as they integrate and conserve the hidden powers of the entire human body . . .

The tenth month is like sitting folks; no more rushing along powered by the greening freshness of life [quoniam viribus suis in veriditate non volat]; the life-warmth subsides. The limbs of trees shed leaves as if to sweat out the cold, as sitting folks hug themselves to escape the effect of the chill [et homo dum sedet se complicat ut frigas evadat], and put more clothes on to keep warm. An example of how people, when they begin to freeze in old age, get wiser, get bored by infantile fads, get a bit more tolerant, avoid the more stupid sorts who only want to exchange ignorances. And desire sinks back, one gets less pleasure from the greening power [ex viriditate jocundus non est] than one once did . . .

The eleventh month comes bent over; builds up the cold; no more summer joys to show; brings the heavy moods of winter. Sleet breaks out and falls on the ground and stirs up the dirt. Folks bend the knee so the cold won't seep all the way in, bend the knee in a sadness, piling up painful thoughts in the heart, feeling like meaningless muck, they can't find upsurge to joy; remembering even in heartache, that the knee is by nature, even in embryo, always already bent . . . That's why this month, as it drips its cold days far from the joys of summer, is like the knee of mankind, which the old ones bend in resignation, as they think back on their genesis, on how their knees were bent exactly like this, when crouched in the womb of the mother . . .

The twelfth month is powerful, cold, the earth hard, freezing. Winter covers the land with iced spume, making it hard and heavy to cross. The month's like the feet, which stamp down and tramp down so much that the earth gets jammed down so it doesn't erupt and you can stand on it. It's cold like the body after the soul's taken off . . . And the soul that remains forgets its own nature. Like Cain with the blood of his brother, it turns away now from God. In anger the blood boils over, the senses rage, people go mad. . . . they grit their teeth against God . . . in their hardening they can't bear the savor of holiness . . . nor strew the seeds of good works . . . they're like a camel weighed down with the stinking load of its sins, forever beshitting itself. . . .[7]

The anticipatory savor of Brueghel in Hildegard's sketch of the seasons does much to prevent any theological meditation to fly too far from the flesh in its search for the meaning of the words. It is this anchoring in tough experience that reveals, especially in this book of old age, the source of so much of her persuasive power; a power that has as much to do with her poetic art as with her mystic theology. But experiential anchoring alone would be merely heavy and sordid without her countering, theological soaring to lift it. And, just to touch for a moment on a parallel concern, as important as Paul was to Hildegard as a model of the hard work of apostolic care and cure, at the center of her capacity for elevation stands the figure and gospel of John. Directly following the Calendar, Hildegard moves the Fourth Vision toward closure with her grand commentary on John's opening chapter, his counter to, and fulfillment of the incipit of Genesis.

Near the end of Book II of her *Vita*, Theodoric quotes Hildegard's reminiscences of key moments of vision. In the seventh, she recalls what for her remained one of the most stunning of them all:

[**mysticam et mirificam visionem vidi, ita quod omnia viscera mea concussa sunt**] I saw a mystical and miraculous vision by which all my insides were shaken, and the powers of bodily senses extinguished, and I knew all of my being had been converted into something never known before. And the

---

7. PL 877–84.

breathing of God was like water-drops raining gently into the knowing of my soul [et de Dei inspiratione in scientia animae meae quasi guttae suavis pluviae spargebantur] just as the Holy Ghost imbued John the Evangelist with the profound revelation which he sucked from the breast of Jesus [cum de pectore Jesu profundissimam revelationem suxit] where the hidden mystery of holy divinity was made known to him [ubi sensus ipsius sancta divinitate ita factus est quod absconsa mysteria] and opens the work beginning "In the beginning was the Word [in principio erat Verbum]."[8]

The charged liminality of the liquid imagery of nursing which embraces Jesus as implied mother suckling the beloved John, even as the Spirit imbues the Evangelist through the astonishingly feminine mediation of the historical Christ, is breathtaking in its artistic and theological risk as Hildegard refreshes anew our sense of her intuition of the vivid centrality of the flesh in the incarnational mystery. It is precisely her feminine refusal to allow successful hegemony on the part of either aspect, Word or Flesh, in their tensive dance of mystical identity that characterizes her gloss in the *LDO* on John's formula:

And the Word was made flesh and dwelt among us [et Verbum caro factum est et habitavit in nobis]

[Verbum enim quod apud Deum aeternataliter ante aevum erat] For the Word which was always eternally with God before all time, and which was God, put on flesh in the uterus of the Virgin by the ardor of the holy Spirit [per ardorem Spiritus sancti carnem de utero Virginis assumpsit]. It drew on the flesh, as the veins enclose and support the body, as they carry the running blood but are not the blood itself. God made humans so that all other creatures would serve them; that is why it pleased him to put on the cloak of human flesh. In this way the Word covered itself with the flesh: Word and flesh become a life-unit together, not as if one had transformed itself into the other, but so they were one in the unity of a person. Just so is the body the covering cloak of the soul, and the soul provides help for the body in its action. The body would be nothing without the soul, the soul could realize nothing without the body, and they are one in their humanity [unde unum in homine sunt] and humanity affirms it. And

8. *Vita*, PL 116B-C.

so this Work of God [opus Dei], that is humanity, has been made in the image and similitude of God. For when the holy breath of God is sent into the flesh, that same spirit and flesh unite in a human being. But the Word took on flesh from the unplowed Virgin, without being fired by any lust for that flesh, in such a way that the Word remains Word, and flesh, and yet both of them are one, for the Word, which both before and after time is always already in the Father, remains unchanged, even as it is clothed in the flesh. [*PL* 889C]

Her prose here is *in extremis,* which is not surprising if one considers the fact that she is using language to create images to capture one of the two great cosmic instances where language exploded perforce beyond its limits: Genesis, where the eternality of the Logos of God put on the dress of human history. Her language is referencing points in imagined genesis where language itself seems to have crossed its natural barrier and entered directly into its own frames of reference. But part of her struggle here is this: in her insistence on the unity of categories she will equally insist on maintaining what she surely felt was their holy/wholly separate autonomy.

This is precisely what makes the incarnation a mystery: if one could solve that mystery, as she says you can't, by thinking of one thing transforming into another, it would not be a mystery, it would be a problem and thus capable of solution. Thus Hildegard's words about the words of John as he speaks of the Word that was at the beginning are always in danger of imploding or leaking away. It is the energy of her own mind as imago Dei, as amalgam of will, memory and intellect, that keeps the syntax bound together in a kind of cold fusion. And we can see, by the heat of the interior conflicts of natural incommensurability of the elements that have been divinely unified, a new sense of the mystery at the center. To close our study of Hildegard's poetics of revelation, we turn to her final vision. And as it is the final vision, in both a literary as well as eschatological sense, we should not be surprised if we find ourselves quite literally at the end of the road.

LDO, Vision Ten: Charity in the Wheel of God.

We'd best look first at the rubric with which the *PL* heads the final Visio of the *LDO*:

[Visio extrema, in qua rota multae amplitudinis ostensa] A threshold [extrema] vision, in which a wheel of great size is revealed which is described with great care [qualis esset diligenter describitur], and the image of charity appears under another schematic [iterumque imago charitatis sub alio schemate conspicitur]. [*PL* 997B]

The very first two words bring irresolvable ambiguity: for the adjective *extrema* insists on referring to two things. First the vision itself is *extrema*. It is either mildly so, as in "the last of a series (this is the last vision, the *visio extrema*, of a group of ten) or, in this case much more likely, this vision is intended to be seen as "at the extreme edge or limit" of its own capacities for depicting anything at all. This is precisely what we shall shortly see is the case about this image, and that itself will justify the oddly disconcerting warning about the need for a "careful description." But *extrema* also insists that what is being depicted in the image is *also* at the edge, and that will prove true as well.

In the figure of the Lady in the Wheel, we creatures of time bump up against an image of the end of time. As we watch the opening maneuvers of LDO Vision Ten, we see God seeking a way to show Hildegard, and she is seeking a way to show us, a set of images that will mediate to us a sense of the ending as closure of what we know, goal (telos, end as in the phrase "means and ends") to which we have come. When things begin to move, as they shortly will, it will also begin to dawn on us that passing through the end will also constitute a new beginning.

But for now the problem of identifying what it is we see is just about overwhelming. The fact that we are made in the image of God, itself a key grounding articulation for all of Hildegard's procedures, guarantees, in this belief system, an unbreakable link with God. But the imago relationship, by its very nature, even as it affirms similitude, denies identity. To be like God, to be made in his image and similitude, is not to BE God. For the 95 percent of the time we move through our days, similitude is more than enough. But when we enter into the liminality of the special five percent of the time, that arena in which we approach differences in kind rather than differences in degree, we have nothing much to go on. Common wisdom, so helpful for 95 percent of the time, has, for the remaining five percent, very little of use for us. We are radically thrown back on our own resources.

How can we see God and live? When we are faced with Hildegard's Wheel of God, what it is we need to see will itself be nothing we have ever experienced; that is why we need to see it. But as we are still living, or partly living, we are still limited by the contingencies of time and space; there is no way to come to us about what we haven't yet experienced other than to present it in the guises of what we have already previously experienced. We can only move to the unknown by steppingstones gathered from the known. Thus in the sort of visionary *extremum* represented by Vision Ten, the parts should probably be recognizable from the domains of our lives; the whole will not. *LDO* Visio X begins thus:

> [**Deinde juxta montem quem velut in medio orientalis plagae conspexi**] Then I saw next to the mountain in the middle of the eastern region a Wheel of wonderful circumference, that seemed like a blinding white cloud: toward the East on the left I saw a dark line like a man's breath reach all the way across to the right. On the middle of the wheel, above this line, appeared another line, shimmering like the morning dawn, that came from the height of the Wheel down to the middle of the first line. The upper part of this half-wheel sent a green brilliance from the left side right to the middle, while from the right side shone a reddish brilliance, also right to the middle, and it all happened precisely so that both brilliances shared the same space. The halves of the Wheel, however, that ran on a bias underneath the line, showed themselves as a whitish color mixed with blacks.
>
> And look there—in the middle of this Wheel I saw on the line I described a figure, who was named to me at the beginning of these visions as Charity. But now I saw her in different adornment than she earlier wore. Her face lit up like the sun, her clothes shone purplish, and hung round her neck she wore a golden band adorned with costly brilliants. She had on shoes that streamed out lightning bolts.
>
> In front of the forehead of this figure appeared a tablet that shone like crystal. On it stood written: "I will show myself in an even more beautiful form shining like silver; because godhead, which is without beginning, shines in ever greater magnificence." Everything that has a beginning is contradictory in its terrible thereness; such a thing can never fully grasp the full meaning of the secrets of God.
>
> The figure looked up at the tablet. And as soon as she did, the line on which she sat started to move. And there, where this line in the Wheel was linked to the left side, the outer part of the Wheel became, due to a narrow interstice, a little watery; and then—over the halves of the divided wheel, which lay on the bias under the line I was talking about, it all went reddish, and then finally pure and brilliantly clear, but then again it turned cloudy and stormy: this happened near the end of that half where the line was linked with the wheel.

And I heard a voice from heaven which said to me: 'O Human, hear and understand the Words of the One who was there and Who Is, without suffering the transformations of Time . . . [O homo, audi et intellige verba illius qui erat, et qui est absque officio mutabilitatis temporum . . .].' [*PL* 998C]

And the vox Dei moves on, saying over and over, gently but firmly, that the familiar bits of images we recognize in the *pictura* indicate this and that about the essentially unfathomable mystery of the unity of divine will. It has already told us that we are doomed to partial knowing as things always are that have a beginning. What we are trying to see from our multiple state of things is the pure Unity of Divine Will. Indeed we may have words to clothe and give some shape to the radical difference, but they cannot by the nature of words form a firm bridge that we can really cross. All they can do is help us begin to see the difference between where and what we are, and where and Whom we seek. In the very next rubric, we hear the vox Dei say that "because the true God is One, I said it was not possible to find in nature anything that is like him [qui Deus vere unus dice non posset si sibi similem ex natura haberet]; so I begin by showing you a circle whose qualities at least foreshadow some of those inherent in God Himself in the way its end meets its beginning."[9] As the voice affirms the ultimate incommensurability between our desiring and its object, it implies that our alternatives are only two: fall back or face the music. But perhaps that is all we need, if not all that we desire.

In any case, here we are, at the end at last: what can we say? One major difficulty seems to lie in the fact that what we usually seem to want in an act of "interpretation" of an image is to move from the image we encounter out to some other structure which we assume that image is busy trying to illuminate. But here we are up against the radical test case, of course, an image of something *that does not move out* to a meaning greater than itself.

Hildegard does her best to help. She suggests that we can view the wheel in two complementary sets of understandings: first as an imago Dei (which has its own delicious irony in that we too are such *imagines Dei*). We can also see in it God's plan for the Salvation of the World. And she proceeds to lay out details of God's will and plan which the elements of the vision can somehow be seen as pointing toward. On reflection, of course, there is nothing so radically different from what we have here as opposed to what we always have in front of us when viewing a picture. The difference really seems to be that here we are

---

9. *PL* 998C-D.

not in the middle of the field, either in terms of what is observed or our capacity for observing it. We are in fact on the very edge of the margin, both in terms of subject and object. To cross over the line would be to cross the limit of our natures as humans; it would be a kind of death. So we linger on the edge of things in a kind of holy suspense, getting as much of it all as we can, with very thin air to breathe, and our networks of support and supply well back behind our lines. Perhaps we need now to seek succor in the critical tradition that has been dealing with Hildegard for centuries. There is no dearth of interest and great value to draw on there.

Heinrich Shipperges, who translated much of this book into German in the mid-1960s, also has things to say about interpretive difficulty here. He notes that although the imagery is nearly "out of control," that the style of presenting and dealing with it is strict and severe. He insists that she distances herself from both the ascetic elevation and ascent models as well as the ecstatic ones, with the result that invites the closest attention of intellect rather than its suppression.

He also says that she is more directed by the impulse to link the things of this world to divine revelation as deeply reconcilable rather than unbridgeable. I would agree with that, but as I have indicated, I also insist that the energy of her imagery and language is contingent on her simultaneous refusal to allow our sense of the natural irreconcilability of these incommensurables to collapse in any way. She will not and does not betray any of the mystery by smoothing it over with the consolation of finding minor similitudes. She is more interested in making us face things as they truly are, rather than as they shall become. So even this vision of the eschaton, or world's end, is a vision of a fulfilled now: it completes what we know and brings satisfaction. It is also clear that something radically different and new is about to start, which brings to many of us tidal waves of fear.

Barbara Newman closes her introduction to the most recent translation of the *Scivias* with a wide-ranging and gratifyingly tolerant review of the extremely diverse approaches taken by recent students of Hildegard. She concludes with a wise and very helpful remark: "all saints are an act of synergy." Like it or not, the synergy of all of Hildegard's readers must be taken together to establish "the record" of readerly encounters with her texts. As we look back, we see many diverse approaches reflecting an honest will to meet the challenge of her legacy, many of which have great value, none of which appears definitive. My own effort here can at best only hope for so much and so little as well. But when it comes to the three great visionary works themselves, and the quest for a way to read them with confidence and full satisfaction, neither the older nor the newer theories of prophecy, the higher criticisms, the more modern fashions involving anthropology, creativism, existentialist Catholicism, essentialist symbolism, or even various kinds of pathologies or psychopathologies seem very promising in terms of providing an exclusive solution. They all help us see that, as usual, one takes what one can find of use and goes back to where one always has to start: the words and the self-imposed frame of encountering the texts themselves. The test of her charism, her gift of prophetic power, remains what it always was. If she is really to move us effectively into any sort of redemption, sacred or secular, she will do so by changing our individual minds, the "reception rooms" of her readers. And to some extent she will do it by making us long for the fulfillment of the visions she is so ardent to show us.

As Hildegard works hard to provide not only the vision, but a range of meanings to help us cope with it, all of which we hear have been validated by divine sponsorship, we are partly grateful, but we also wonder, if part of the work we are encountering is the explication of its own meaning. What is there really left for us to do? Are we to test her own explications? Against what, pray tell? Or generate alternative explications of symbolic reference? At the moment that seems an unpromising procedure. What else can we do, what new tack can we take?

As I go back over the images of Charity in The Wheel of God, I am struck particularly by the act of the imaginary movie director I find myself forced to imitate when I read: "The figure looked up at the tablet. And as soon as she did, the line on which she sat started to move. . . ." At this point, the somewhat depressing feeling of being daunted by this edifice, of being the passive victim of good-willed exegetical imposition begins to lift.

We are no longer fixated on what, beyond the image, this all means. Rather we begin to picture in our minds a circle of precise description, and then we start to make one of the lines move, and one of the sectors starts to palpitate and change color. We suddenly find ourselves called upon to participate, and we ask, not what does it mean, but what happens next? When things underneath the *figura humana* of love get suddenly reddish, than radiantly clear, then turbulent and stormy, what is happening? Is the turbulence a bad sign? A good sign? And then I look over at the glossy photograph of the manuscript illumination that accompanies, not the text in the *Patrologia* that I am actually working with, but Schipperges' German translation. Even as I know that the illumination, however gorgeous it is, and it is gorgeous, comes from Lucca and can have no direct, unmediated line back to Hildegard's mind or imagination—even so, I still see that the artist who produced it was also drawn, like all of us, to appropriate this verbal image into a *pictura* that could be made first one's own, then compared with Hildegard's words, and then shared. How did the artist manage to get Charity's garment to "shine out in purple?" Although one cannot be sure from such reproductions as we have, the solution seems to have been in making the greenish gown appear irridescently purplish among its folds. But where are the lightning bolts flashing out of the shoes? Not here. Why not? Etc., etc., etc. Such stabbings into the dark, such painfully partial answers. But it is nonetheless a true engagement of mind and of heart at the end. What can we do otherwise? Perhaps, given the situation, there is something finally right about this giddy balancing act of memory and desire, of fear and hope.

We have seen that Hildegard deployed an impressive range of feminine modes of synthesis; they are always energetically present in her minor works and fully figured in the three great visionary books. Everywhere we can see the process by which she worked to reveal the reciprocal illuminations by and through which, for her, eternity can and does shine in and through the ticking of mere chronicity, and reveals, of a sudden, the tongued fire of the Logos speaking through the fleshly exigencies of time. But there is in all of her work no sure sense of final rest for the truly living, unquietly augustinian heart. For she also refuses us, we sense with a smile, any final ease of reaching satisfactory closure to our quest for meaning; she implies that although we shall never complete the project, neither can we ever abandon it. Thus she keeps us alive, which is, after all, true enough to our current state. Her visions did not put her to sleep, nor do they put us to sleep. Her modalities of flashing ahead, of looping back, of soaring up, diving down, her moments of sudden and vulnerable candor, her capacity to pierce our minds and hearts with a fiery imagination, always accompanied by diamond lucidity, wake us up and keep us awake. In front of her work we remain poised on the edge for the lift-off. For many of us, there is finally not much to say as we wait for the end with our eyes wide open. Perhaps the last words of the Revelation according to John will echo in the chambers of our waiting memory, and a voice in us will respond: "Even so, come quickly."

CHAPTER 4

◇   ◇   ◇

Julian of Norwich
and the Via Negativa

*A*fter collecting a few items of background information regarding Julian of Norwich and her *Shewings*, we will broach some central issues relating to a style of writing she developed to answer adequately what she felt was a God-driven imperative to share her visions. This preliminary discussion will suggest that the modalities Julian found to communicate her revelations to her fellow Christians comprise a crucial and fulfilling contribution to the feminine poetics of revelation that we have been examining here. Important aspects of this style were initiated by Vibia Perpetua and her diary of martyrdom. And, as we have seen, the range and modalities of Perpetua's "feminine style" of inscribing revelation was immensely expanded nearly a millennium later by the cosmic visions of twelfth-century Hildegard of Bingen, and by the extraordinarily wide range of doctrinal, political, and personal applications through which she was able to channel her revelatory powers.

In the hands of late fourteenth-century Julian of Norwich, this feminine mode of generating meditative discourse led, by an alternative route, to an equally stunning illumination of interior reality. We shall see, in a detailed examination of Julian's *Shewings*, that the feminine style is capable of maintaining its essentially synthesizing integrity in the service of both the negative and affirmative ways to illumination.

If Hildegard of Bingen was driven to an incessant, often boisterous, and always affirmative bestowal of the sheer plenitude she felt herself empowered to embrace and share through divine vision and angelic calling, Julian of Norwich moved more slowly, carefully, quietly, and yet tenaciously inward, pursuing a pilgrimage to inner illumination that lasted nearly as many years as the more public pilgrimage of Hildegard. Julian's record of the journey in and through the vernacular particularity of her own mystical experience is in many ways consonant with the negative theology of pseudo-Dionysus the Areopagite, then undergoing translation and recuperation in England, and available to Julian and her colleagues in the Middle English recension known as *Deonise Hid Diuinite.*[1]

In addition, her feminine style contributes an important, but ultimately contrapuntal alternative voice against which it is fruitful to read the "male" styles of her fellow fourteenth-century English mystics: Walter Hilton, Richard Rolle, and the anonymous writer of the *Cloud of Unknowing.*[2] Like her male contemporaries, Julian's discourse, when speculatively considered, glows with a quiet but brilliant sophistication; but in contrast to the men, her work was designed more in the mode of what her contemporaries would have called practical rather than speculative theology. Her voice is always English, intelligent, critical, clear, intimate, warm, generous, consolatory, and embracing: everything that warranted her contemporary, unofficial title of "Mother Julian." But in creative tension with her natural wit and warmth, and even more importantly, with her captivatingly sinuous weaving of language into the fabric that comprises her texts, she maintains a breathtaking severity of focus.

Two more comparisons with Hildegard help complete our sense of the fundamental difference between these two women as well as their shared femininity. Hildegard experienced revelation from the age of three until her last days, and was always confident of her ability to "look into the living light." Julian experienced all but two of her "shewings" on a single day of her life. From Hildegard we have three major works, each huge in scale, each devoted to a host of divine revelations ranging in their illumination from the creation of the world to the end of time itself. We also have additional writings of autobiographical recollection, over three hundred letters, records of an obscure adventure in a secret language, over seventy poems, dozens of manuscript illuminations that

---

1. Edited by Phyllis Hodgson, EETS, no. 231 1955 (for 1949) (London: Oxford University Press, 1955). The two ways of the *Mystica Theologica* are often construed quite strictly in order to construct very specific meditative exercises for very specific purposes. I am not suggesting that either Hildegard or Julian found in dionysian theology any such specific, systematic program. I am suggesting that in the course of their lives, each revealed at the heart of their encounters with the world what we can in hindsight perceive as an intuitive affinity with one of the two ways. Hildegard embraces, affirms, appropriates, and synthesizes all she encounters as she moves rapidly forward from station to station. Julian stays still; her mind anatomizes the intricate defense structures revealed by the layers of the onion or the petals of the rose enclosing the secret of God; but she always moves carefully, intellectually, tentatively, so as not to mar or mutilate, but rather to celebrate the complexity of the organism. It is perhaps more a habit of mind and heart than a strict method of procedure that best characterizes the relationship of these women to the modal complementarities of Dionysian theology.

2. My inquiry into "male" visionary and literary contextualities surrounding both Hildegard and Julian is underway and awaits completion of this project prior to continuation. See Select Bibliography for suggestions for further reading.

were to some extent crafted under her direction, musical notations of a symphony and a setting for a miracle play, several biblical expositions, two compendia of the causes and cures of myriad physical and mental discomforts and disorders, as well as "official" biographies she wrote celebrating the lives of two other saints. From Julian, on the other hand, we have two, at the very most three, recensions of a single work devoted to one particular set of visions that she experienced on one particular day.

From the beginning, the plan of this book has been to encounter these women through their texts. With Hildegard the choice of texts was richly problematic. For Julian we read, perforce, her *Shewings*; the only question is, which redaction. I have decided to present a close reading of a glossed modernization of Julian's *Shewings* that I prepared especially for this book. Our text is based on everything inscribed in folios 72v through 112v of the unpublished Westminster Cathedral manuscript of Julian's *Shewings*, using a procedure that alternates sections of modernized text keyed to the original manuscript folio numbers, with extended, often highly speculative commentary of my own.

According to her own record, it was shortly after Easter, on the eighth day of May in 1373, that Julian of Norwich, thirty and a half years old, lay on her deathbed in excruciating pain, paralyzed with an illness that no one understood. Her priest had brought, for her comfort, a small crucifix on which hung a simulacrum of Christ in his passion. As she fixed her eyes on that image, a strange light shone, and she was suddenly released from pain as she saw blood begin to flow from underneath the crown of thorns. She fell into the grip of holy vision and suffered sixteen "shewings" that lasted, in bursts, for fifteen hours. And except for two aftershocks that she reported much later as occurring separately (one in 1388, the other in 1393), she never experienced a like visitation again.

With the overwhelming imposition of holy vision came an attendant imperative to share it. For at least twenty years, and a few recent scholars, including this writer, have begun to feel it was more like forty, she spent much of her life as a recluse in a systematic attempt to deal with her unique (and hence unsharable) shewings by converting them, with all the attendant losses and gains of such a conversion, into the problematic, partial adequacies of a sharable, "authoritative" text. As we learn to read more adequately the recensions of her work, we become convinced that it was the process as much as the product of this conversion of divine vision into English words that both embodied and figured forth what it was her vision finally meant to her, and, by extension, to us. Recuperating a viable sense of this "double" or "mirrored" conversion process will constitute both subject and goal of this chapter.

Scholarly consensus has for some time agreed that Julian's years of converting recollected vision into written text eventuated in two redactions: the Short-text (S), which occurs in only one manuscript (British Library Additional MS 37790) and the Long-text (L), which occurs in three (B.L. Sloane MS 2499 [LS1], B.L. Sloane MS 3705 [LS2], and Bibliothèque Nationale, Paris, fonds anglais No. 40 [LP]). There are two additional manuscripts which current consensus asserts are mere "compilations of extracts drawn from L." One has been dated as early as 1500, and is on deposit in the Library of Westminster Cathedral, London (Westminster Treasury 4, folios 72v–112v); the other dates from the seventeenth century and is located at St Joseph's College, Upholland.[3]

Recently a former colleague of mine, now Sister Julia Bolton Holloway, CHF, took a considered look at the Westminster manuscript (W) and became convinced that the forty folios in W devoted to Julian's *Shewings* are no mere compilation, but in fact have the earmarks of a separate, independently composed redaction, which she refers to as the "First Text." Sister Julia reports that she is currently preparing an edition of these Julian folios with full scholarly apparatus to explore and prove her assertions.[4] She was also kind enough to provide me with a photocopy of her transcription of the Julian folios of W.

At this distance, I am not in a position to fully assess Sister Julia's assertion that W is a separate redaction composed by Julian herself. But close study of her transcription suggests that she could well be right. My sense is that the major argument in favor of Sister Julia's intuition, and certainly the major point for us, is that whatever its provenance, the Westminster "version" of Julian's *Shewings* is far too unified a text to be considered a mere compilation. If W was not actually composed by Julian herself, we must at least stipulate that it was culled, emended, and pieced together by a scribe who was a close collaborator of Julian's, at least in spirit, if not in actual historical time. As we shall see, W is driven by structuring principles which contribute to a coherent style and rhetoric, and a controlling curve of implied and fulfilled intention, that gives the text a highly burnished sense of finish all its own. If one knew nothing at all about the existing manuscript tradition of Julian's writing, W would stand alone as an inde-

---

3. See Select Bibliography for a full list of the standard editions and the major secondary texts relevant to Julian of Norwich.

4. Sister Julia Bolton Holloway reported her preliminary findings in a talk given at the University of Colorado at Boulder, May 1993. The rest of the folios in W are devoted to other contemporary English mystical writings; a technical description of W can be found in Colledge and Walsh's introduction to their Toronto edition of the *Shewings*, which they have titled *A Book of Showings to the Anchoress Julian of Norwich*, Part I, 9–10.

pendent work of fourteenth-century English mysticism of the first water. As it is, with the access we in fact do have to the content, shape, and webs of concern informing the other manuscripts, W appears, if anything, even more illuminating: not only in terms of what is present in the manuscript, which is a great deal indeed, but perhaps just as significantly in terms of what is absent.

W has never appeared in the kind of scholarly edition that Sister Julia envisions, only in a modern English translation of the entire W manuscript, now long out of print.[5] It is high time to make W more available, and in a version that brings us much closer to the actual manuscript than modern idiom usually allows. Our own need for a base text for this study provides an ideal occasion, for W is short enough to handle in the scope of our study, and yet sufficiently representative and rich in detail to serve as a reliable textual foundation for analysis.

To prepare for a systematic presentation and reading of W, it is useful to review briefly the kinds of problems Julian faced as she converted recollected private vision into an authoritative public text to be read by her "evencristen" (that wonderful Middle English word for fellow-Christians). We shall also consider some hypotheses regarding her resulting strategies as we shall later see them figured in the shape and pitch of her work.

THE KENOSIS OF CHRIST AND JULIAN'S FIELD OF PLAY

> [One must have a mind of winter . . . not to think
> of any misery in the sound of the wind . . .
> For the listener, who listens in the snow,
> And, nothing himself, beholds
> Nothing that is not there and the nothing that is.
> Wallace Stevens, The Snow Man.]

The shewings in the standard editions of both S and L begin with the bleeding crucifix. As Julian recalls for us a crisis of illness and prostration, she reports her shock, while gazing on a crucifix, to see the carved head of Christ abruptly begin to bleed. And as we imagine her watching with horror, we see in our mind's eye a highly conventional image of Christ partially transform itself from the status of sign back into that of signifier, from the status of the relative safety of a comfortable, everyday piece of medieval household furniture back into that moment

---

5. *The Knowledge of Ourselves and of God*, Edmund Colledge and James Walsh, editors (London: Mowbray, Fleurs-de-lys Series, 1961).

of "love-daungere" that was always already happening fifteen hundred years ago at Calvary on the cross.

But here we must move with circumspection: what she says she saw is not what it was she saw. I am not suggesting any raving delusion or any calculated perfidy on her part, but rather wish to call into discussion something of which Julian herself was very much aware: the inevitable ontological gap between what it is we perceive, and our perceptions and depictions of it. For Julian, it is precisely in that gap of transaction between what is seen and what is said that we can, with love and good will, discover what we are really looking for. Julian's verbal strategies, in converting whatever it was she saw into the imagery that she wants us to read and see, are not only beautiful and powerful in and of themselves, but crucial for any adequate understanding of her program.

We turn for a moment to L's report of the shewing of the bleeding Christ, noting that although the image of the bleeding head is of foundational importance in all versions of S and L, it is conspicuously absent in W. Here is the shewing drawn from the text of *LS*:

> The great drops of blood fell down from under the garland like pellets seeming as if they had come out of the veins; and in the coming out it was brown red, for the blood was full thick; and in the spreading abroad it was bright red; and when it came to the brows, then it vanished. Notwithstanding, the bleeding continued till many things were seen and understood. **The fairehede and the livelyhede is like nothing but the same** [The fairness (but also the fair head and the forehead), and the liveliness (but also the living head) *is like nothing but the same as that which it was*]. The plenteousness was like the drops of water that fall off the eaves after a great shower of rain that falls so thick that nobody may number them with bodily wit. And for the roundness, it was like the scales of herring in the spreading over the forehead. . . . pellets for roundness in the coming out of the blood; the scales of herring in the spreading on the forehead . . . the drops off eaves for the plenteousness innumerable. **This shewing was quick and lively, and hidouse and dredfull, swete** [sweet, but also a resonance here with "sweaty"] **and lovely.**[6]

6. All translations, glosses, and emphases are mine. For the ME text of this passage, see Glasscoe, Sloane Long Text, 7. In all quotations from the *Shewings* I render key words and problematic phrases in the original Middle English and provide a gloss for them in square brackets. This reverses the procedure used for Hildegard's Latin. It is necessary because the kind and range of ambiguity are not only extremely rich in Julian's English,

What are we to make of the authorial intrusions by which Julian speaks to us *about* what she saw, even as she tells us what it *was* she saw? How understand that the head of Christ in its livingness was "like nothing but the same" as what it was. And how deal with the dislocating effect triggered in us by the apparent contradictions inherent in the affect of the shewing: "quick and lively," but also "hideous"; "sweet and lovely," but also "dreadful?"

Let us first probe that sense of contradiction and resulting dislocation. The adjectives come at us in pairs, each of which can be seen as dealing with three different domains of experience. The first, "quick and lively," reports Bonaventure's *extra nos*, we "see" the vision as it displays purely exterior phenomena, i.e., the way that the carved figure of Christ on the crucifix appears, by its bleeding, to be suddenly alive. The second, "hideous and dreadful," signals the realm of *intra nos*, the interior domain of response: we "see" the effect of the bleeding upon Julian's observing sensibility. The third pair, "sweet and lovely," appears more meditative: we "see" the result of an analysis, one that can be construed as exegetical in terms of the revelation of divine intention lying above and behind the shewing [*supra nos*].[7]

But such "domains" should not be mistaken for "explanations": they neither do nor should resolve our sense of dislocation.[8] On the contrary, noting them helps us better see how Julian's very conflation of these domains creates an ambiguity of response that in turn triggers a sense of distortion and disorientation in us as readers. The fact that we see her collapse domains of experience that are normally kept carefully separate should excite, not mask, our sense of their being telescoped by Julian into a special kind of narrative simultaneity.

Our challenge is then to ask why Julian engaged in such disordering of normal modes of discourse in the first place. I suggest she collapsed these orders to help us fully appreciate the tension she saw operating between the divine signifier (God) and his human targets (us). She excites our interest and concern, and even our curiosity by her multiple modes of "receiving" the imaging-forth of Christ's *kenosis*, his self-

---

but an intrinsic part of her literary program. By using this method we can more efficiently test the range of meanings of her many code words as she weaves them into a system of multi-layered signification.

7. The taxonomy of *extra nos*, *intra nos*, *supra nos*, already raised in the discussion of Hildegard, is derived from Bonaventure's *Itinerarium mentis in Deum*.

8. Vincent Gillespie and Maggie Ross, who drew my attention to this passage, agree: "Julian makes no attempt to resolve the paradoxes of this description, instead she allows them to imply the different perspectives which simultaneously coinhere in the showing." See their "Apophatic Image: The Poetics of Effacement in Julian of Norwich," in *The Medieval Mystical Tradition in England: Exeter Symposium V*, ed. by Marion Glasscoe (Cambridge: D.S. Brewer, 1992), 62.

humiliation and self-emptying on the cross, and so we become more active, participatory readers. In a sense, we are being taught a medieval lesson in reader-response theory. As we gradually discover that our awakened, critical sense of dislocation is part of her design, we realize that it is only when our energies as participatory readers prevail and create more vivid and participatory encounters with her text, that Christ's promise can also be read as her own: "all shall be well, and all manner of thing shall be well."

Turning now to the phrase which asserts that the **fairehead and the livlihed** are "like nothing but the same," we find that whatever difficulty we may have in reconstructing the image of what Julian saw, the implications of this observation of hers are in fact pretty clear: Christ is NOT LIKE anything but that which he is. By describing the head of the bleeding Christ as both an objective ("head"-as-bleeding-body-part) and as abstract ("head" as a suffix marker for "superiority," "quality," or "quiddity" (cf. "woman-hood," "man-hood," "maiden-head," "God-head"), and then couching that "head" in the mixed terms of "hideous," and "lovely," Julian leads us directly into St. Augustine's "land of un-likeness." We recall him saying to his own longed-for Christ: "The radiance of your aspect reverberated violently within my weakness, **mixing love with horror**; and I knew that for a long time I would find you only in the land of unlikeness [et reverberasti infirmitatem aspectus mei radians in me vehementer, et **contremui amore et horrore**: et inveni longe me esse ad te in regione dissimilitudinis] (*Confessions* 7.10, my translation and emphasis). In a landscape that is totally familiar there is nothing new to learn. It is precisely (and only) in such regions of unlikeness that revelation becomes possible, for it is only the recognitions of those ironclad and intransigent facts of dissimilitude, residing exactly at the center of any assertion of similitude, which can trigger new awareness.[9]

When Dante says of his teacher Brunetto Latini, "and he ran the race like a winner, not like a loser" (*Inferno*, 15.124), he is demonstrating two things at once. Even as he asserts a similitude, he denies an identity: the subtext lying under the words, "not like a loser, but like a winner," reads "but of course he was in actual fact a loser." The word "like" is NOT the word "is"—that is one of the most important things about it.[10] By the very nature of discourse itself there is always some factor of difference in assertions of similitude. And as the words uttered "in consort" can create as well as reflect worlds, we should probably see

9. See my chapter on the tensions in Augustine between like and unlike in *Now through a Glass Darkly*, esp. 55–59.
10. See my digression on the special case of infernal figuration in *Glass Darkly*, 175–78.

this linguistic situation as central to the human condition. In medieval theological terms, only God *is* God (Yahweh Yahweh), whereas it is we who are LIKE God. Our redemption stems from the fact that we were made *ad imaginem Dei*; but the gap of difference between the fallen image and the Original, even within the mutually redemptive embrace of human freedom and divine design, remains ineluctable. It is to help us see and deal with this proto-tragic, yet also potentially revelatory and redemptive gap of unlikeness that partly accounts for the design and strategy of Julian's discourse.

So if the principle of similarity (and not identity) ordinates the meaning(s) of difference, it is precisely within this sense of gap and contradiction, as opened up by Julian's discourse, that we not only can, but must, with eyes wide open, walk our chancey pilgrimages as careful readers. Any attempt on our part at premature resolution of meaning (any indulgence in, say, what Richard Rorty calls a "final" vocabulary) would be a kind of intellectual foreclosure, tantamount to a moral and ethical, if only figurative suicide.[11] Such a concession to the seductions of finality might well "perfect" our quest, but only in the grammatical sense of "bringing to an end" our "sentence"—our pilgrimage toward meaning. We learn that meaning for Julian, and by extension for her readers, is not so much structural, nor teleological in any severely construed sense of that word, but rather ongoing, gerundive, processive; never over with until death does in fact us part.

So when we "see" within Julian's discourse an image of Julian "seeing" Christ—who is figured to her first as signified, and then revealed as living, originating signifier, we begin to see that the appropriate direction for seeking meaning here is not from the sign out into the implied otherness of the world, but rather the reverse: through the sign back into the implied signifier of the words.

As we watch Julian learn to cope with these disorienting senses of what it was she saw, we must learn to read "for love" the disturbing and disruptive ways in which she provides us with verbal mediations of her sense of things. As we seek to unpack her discourse, we shall see that she has composed her language so that the act of reading it becomes a simulacrum of her own act of encountering her shewing. The way we learn to cope with her text grows into a mirroring analog

---

11. See Rorty's *Contingency, irony, and solidarity* (Cambridge: Cambridge University Press, 1989), esp. "The Contingency of language," 3–22. I would argue that Julian's programmatic resistance to the strategies of closure in her discourse reflects not only a poetics of "self-effacement" (see Gillespie and Ross, "Apophatic Image,") but also her deep and empowering sense of irony, as well as a healthy, life-furthering respect for contingency, which comes to her as she intuits the discrepancies of knowing that she sees as obtaining between reality as seen by us, and reality as she believes it is seen by God.

of her own epistemological processing, of the way she learned, over the years, not only to cope with, but also to share her vision: two acts which, in an important sense, become one as we complete our reading of her text. And we begin to see that creating a "feminine" style adequate to the fulfillment of this mirroring task became, in her hands, a primary means of converting her readership.

As we try to develop more adequate modes of reading Julian's discourse, we are led, by sound academic instinct, to seek the help of contemporary medieval theories of textual interpretation. There we find that, of the standard exegetical programs, the dominant one of "reading" or interpreting the literal sense of the image (*sensus litteralis*) outward in search of a spiritual sense of the image (*sensus spiritualis*) is the wrong program for us. It works the wrong way around, and directs and carries us away from precisely where it is we wish to arrive. We need a different program, one that more fully assesses the "literal level" on its own grounds and on its own terms. And we find it in a mode of reading scripture that also has an important history in medieval culture: "reading for the letter": *ad litteram*. This was a program of crafting expositions of biblical texts that sought deeper and richer understandings of the *sensus litteralis* by construing the words given on the page as *already constituting* a "spiritual" sign, and then proceeding to read it "backward and inward," hoping to capture a sense of the originating act of signifying. This is a kind of "de-reading," perhaps we can even call it a "deconstruction" of the "spiritual" image as given to us on the page in the search of the originating gesture that impelled and occasioned it.

We find, in this process of de-reading Julian's discourse, that the meaning of the word "meaning" in the *Shewings* becomes not only a tantalizing, but also an illuminating issue all by itself. If we turn to the *MED*, we find that the word **menen**, in its many verbal and nominal forms, ranges over an extremely wide semantic field, from **intention**, through **mediation**, to the completion of intended acts of **agency** (more detailed glossing is provided in the commentary below). This kind of linguistic evidence helps us resist capitulation to the domination of the centrifugal, and we can feel more justified in exploring those ways of meaning in and by which images implode, move in, and back upon themselves.

This inward direction of signification is actually as ancient as it was medieval, and remains post-modern. As I have already suggested, it is even reflected in the etymology of the Greek word for "symbolize" itself: syn + ballein: a throwing or falling together, a condensing, compacting: something a potter does when throwing a pot, or a cook when throwing dinner together. As we approach a well-made pot, we have a primal, healthy desire to touch it, fill it, lift it, and hold it, in order to sense more fully its function, scale, shape, and heft. And as we watch a good cook cook, we have not so much the desire to learn what the dinner means, but to dive in and eat it. So it is with Julian's discourse. Of course we want to know what it means, but that includes our desire to explore it on its own terms, to test it, touch it, and taste it fully with our "sensualyte" (an important, and favorite term of hers)—in order to get into its "substance", so that we can fully appropriate it and make it our own. This we discover, as we analyze her discourse, is precisely what she had in mind.

So when Julian says that the bleeding Christ she saw was not LIKE anything but "the same that which it was," we must think, not of an image referring outward, but of an image that, at least for the time she saw it in her moment of visionary crisis, was exquisitely **in vivo,** and therefore purely self-reflective. And even though existentially this was for her a "suspended moment" in time, there is still an implied narrative in the way we read her report, as we watch Julian watching a statue of Christ undergo a metamorphosis back over fourteen hundred years into the event that impelled its carving.

What can we call this sort of image, this image that even more than radiating out beyond itself to the world that is other than itself, actually shines back onto itself and into its impelling moment, providing its own back-lighting? Recently, Gillespie and Ross, in the title of an article just cited, suggested a name for it: "the apophatic image."

In Lewis and Short's monumental *New Latin Dictionary* (1879), we find the Greek word *apophasis* cited as a rhetorical figure; here is the entry in its entirety: "apophasis (denial), rhet. fig., whereby one, as it were, answers himself, Jul. Ruf. 8." Now if it is true, at least for dictionary makers, that what a word really means is a result of a committee show of hands, let us stipulate that for our purposes, "apophatic" refers to that aspect of any image that refers inward to and on itself, especially in cases where such reflexivity or self-referentiality is the dominant mode of signification.

We can summarize all this by returning again to the image of the bleeding Christ. Julian gives us two takes: first as it shewed itself to her; second as she figures the analog of that shewing in the act of textualizing it for us. We cannot see, in any unmediated way, what it was she saw, nor can we really reconstruct what happened in Julian's head when she saw it. We can do much better with what she gives us to read. My perhaps overly labored point here is that what **we** are seeing is not what Julian saw, but what Julian crafted as a considered scenario for our own **act** of seeing, a complex verbal icon constructed of language that she hoped could trigger in our heads the **kind** of transformation that the original shewing triggered in hers. As we look at her text, we see an image of certain carefully chosen words (as opposed to words not chosen) deployed in a certain carefully chosen order (as opposed to an order not chosen). It is in this verbal icon of ordinated phonemes, lexis and syntax, that we must learn to see, however darkly, her figure of the incarnated Word.

So much for the literary aspect of both the text and the originating phenomena comprising Julian's shewings. What makes this all theologically cogent has to do with two aspects of the suffering Christ: his hypostasy, or dual nature, by which he participates in the domain of humanity as well as that of divinity, and his kenosis, his self-emptying, his partial self-sacrifice of his divinity by assuming our humanity in the Incarnation, a self-emptying that is both reversed, parodied, and culminated in his "noughting for love" on the cross.

How does she make a language that figures forth both Christ's hypostasy and his kenosis? How does she make her language more apophatic? It is important to feel to the bone the truth of the assertion that language signifies both centrifugally and centripetally. Of course ALL words, including all of Julian's words, refer outward—they signify to a world beyond themselves. But all words also refer inward in and upon themselves: the word *cat* not only refers outward to four-legged furry creatures, but also inward to a concatenation of syllables, phonemes, and tonal colorations. Julian raises the apophatic ante by making more dominant the centripetal, inward-pointing power of her discourse. How?

One primary strategy is lexical. She uses a small group of key words each of which has many meanings; she then repeats them very often together in order to create complex patterns, concatenations, and interlacings whose own denotative (as well as connotative) range is so rich and strange as to appear at times self-contradictory, disjunctive, even, at times, dysfunctional. The attentive reader of such a risky and apparently unstable lexicon remains far less passive than usual, becomes radically more participatory, and because of that, can easily learn to feel greater personal responsibility for the act of reading her discourse more adequately.

Julian's second primary strategy is syntactical. She orders her phrases so as to avoid, wherever possible, the kinds of implied interdependencies and hierarchies among parts and wholes that lead to sentence closure. In Julian's discourse each phrase seems to generate, or at least link onto, or into, the next—and actual grammatical closure is for long stretches programmatically avoided and, when it does finally occur, seems almost "accidental." And that is because it usually **is** accidental, at least in the medieval sense of that word.

Normally impending closure is signaled, not only by word order, but also by such supra-segmental markers in the manuscript as punctuation: particularly periods and capitalization. In W, both periods and capitalization are used generously—but not consistently. Eventually this inconsistency must be laid to the hand of the scribe; what is interesting is that such scribal vagaries ironically reinforce Julian's general program of chipping away at the usual "male" horizon of expectation regarding orderly moves toward closure.

In many ways the act of reading the *Shewings* involves active collaboration with Julian to defer our itch for closure, in favor of the pleasures of participating in a kind of verbal dance, in the weaving of an endlessly elaborating textile (Lat. *textus* = "fabric" as well as "text"), in which the discourse, in the very process of our reading it, weaves in our mind complex figures which curl forward, reach out, but also loop back on themselves, creating a syntactic image of their speaker's own assaults and reversals. It thus becomes very clear, very soon, that Julian's design for us in the reading of her writing is not that we reach any conclusion, but that we continue our encounter with her text as a co-celebration of the life-generating and life-furthering energy of the divine logos itself.

We will see this in much greater detail as we attack the particularities of her text. As we move into that process, let me complete this first pass at Julian's feminine style of visionary writing by saying again that she crafts an apophatic discourse that "stands" as an analog of the apophatic vision she herself saw. Thus our act of reading her words becomes an analog of her act of seeing her shewings. And as we watch her "unpack" the living "verbum" of Christ as he reveals himself to her in and as his own signifying *res,* or person, we also watch our own unpacking of Julian's "verbal icon" become a linguistic version of the *imitatio Christi.* In more participatory acts of reading Julian's discourse, it seems to transform before our mind's eyes and ears from received text to living voice, and reading it becomes, in our delight in its endless elaboration, a kind of prefatory reflection of the long-desired, long-promised encounter with the living Word.

READING THE WESTMINSTER *SHEWINGS*

The unpublished Westminster Manuscript

The Westminster Manuscript, as indicated earlier, has a set of organizing principles and rhythms all its own. Whoever was responsible for this text, whether Julian in a separate rescension, or some now anonymous scribe compiling from one or more now missing manuscripts, W has a unity of design and purpose that goes far beyond that implied by calling it mere compilation.

Perhaps one of the most important characteristics of W is its seamlessness. There are no formal indications of division, no rubrics, no interior catchwords in the margin. But a strong sense of an ordering principle surfaces nonetheless. On analysis one finds oneself carried along in a kind of cursive fluidity, crested by seven major surges of thematic concern, which I have, for strategic purposes, artificially highlighted by dividing the whole into subsections.

A second feature that makes W unique is the way the beginning, middle, and end are deeply in accord with each other, forming a unified whole, and yet differ considerably in strategy and effect from S as well as either version of L. This extraordinary document of a rising and falling rhythm of interior meditation and exhortation opens with a visionary tableau, not of the bleeding crucifix, but of Mary in the posture of the *stabat mater,* in the still and quiet act of beholding her son. From that image of an adoring and expectant woman all begins. After forty folios of flowing discourse, W ends with a very short sentence, voiced in a suddenly distanced timbre: "It is godis wyll that we sett the poynt of our thought in this blessed beholdyng, as often as we may, & as long." As we shall see below, in any sense that finally matters, this is no "ending" at all: neither grammatically, rhetorically, nor thematically—yet it has the feel of credible, even appropriate closure. Here in W, at the point of valediction, is no envoy to the reader, no prayer for the speaker, the writer or the reader: no Amen—but an admonishment to continue indefinitely with Julian in her meditation, perhaps by starting again at the beginning.

Contrary to the unbroken interior design of W, I have decided, as I said, to present the Julian section of the manuscript, for greater ease of study and analysis, in eight major parts, with precisely the sort of rubrics that are not present in the manuscript. That, along with the occasional resulting interruption in presentation of a given folio, is the crucial, but sole deviation between my "male" presentation here, and the "feminine" format of W in the manuscript. Otherwise each section below, identified with folio numbers, represents what is actually on the identically numbered folios, or pages, of the W manuscript. If a sentence, or even a word in the manuscript continues onto the next page, it does so here as well.

At those moments that seem to me to indicate the trough of the wave, indicating the move of Julian's mind from one thematic surge to another, I break presentation of the text and enter into commentary, as one can see by the shift in format. Like any good commentary, this one should begin to exhaust its own necessity long before the end of the work it seeks to illuminate; therefore there is much more of it in the first half of the *Shewings* than in the latter half. Structural symmetries may be appropriate in the work under observation, but they seldom have any useful function in explication. So as we move toward the end of the *Shewings*, my intrusions will subside somewhat in what I hope is an appropriate act of self-effacement, and the voice of Julian will sing at the end with less encumbering accompaniment.

A preliminary note on language(s)—

Many fourteenth-century words had a wider denotative as well as connotative range than they do now, and in the development of English over the centuries, some of that range was naturally diminished, dispersed, and sometimes transformed altogether. Part of the challenge of reading an older form of our own language derives from the impact, over time, of that natural lexical evolution. As we look back, we see there is often a kind of reconstructive project we need to undertake. We must seek to regather meanings now more widely dispersed throughout our lexicon and repack them back into a semantic construct that more closely resembles what the word in its earlier state meant to a contemporary who spoke or wrote it. There are about two dozen such words of special importance in Julian's core lexicon for which we need to do this; one of them, as we shall see, is the word **menen**, or "meaning" itself.

Near the end of L, Julian reports the result of her second visionary aftershock, which she experienced in 1393, and which helped her better see the implications of what was shewed to her in 1373: "Woldst thou wetten [know] thy lords **menen** in this thing? Wete it wele: love was hys mening." (LS 102.12–13). But before we leap to any conclusions ourselves about **hys menen**, we must know that the meaning of the word **menen** for Julian was not limited to mere "lexical signification." We must realize that it also meant "modes of agency" (as in the phrase, "ways and means"). The answer to the question becomes significantly expanded as one scans the denotative ranges of the word **menen**: Love was not only his "intending," but also his "mediating," "transacting," and his "doing."

Once we suspect the presence of such "portmanteaus" at the core of Julian's vocabulary, the question arises: how can we reconstruct, with any sense of confidence, their full medieval semantic range? Fortunately, we have two lexical reference works at our disposal which track historical usage in impressive detail. In addition to the *Oxford English Dictionary* (OED), we also have the nearly equally massive *Middle English Dictionary* (MED), which, though still in progress, is now complete through most of the letter S.

Each of the ME "code" words identified here as belonging to Julian's core vocabulary has been traced, first in the MED and then, as an additional check, in the OED, tracking their semantic development from roughly the twelfth to the fifteenth centuries. The more highly differentiated modern meanings of these core words are placed in square brackets, after their occurrence in the text, and the words themselves are given in their original form.

* * * * *

THE TEXT, WITH GLOSS AND COMMENTARY
THE SHEWINGS OF JULIAN OF NORWICH

Incipit: "the soule of oure blessed lady" (fols. 72v-mid 73v).

[72v] Our gracious & good lord God **shewed me in party** [revealed to me in part] the wisdom & the truth of the soul of our blessed lady, saint Mary, wherein I understood the reverent **beholdynge**, that she **behelde** her God that is her **maker**, marveling with great reverence that he would be **borne of** [born of, borne by] her that was a simple creature of his **makyng**. For this was her marvelling, that he that was her **maker** [maker + echo of **make** (spouse or peer)] would be born of her that is **made** [created, fore-echo of **maiden**]. And this wisdom & truth, knowing the greatness of her **maker**, and the littleness of her

[73r] self that is **made**, caused her to say full meekly unto Gabriel: **Lo me here** [Look at me here], God's **hand maiden** [hand-maid, (hand-made)]. This wisdom & truth made her to behold her God so great, so high, so mighty, and so good that the greatness & the nobility & beholding God filled her full of reverent dread. And with this she saw her self so little & so low, so simple & so poor in regard of her God, that his **reverent drede** filled her full of meekness. And this: **by this grounde** [for this reason, on these grounds] she was filled full of grace & of all manner of virtues, and passes over all creatures. In this

[73v] sight, I understood truly that she is more than all that God made beneath her in worthiness & in fullness, for above her there is no thing that is made but the blessed manhood of Christ, as to my sight. And this our good lord shewed to

my understanding **in lernyng of us** [by teaching us about ourselves].

72v–73v. The Shewings of W open with a vision of the Virgin Mary in a posture of cynosure: gazing on the Deity that is both God her Maker and her Son. Other versions open with the suddenly bleeding head of Christ upon which Julian gazes in her grave illness. W begins with Julian, with no mark of illness, gazing at the gazing Mary: and there is no specific image made available to us of the form of the deity on which she gazes. We see Julian seeing Mary, but not what it is that Mary sees.

72v. —Shewed me in party—showed me in part. ME **shewing,** as both participle and noun, had a wide field of denotation, ranging from the general indicative sense of the modern words "showing," "relating," and "informing," to the more technically perceptual, often theological senses of "vision" or "revelation." As we shall see, Julian used, as a fundamental strategy in her compositional procedures, the entire denotative and connotative range of all of her key words, and she did so most of the time. At frequent intervals, she repeats these key words (e.g. not only **shewing,** but a string of other words as well, such as **lykyng, besekyng, mening, kynde**, etc.) in rhythmic patterns of verbal concatenation, imagistic interlace, and phonic cantillation, patterns whose theological as well as literary impact we will need to examine rather closely.

As we note these special moments of concatenated repetition of key words, we sense rather keenly the centrality of a select master lexicon driving her discourse. As we sense a style characterised by a sharply reduced range of repeated lexical items, we also sense a style that is carefully orchestrated in terms of its range of effect. We feel the ordinating pressures of her style narrowing us inward in terms of intellectual focus, guiding us ever more deeply into the hidden implications of her text. And there are several reasons that we feel moved by the flow of her discourse, not so much toward the severance and release of closure, as into the welcoming embrace of enclosure.

As we reflect on this sense, however gently imposed, of readerly manipulation, we discover that Julian's style, like that of both Vibia Perpetua and Hildegard of Bingen, employs important techniques of avoidance as well as commission. For example, she avoids, in her feminine style, many of the conventional modes by which male medieval writers establish clear senses of division, and thus of spatial, temporal, causal, and even hierarchic relationships, those divisions which keep our minds moving in a relatively linear fashion through a sense of discourse primarily as a matter of structure rather than process. In the dominant mode of medieval discourse formation, which Julian avoids, we are always impelled by and drawn to the desire for periodic and gratifying moments of severance. It is this linear, hypertactic mode of a writing that rushes to closure that we have come in this study to identify as an aspect of the male style.

In addition to avoiding such signals of division and immanent closure, Julian's feminine writing selects and deploys its own conventions for generating the expectation of continuance. She establishes sometimes curvilinear, sometimes phasic ("chaotic" or nonlinear) senses of flow, of loop, and of surge. This capacity of Julian's feminine discourse to proceed without generating a countering pressure to cease, to coil and curve, advance and return, bunch and disperse, can easily and frequently collapse our expectations of discursive clarity as somehow dependent upon the more masculine manipulations of distance and proximity: starting and stopping, domination and subordination.

Finally, we shall discover that Julian's feminine style of writing is extremely effective in establishing a programmatic ambiguity that results, not from any urge to occlude or deceive, but from a resistance, in the service of candor, to select and privilege one item over a range of items, and thereby reduce the inventory of possibility. This inclusionary aspect of the feminine style is also shaped, and our resulting sense of its non-linearity is enhanced, by forwarding strategies that generate the effect of a limitless source of energy, as we engage in revising our interior constructions of space and time in response to her discourse. In the arsenal of a will as committed and dedicated as Julian's, this feminine style is well-suited as an art of radical persuasion. It can convert our perspective on the mystery of things by radically converting our horizons of readerly expectation. And it allows her to achieve a startling edge to her voice, even as she seeks to recruit, embrace, and console us.

—shewed me . . . There is a long and useful tradition, continued here, of referring to Julian's text, as well as the visions she received, in the ME form of the word *"shewings."* The most important reason for this spelling convention is to keep a steady reminder in our eye of the fourteenth-century sense of what the word meant. Here she means all that **shewed me** *can* mean: the "lord God *shewed me in part* [both 'informed me in part about,' as well as 'sent me a holy vision containing a part of'], the wisdom and the truth. . . ."

—in party. In addition to the familiar, colloquial sense of "in part," there is a strong resonance with, if not an actual allusion to, Paul's famous formula that captures our sense of being doomed to partial knowing in this life: "Now I know *in part*: then I will know as I am known [nunc cognosco *ex parte*; tunc autem cognoscam sicut et cognitus sum] (1 Corinthians 13.12). Paul's doctrine of partial knowing is crucial to an adequate understanding of what it is that Julian is telling us about what she saw—and it is fully figured in what she has given us to read. Of course, the fundamental authority of her vision as divinely inspired remained for her unquestioned; but she was always more than merely aware of the fact that her own adequacy in the face of revealed truth could only be partial, if only because of the contingencies defining the fallen human condition.

Paul's *ex parte* has another sense that even further enhances the existential reach of Julian's phrasing: not only "to know a part **of** it," but also "to know while being apart **from** it," to know as an outsider. In this life our intelligences, which appear to us so central in everyday life, are marginal in relationship to the mind of God; we are outsiders looking in. And this direction of "looking in" from the outside is precisely the exegetical direction we must pursue in our reading of Julian's writing. We find that to participate actively in the parsing of her sentences is to uncover an epistemic gap, and thus enhance our understanding of the fact that our current knowledge is and can only be partial: that only on the other side of death shall we know "then" as fully as we are known "now."

73v.—**Lo me here.** "Look at me here." Only in W does this vision of the Virgin Mary play such a central mediating role. In S, Julian is first shewed a vision of the bleeding figure of Christ, then a "ball the quantity of a hazelnut," and then, beholding her maker, the Virgin Mary. L also begins with a vision of the image of Christ suddenly bleeding, but the "presence" of Mary is significantly deferred. The focus of the shewings in L remains steadfastly upon Christ until the eleventh shewing, when Christ, by looking down at his right, "brings to mind," not the Virgin, but the place where our Lady, according to the traditional *stabat mater* iconography of the Crucifixion, stood "at the time." In L, Christ asks Julian, almost teasingly: "Wilt thou see her?" And although Julian answers in the affirmative, she never reports that a vision of the Virgin was actually brought to her.

The decision in W, then, is not to follow L, but rather to enhance the strategy of S. By opening this section with a sustained vision of Mary beholding her maker, rather than with the horrifics of the head of the bleeding Christ, W creates a major shift of emphasis and perspective: from the thing seen to the act of seeing the thing. The image of Mary as Mediatrix beholding Christ lets us see his suffering in the mirror of her own maternal eyes, and this renders the scene as a tableau of the gaze, of cynosure, and renders it paradigmatic—both foreshadowing and contextualizing Julian's beholding as well as our own.

Surrounding the shewing of the Virgin is a dance of rich and illuminating wordplay that enriches her mystery: "Lo," and "behold," and their root verbs, "look" and "hold," are concatenated with the words "maker," "made," and "maiden." Julian suggests, in her opening image, that at the portal of our genesis stands our innocence, our own virginity figured in the expectant, lady-in-waiting, maid Mary, who at and from "the beginning" of this revelation of love both "beholds" and "holds" her maker. If we read the words aloud, we hear phonic cantillation as well as thematic concatenation. The phonetic "music" derives from the strong resonance **maker** (mAHkehr) and **made** have with the ME noun **make** (mAHkeh), the word for "spouse" or "peer." This phonic resonance sounds a quiet, ironic echo that anticipates something even more piquant: the ludic echo reverberating between **made** and **maiden**. For although there was a phonetic difference in Middle English between the /ah/ of the past participle **made** (mAHde) and the /eye/ of the noun **maiden** (mEYEden)—the sounds of which are nearly identical in modern English—there was nonetheless sufficient resonance for the like sounds of these two differing words to signal the looming of a sexual pun long and deeply embedded in English-speaking culture.

Mary, an adoring and expectant mother, is depicted at the same time as a "made" maid, a pure and receptive vessel created as always already filled with light and vision, beholding her son and maker, and saying to the angel Gabriel: "Look at me here, God's hand-maiden, made in God's image and by God's hand." In ME, **Lo** is colloquial intensive of the imperative form of the verbs "look" and "behold" (MED). And **beholden** is in turn an intensive form of the verb **holden**, which has a very wide range of denotation, only one aspect of which has to do with acts of looking or seeing. And we need to know that another important sense of ME **beholden** is very close to the modern German *behalten*—to possess or retain. So Julian's imperative to Gabriel, **Loo me here** generates an echo chamber of subtexts that includes not only the imperative to "Look at me here" but also a richocheting set of enriching, interweaving minor signals: "Look at me here, Hold me here, Hold on to me here, Possess me here, Retain me here, even as I am: God's hand-made handmaid."

Here, in the riffs that Julian plays on the various senses of "holding" and "beholding" Christ, we discover that we can only appropriate him (make him our own) by correctly reading (seeing) the entire process of the "meaning" of Christ's self-willed suffering. The intending, transmitting, and effecting of his shewing on the cross is indivisible (or as Julian will later say, "unparceable"), and the apparent dichotomy between signifier and signified must be resynthesized, by means of a new appropriation of the sign, into the interiority of the "seer" who is Mary, Julian, and ourselves. As we work through Julian's discourse as a simulacrum that imitates her own working through her shewing, we realize that we have "beheld" or read well when we begin to sense we have possessed and retained well. The test, of course, is a felt sense, as well as an intellectual appreciation, of a reformed, or at least realigned interiority. Revelation here is no easy, ecstatic escape from the severe demands of critical thought. Julian's impulse when encountering holy vision is never to abandon or escape the powers of intellect and memory, but rather to seize and use those "medieval faculties" of mind in ever intenser modes of application. The eye of Julian's vision now moves from the generalized image of Mary, to an even more intellectualized image of Christ: seen not in picture, but in words. He in turn shows Julian "a lytil thing."

God and the Cosmos: "He shewed me a lytil thyng the quantity of a hazelnut" (73v–76r)

[73v (cont.)] Also I saw that our good lord is to us every thing that is good & comfortable to our help. **He is oure clothyng,** which for love wraps us & winds us, helps us & **ablyth us** [enables/(clothes) us] and hangs about us for tender love, so that he may never

[74r] leave us. And so in this sight I saw that **he is al thyng** that is good, according to my understanding. And in this he shewed me **a lytil thyng the quantite of a hazyl nott** [nut] lying in the palm of my hand as it seemed, and it was as round as any ball. I looked upon it **with the eye of my understondyng,** and I thought what may this be. And it was answered generally thus. It is all that is made. I marveled how it might last, for I thought it might suddenly have **fallen to nought** [fallen to nothing, into nothingness] **for littleness** [for being so little]. And I was answered in my under

[74v] standing. It lasts & ever shall for God loves it, and so has every thing its beginning by the love of God. In this little thing I saw three **propertees.** The first is, that God made it, the second is, that God loves it, and the third is that God keeps it. But what is this to me? **Truly, the maker, the keeper & the lover.** For until I am substantially **oned to** [united to, unified with] him, I may never have full rest nor true bliss, that is to say, that I be so fastened to him that there be no thing that is

made between my God & me. This little thing that is made, I thought

[75r] it might have **fallen to nought for littleness**. Of this we need to have knowing that **it is like to nought all thyng that is made** [it is like negating everything that has been made] to love & have God that is **unmade** [himself uncreated]. For this is the cause **why that we be not all in ease of heart** [why we are uneasy in heart] & soul: **for we seek here reste**, in this **thyng** that is so little wherein [there] is no **reste**, and **know not** God that is almighty, all wise & all good, for he is true **reste**. God will be known, and he likes it that we **reste us** [place ourselves, dwell, find peace for, and extension of, ourselves] in him, for all that is beneath him suffices **not** to us. And this is the cause why no soul is **rested** [rested, at rest, left, left to be dealt with, but also silenced, seized, or taken into custody] till it be

[75v] **noughted of** [set at nought regarding; despised, ignored, insulted by, refrained from, undone by, annihilated by, self-emptied of, self effaced by, but also freed by and freed from] all that is made. And when **he** is willfully **noughted** [self-denied, self-emptied, freed] for love, to have Him that is **all**, then is he able to receive **goostely** reste [spiritual quiet, but also silence, freedom from trouble, interruption, self-restraint, resolve, decision, purpose, cessation, exemption, continuation, remaining portion, extension, self-fulfillment]. Also that **she** wed our lord, that is full great pleasure to him, that a happy soul come to him nakedly, plainly & **homly** [intimately, vulnerably], for this is the **kynde yerning** [natural yearning, erotic desire, but also compassionate turning] of the soul by the touching of the holy ghost, as by the understanding that I have in this shewing. God for thy goodness give unto me thyself: **for** [except] thou art, I **noughte** [am nothing] to me, and I may ask no thing that is less that may be full worship to thee. And if I ask any

[76r] thing that is less, ever will I **want** [lack, desire], but only in thee have I all. And these words **God of thi goodnes** are full lovesome to the soul, and **full nigh** touching the will of our lord. For his goodness comprehends all his creatures & all his blessed work, and passes over without end. For he is the endless **hed** [person, head, quality, essence, being], and he has made us only **to hymselfe** [like unto, for the sake of him-

self], and restored us by his precious passion, & ever keeps us in his blessed love, and all this is of his goodness. This shewyng is given to my understanding to teach our souls wisely to cleave to the goodness of God.

73v–76r. In effect, this section brings two shewings to the eye of Julian's mind: neither of which can be pictorially represented as physically possible. The first is a general image of ourselves as clothed in Christ. The second is the entire universe presented as a ball the size of a hazelnut. The substance of the section is comprised of Julian's meditations on what her shewings signify: the cloak of Christ leads to an attempt to understand the implications of the Incarnation and the way in which we are created in the image of God. The vertigo triggered by seeing the universe as having the size of a hazelnut launches a concatenated meditation on negation as a way of moving closer to the real.

73v. —He is oure clothyng. Christ clothes us, presumbly by means of himself, using his dual nature to do so. For love he **ablyth us** [enables us, but also "suits us" (in the sense of dressing us in clothes, cf. Old French *habiller*)]. Two things of importance stand out here. First, there is the choice of the image of the cloak itself, an "integumentum" or "palliatum" that hides, protects, encloses, and warms something: presumably us, which includes our naked truth. Such an image of "fabrication"—of a stuff that both reveals the "outline" of what it conceals even as it protects and warms it, is extremely appropriate when the seer speaks a discourse designed to deal with apophatic vision.

Julian's use of the image of the cloak also suggests an exegetical situation in which we need to move inward as we seek the meaning. This use of an image to suggest directional emphasis is not anachronistic, no invention of yesterday: several similar (and popular) medieval images come to mind: the chaff enclosing the wheat-kernel, the nutshell enclosing the meat, and, one of Julian's own which we shall see later on: the **hart in the bouke** [heart in the belly].[1]

Second, we should also note the apophatic identification of the palliatum as Christ. The idea of Christ **as** a protective cloak sets up a horizon of expectation of Christ as encloser and protector. This proves especially helpful later for dealing with Julian's famous identification of Christ-as-Mother, and prepares us to read more adequately the stunning vision in f.87r below, in which, by peering with the smiling Christ-Mother into the vaginal wound of his/her crucified side, we see our future selves somehow always already new-born and at rest in the sa-

---

1. See my chapter on medieval commentary in *Glass Darkly,* 83–114.

cred heart of the heavenly city. It also prepares us for the final folios of W, in which Julian tells us that our souls are so deeply enclosed in God that **we have to know God before we can know our own souls.** The central message that Julian "enclothes" with this string of images of divine enclosing is that we must learn to know the palliatum, the literal sense of things, for all that it can be as well as bear in terms of meaning before we can prepare and credential ourselves sufficiently to find the truth that resides within it.

As we contemplate Julian's Christ as both Word and Clothing, we see that she has privileged the letter almost infinitely. One traditional way people thought exegetically about such images in the middle ages was to consider their literal sense, i.e. their "palliatum," with some disdain: as we today value the chaff or the nutshell as itself relatively worthless, even as it holds, hides, and protects what is valuable within. Hugh of Saint Victor warned his students (and the readers of his *Didascalicon*) of the seductive dangers of such attitudes of the allegorist: it can all too easily diminish the created sanctity of the sign-as-thing in favor of its meaning as sign-as-signifier. Julian asks us here, along with Hugh, rather to see the palliatum as capable of having just as much, and in this special case even "more" meaning than the secret it encloses. In Julian's image the palliatum is the living Christ, in that aspect of his hypostasy that he shares with us, our human nature, busily hiding, protecting, and clothing us. In terms of this image of Christ as Cloak, to know Christ is to know both his human, as well as the divine nature well enough to be able to see and know the divine aspect of ourselves hidden and protected within him. Finally, with further regard to Julian's "apophatic style," it is not a case, any more than it was for Hugh of Saint Victor, of either/or. Ultimately she, like Hugh, pushes and pulls us in both directions of signification simultaneously: centrifugally as well as centripetally. The gravitational power of both directions of her will helps us keep our own balance, keeps us in that middle position and distance between is and like, and between like and unlike, in a word, keeps us from falling asleep in Augustine's land of unlikeness. We are carefully suspended in our own mental air as we try to imagine a Thing that was so small, that It could fit into the palm of her hand (which it couldn't), and see It as having the quantity of a hazelnut (which it hasn't), and at the same time see It as "all that is made" (which it is).

74r. —a lytil thyng the quantite of a hazyl nott. The hazelnut passage is one of Julian's famous set-pieces. The apophatic "thing" at the center of the image of course is **not** a hazelnut: it is a "thing" that has the **quantity** of a hazelnut, and yet is "all that is made." Like any reader, I too am concerned about what the image means. But in this study I am most concerned with the way that her depiction of the image leads to and is extended by the verbal/phonic concatenation in which she situates it or inscribes it, in which she plays together for our ears to hear, almost musically, the sounds and referential powers of these particular words: **notte** [nut] plus **thynge** [= **nothing**] plus **nought** plus **one** plus **oned** [unified] plus **reste**. Contemplation of this extended verbal/phonic display links an image of Universe-as-size-of-hazelnut with an attending descant on "not-one-unified-thing-at-rest." This leads us to re[en]vision and so reconfigure our normative ideas of space and scale by and in which the human condition both exists, and figures itself forth, within a divinely instantiated cosmos.

74r. —with the eye of my understonding. Here she names one of the three perspectives from which she says she views her shewings, and for which she believes they were designed. Here is her trinitarian taxonomy of vision: the "eye of my understanding" is the eye of the intellect fed by words. There is also "bodily sight"—by which she seems to mean the normal physical act of seeing, and "gostly sight," a more spiritual kind of knowing. She also refers to domains of experience from the point of view of the category of objects, often as "three properties" (see 74v below). By using these terms she lightly orders the process both rhetorically and intellectually, but without forcing us into an atmosphere of undue schematic abstraction. One stretches the mind as one hovers around the interior image of an infinite cosmos which we try to "see as" having the size of a hazelnut.[2] And that seems to be the point: for us actively to stretch the capacity of the mind for new senses of scale and dimensionality.

74v. —thre propertees. As suggested above, these aspects of the object reflect, from the point of view of the thing seen, three ways of seeing them: bodily, ghostly and intellectual sight. There are further reverberations.

First, we should note the trinitarian rhythm: Julian's impulse to couch things in threes has both theological as well as psychological resonance.[3] In the Bible, the link between the divine and human do-

---

2. One sometimes feels in Julian's talk about seeing things medieval anticipations of Wittgenstein's "seeing as" and Vaihinger's "as if" [*als ob*]. It is as if our modes of visual perception were not only useful for literally seeing where it is we are, but also, however tentative and contingent on the moment, as modes of intellectual perception.

3. In the middle ages, there was no meaningful distinction between theology and psychology. The latter was not even a word, though its etymon would have been clear: psychology would have meant the logics of the soul, as theology would have to do with

mains was guaranteed at the point of our genesis: we were all made in the image of God (ad imaginem Dei). Augustine argues in many places that as we seek a better understanding of the "imago Dei" relation, it helps to see it as a matter of "psychological" imaging.[4] We were obviously not made in his physical image, our warts are not an image of God's warts. But our mental interiority, the three faculties of intellect (*intellectus*), will (*voluntas*) and memory (*memoria*) integrated in one mind (mens), **was** so structured as to "image itself back" to the originating mystery of the Three in One of God, which Julian here unforgettably figures as the Maker, the Keeper, and the Lover of "this lytel thynge"— all that is made.

Second, we note that the range of connotation of the "three properties" enhances our double sense of foundation, that hypostatic link between the domains of the human and the divine. This dualism is reflected in the two major semantic fields of the word "properties" which then (as now) had both mercantile and legal ("human") as well as philosophical and theological ("divine") frames of reference.

75r. —fallen to nought for lytelnes. This image of the immensity of the universe falling into nothingness because of its insignificance relative to its maker is repeated twice; it evokes a striking kind of fear in Julian, an anxiety that arises out of charity. She worries for the vulnerability of this "thyng" that is both so tiny and "all that is made." This is a beautifully nuanced projection of cosmic vertigo in the face of a vision in which the macrocosm fell into the microcosm, just as the divine nature of Christ "emptied itself" into his historical body.

75r. —why that we be not all in ease of heart . . . for we seke here reste. We hear the echo of the famous opening of Augustine's *Confessions*: "and unquiet is our heart, until we rest in thee [et inquietum est cor nostrum, donec requiescat in te]." Obviously in the word **reste** we have the sense of "rest" as respite for the unquiet: but another sense of "rest" is also present, as in the "remaining portion." And we note both of these, as well as many other associated meanings, as we engage the intense concatenation that flows from the phrase: **"we seke here rest."** "We seek rest," but also "we sick ones find rest here" in this thing, this cosmos. But this is a cosmos that is also so little that inside of it there can really be no **reste**, no peace, because of the nothing that

---

the logics of God. For the medieval world, the logics of the soul were precisely at the heart of the theological game of love played out between medieval men and women and their God.

4. See particularly the last three books of *De Trinitate*.

is left within it; and we shall not find **reste** until we know our God who is almighty, who himself *is* veritable **reste**: not only the peace and quiet that passeth understanding, but also rest that is a remainder, that *does* remain: i.e., fulfillment, quintessence, divine presence. In this continuing concatenation, we must also track the subtext that Julian slowly builds up under the surface by her rich and playful repetitions of the words "made/unmade," "nut," and "nought" in which the negative "nought" phonically careers and caroms off the positive "notte" of the hazel. These signal a radical mixing and re-identification of negativity and positivity, creating an atmosphere that readies us for Julian's mystical ascent, via her assent to the *via negativa*, which is her own self-image of the ironically self-fulfilling kenosis of Christ, his self-emptying on the cross.

75v. **—nouhted for loue**. Julian engages in a most serious game of apophasis with the word "nought" throughout these folios, using it in its fullest inflective range: not only as noun, adjective, and adverb but also, in a move close to coinage, using "to nought" as verb (reflexive and transitive). So in **nouhted for loue**, she weaves a sense of self-emptying that paradoxically feeds into the fulfillment of everything. And as the sounds of "nought" flow on in rich repetition, the "ought," which is the *mot sous le mot* undergirding the word "**nought**," brings to the ear the insistently reverberating sound of O, the Omega, which is not only the zero as positive number, but also the letter, the circle, the prime figure of God in the medieval imagination.

So when she says with approval that Christ's lover has "noughted himself for love" it is because Christ has done so as well. And this begins to mean that it was by the very means of self-denial that Christ self-emptied into glory, and offered us a means, by the mimetic form of the imitatio Christi, to empty ourselves in order to find him: our peace, self-extension, and our final self-fulfillment.

Near the end of this extended concatenation (75v) there is, in addition, an important "contaminatio" of gender as well as pronominal reference, a cross-usage of pronouns that implies an apparent substitutability of masculinity and femininity, as well as a collection of "hims" and "hes" for both Christ and his lover, indicating in the subtext an androgynous subject/object coalescence in which Christ's Lovers (as men and as women) and the Beloved merge identities of gender and reference. This blurring of gender barriers is an effective technique of the feminine style when it seeks new syntheses by collapsing conventional oppositions.

75v. **—kynde yerning**: "natural, erotic desire," but also "compassionate turning." The phrase signals the presence, which continues throughout this part of the *Shewings*, of the slightly heady mix of the erotic shimmering midst the spiritual that we further sense in her word choice of "**naked**," and "**homly**" (intimate), etc. We must feel how "right" this is for the desired intimate, yet multiple sense of things. As she shortly says, "and thus I saw him & sought him & I had him & wanted him. And this is & should be our common working in this life, as to my sight"(80r-80v). And she also says that to ask for less is to ask for nothing, and by that to extend infinitely, by the failure of nerve and the cowardice of the negative will, the domain of unfulfilled lacking and desire. If we are to have any of it, we must ask for all of it.

76r. —**he is the endless hed.** As we reflect on the carved image (in S and L manuscripts) of the head of Christ bleeding in the sight of Julian, we also recall that "head" is not only the noun reserved for the body, it is also a key suffix, indicating superiority, quality, and ultimately quiddity. So the head of Christ is not only the *caput* of his own corpus, he is the leader of the Church (cf Paul: we are all members of the body of Christ). His "endless head" is also the infinite extension of all quantity and quality, and, at the last, essentiality or "isness" itself. Julian now turns her attention to prayer.

On Prayer: "He comes down to us
to the lowest part of our need" (76v–82r).

[76v] And in that same tyme [Easter] the custom of our prayer was brought to my mind how that we use, for unknowing of love, **to make many meanys** [make complaints and moans, but also to make meanings, exert means, and engage in mediations]. Then I saw truly that [it] is more worship to God, & more a very delight, that we faithfully pray to him of his goodness and cleave thereto by his grace with true understanding & steadfast belief, than if we made all the **meanys** [complaints to him, but also good intentions toward him] that heart may think. For though we make all this **meanys**, it is too little & not full worship to God, but in his goodness is all the whole, and there fails no thing. For this as I say

[77r] came to my mind at the same time we prayed to God for his holy flesh & for his precious blood, his holy passion, & his **dereworthi deeth** [precious death], his worshipful wounds, and all the blessed **kyndeness** [kindness, but also his essential nature]. The endless life that we have of all this, **it is of his**

goodness. And we pray him for the love of his mother that bore him, and all that help that we have in her. It is of his goodness. And we pray for his holy cross that he died on, and all the help & virtue that we have of the cross. It is of his goodness. And in the same way, all the help we have of special

[77v] saints, & all the blessed company in heaven, the **derewor-thi loue** [precious, prized, excellent love] and the holy endless friendship that we have of them, is **all of** [all belongs to, is a result of all, has all to do with] his goodness. For God of his goodness, for God of his great goodness hath ordained **mea-nys** to help us in [a] most loving & blessed manner, of which the chief & principal **meane** is the blessed **kynde** [nature, kindness] that he took **of** [off, from, regarding] the **mayden mary** [maiden (created) Mary], with **all the menys** [means, moans] that go before, & come after, **whiche ben longing to** [belong to, are longing for] **our salvacion**, & endless redemp-tion, wherefore it pleases him, that we seek him & worship him by **menys**, understanding & knowing that

[78r] he is goodness of all. For to the goodness of God is the highest prayer, **and he commyth down to us, to the lowest party of our nede** [need]. It quickens our soul & brings it **on lyf** [alive], and makes it to wax in grace & in virtue. It is nearest in **kynde** [nature] & readiest in grace, for it is the same grace that the soul seeks, and ever shall till we know our God verily, who has us all in him **beclosed** [enclosed, brought to an end]. A man goes upright, and the soul of his body is **sperd** [closed, shut, speared, fastened, stored, blocked, kept apart] as a **purse ful feyre** [beautiful purse], and when it is time **of his necessary** [at his call, by dint of his decreed neces-sity] it is opened and **sperd** [spared, kept] again, **well honestly** [quite fittingly]. And it is

[78v] he that does this. He **shewyth** that he sees. **He commyth downe to us, to the lowest party of our nede,** for he has no **dispyte of** [contempt for] that which he has made, neither has he any disdain to serve us in the simplest office that **longith to** [belongs to, longs within] our body **in kynde** [by nature], for love of the soul, that he has made **to** [according to, into] his own likeness. For as the body is clad in the cloth & the flesh, and the **harte in the bouke** [heart in the belly], so be we soul & body clad & closed in the goodness of God. Yea & more **holi**, for all this may wear and waste away, but the goodness of God is ever **whole**, and near

[79r] to us without any sickness. For truly, our lover desires that the soul climb to him, with all our might, and that we be ever climbing to his goodness. For of all thing that heart may think, it pleases most God, and soonest speeds. For our soul is so preciously loved by him that is highest, that it **ouerpassith** the knowledge of all other creatures, that is to say there is no creature that is made, that may know how much & how sweetly & how tenderly our maker loves us. Wherefor we may with his grace & with his **hooly ston**

[79v] **dyng** [holy presence, support] seek him in **goostly be-holdynge** [spiritual beholding], with everlasting marveling, in this **overpassing** unmeasurable love here that our lord has for us out of his goodness. And therefore we may ask of our lover with reverence all that we will. For **our kyndely wyll** [natural will] **is to haue god**, and the good will of God is to have us. And we may never stop in willing nor in loving, till we have him in fullness of joy, and then may we desire no more. For he will that we be occupied in knowing & loving him, till the time come that we shall be fulfilled in

[80r] heaven. For of all things the beholding & the loving of the maker causes the soul **to seeme left in his owne sight**, and most filled it [is] with reverent drede & true meekness, and with plenty of charity to its **evencristen** [fellow Christians]. Furthermore, we be now so blind & so unwise that we can never seek God till that time that he of his goodness **shew-yth** himself to us, and when we see anything of him graciously, then are we stirred by the same grace to seek him with great desire, to see him more blissfully. **And thus I saw him & sought him**

[80v] **and I had him & wanted him. And this is & should be our common working in this life, as to my sight.** For the continuing seeking of the soul pleases God full much, for it may do more than seeking, suffering & trusting. And this is wrought on each soul that has it by the holy ghost. And **the clerenes of fyndyng** is of a special grace of God, when it is his will. The seeking with faith, hope and charity pleases our lord God, & the finding pleases the soul, and fills it full of joys. And thus was I taught to my under

[81r] standing, that **the sekyng is as good as beholdyng**, for the time that he will suffer the soul to be in **traueyle** [labor,

pain, passage, pilgrimage]. It is God's will that we seek into the beholding of him, for by that shall he **shewe** us himself of his special grace when he will. And how a soul shall have Him in His beholding, he shall teach himself, and that is most worship to Him, & most profit to the soul. And it most **receyveth of** meekness & virtues with the grace & leading of the holy ghost. For a soul that only **fastneth hym** to God with true trust

[81v] either in seeking or in beholdying, that is the most worship that he may do, as to my sight. It is God's will that we have three things in **our sekyng of his yefte** [gift]. The first is, we seek willfully & busily without sloth, as it may be with his grace, gladly & merrily without unskillful heaviness & vain sorrow. The second that we abide him steadfastly for his love without grouching & stirring against him until our live's end, for it shall last but a while. The third is that we trust in him mightily with full sure faith, for it is his will that

[82r] we shall know that he will appear suddenly & blessedfully to all his lovers, for his working is private and will be perceived, and his appearing shall be very sudden, and he will be believed, for he is full **hende** [noble, but also clever, handy], **homly** [intimate, comfortable] and courteous, blessed must he be.

[76v–82r] In this section Julian meditates on the difficulties and risks involved in summoning up the courage for prayer. As she weaves her way among related issues, she engages in suggestive, and ultimately illuminating word play on the words "means," "kindness," "beholding," "belonging," and ME **sperd.**

76v. to make many meanys. Julian moves naturally enough from her powerful image of God as the Maker, Keeper, and Lover of the Cosmos to the grounds and motives for prayer. Over the next twelve folios, she weaves an extended concatenation of the words **meanys, dereworthi, kynde, shewing, beholding, sekyng, fyndyng, and yefte** [gift], into an elaborate discourse on prayer that reflects the grounds, strategies, modalities, and forms of prayer itself.

The season of Easter brings to her mind how we are drawn, when "unknowing of love" [neither feeling its presence nor knowing its nature], to **make many meanys. Meanys** is another of Julian's key words, both extremely important in function, and multiple in its range of denotation. Here the word seems to bear primarily the force of "complaints", or "moans"—and if the word appeared only once in this particular articulation, there would be nothing more of interest to say about it. But she uses the word **meanys** and its variants nearly a dozen times in as many pages, perhaps most notably, and in very short order, in f.77v below, and there in the more usual and neutral senses of "intention", "modes" (as in ways and "means") and "mediations": "God . . . hath ordayned **meanys** to help us . . . of which the chief **meane** is [his] blessed **kynde** [nature]. There, in 77v, the words **meanys** and **meane** can have little sense of "complaint" or "moan," but it is precisely that meaning of **meanys** that is present here in 76v, just two folios earlier. So one particular meaning after another leaps to mind as the contexts shift, and eventually all the meanings are called forward in the process of concatenation. They form an aggregate that functions as a kind of readerly/writerly pallette or inventory of semantic backgrounding. And Julian's discourse, by insisting on the widest range of differing meanings keeps us resistant to any desire to settle on one of them. Her writing begins to lose the conventional function of communicating to some specific end of meaning, and rather begins to reveal itself as an analog of the never-ending process of meaning itself.

77r-77v. **and all the blessed kyndenes**. Here is the first appearance of **kyndeness**, one of several forms Julian uses of the key word **kynde**. The basic denotational range of **kynde** moved from "sort" or "genre": the category that a thing "naturally" belongs to, to the "nature of something", to "nature" itself. It also, perhaps by extension, meant "kind" or "kindly," "gentle," "humane," and "compassionate." Seldom in Julian does the word appear with the force of only one of its meanings. Thus in this phrase it is both the kindness and the very hypostatic nature of Christ as Logos that grounds, along with his blood, passion, death, and wounds, our impulse to pray to him.

77r. —**it is all of his goodnes**. Everything comes out of his goodness, but the effect of repeating this phrase so often in such short shrift (three times in this folio alone) and the fact that the vowel sounds heard in the words "good" and "God" were much closer in ME than now, we also hear the phrase meaning "out of his "God-ness," his blessed **kynde**, his divine nature. Indeed the two words appear together, one modifying the other, at the top of 78r below: "**for to the** *goodnes of god* **is the hygheste prayer.**"

77v. —**all the menys . . . whiche ben longyng to oure salvacion**. Julian takes wonderful advantage of the fact that "belonging" has the double sense of both desire and possession, of both "longing for" and "belonging to"; and she links it to that equally fecund double sense of **meanys** as "moans" as well as "means" and achieves a breathtaking economy, capturing in a single phrase both the need for and the way to our redemption: "with all the **menys . . . whiche ben longing to our salvaction**: ["with all the moans which are longing for" as well as "all the means which belong to" our salvation]. The capacity of language to say both these things at once reflects the promised "double-meaning" of Christ-as-Word: that the turning of the will toward God in desire is sufficient for the accomplishment of that desire, a reminder that Christ is both the goal and the way.

77v. —**the cheyff & principall meane is the blessed kynde.** The extended concatenation linking these folios demonstrates, more than argues, its theological point: The very **meanys** of Christ reside in his **kynde**: his hypostatic nature encloses and effects all mediation and meaning: his goodness is inherent in his godness, his godness in his goodness.

The tiny prepositional particle "**of** " plays a special role within this concatenation: its various meanings (about, concerning, belonging to, etc.) play out their full range here.

The dazzling uses of anaphora itself, the insistent repetitions of "**for god in his goodnes,**" "**for god in his grete goodnes,**" "**it is all in hys goodnes**" helps establish our sense of the godness in the goodness—this *repetitio* is not mere "dittography," as some scholars argue, but reflects the great power of Julian's rhetorical gift and cuts to the bone. Colledge and Walsh prove, in their lists of Julian's use of rhetorical figures (Toronto edition), that Julian generously exercised her great range of control over the standard techniques of persuasive rhetoric throughout the *Shewings*—although they do not do much in the way of functional analysis. We have here a detailed example of precisely how she puts those figures to higher theological, rather than merely logical and rhetorical uses.

78r. —**the soul of his body is sperd . . . and sperd again** [speared, spared]. In yet another central image of enclosure deriving from that of the soul in the body, the soul is imagined as a treasure in the body of a precious purse, which is first **sperd** [speared, but also shut, hence kept apart, stored up], and then, when it is time, opened and **sperd** again [this time in the sense of spared or saved]. The use of the multivalent meanings of a purse as **sperd** also marks the first example of what will become a major cluster of monetary imagery of marketing, currency and exchange that is shortly to dominate several folios of W, as Julian surges forward from domain to domain of familiar areas of experience in her attempt to ready us for the illuminations of something new and unheard of.

78v. —he commyth downe to us to the loweste party of our nede. This image of descent reflects Christ's kenosis, his self-humiliation in the Incarnation, in which the logos descends into the flesh, down to the lowest part of our need. Grace stoops to conquer. **Harte in the bouke:** "heart in the belly" (bouke: cf. Ger. *Bauch*). Another palliatum image: the soul in the body, but, like the money in the purse, a more emphatically physical image. **In kynde:** "by nature." There is a nice insistence on the semantic relationship between "holy", "wholely," and "hale" ("Hale" phonetically a lot closer in ME to the others than currently): holy because hale and whole.

79v. —our kyndely wyll is to haue god. Again Julian insists that our desire for the possession of God is different than, but nonetheless reverberates in, its dynamics with the domain of erotic passion; this is in itself good because it is part of our "natural will."

80r. —to seme left in his owne sight. For the reluctant lover, Christ **"causith the soule to seme lefte** [left alone] **in his owne sight, and moste fyllit it** [feels the need to fill that soul] **with reverend drede."** This is the gift of fear that allows us to begin the journey to wisdom; it leads up the liberating ladder of love as sketched in the gospel and epistles of John. If we imagine ourselves emptied of everything other-related, we imitate in that exercise Christ's kenosis, and we "come down to the lowest part of our need" which for most of us is the nada that lurks in the soul when completely emptied of the Other. At this nadir of the negative way, we feel appropriate fear and self-loathing: "reverend dread." If lucky, we feel so drenched in holy terror that we reach out for help: and this is the turning point: for that very reaching out from the self to the other is the beginning of love—which is also the beginning of wisdom. This lowest part of our need is where, as Yeats put it, "all the ladders start/ in the foul rag-and-bone shop of the heart."

As we begin, in our fear and anxiety, slowly and tentatively to climb that ladder of love, our faculty for loving gradually improves, and we begin to achieve some portion of real wisdom. Finally, as we near the completion of our course in love, we reach the threshold of "perfect love," which, John assures us, "casts out all fear." This process gives a new and redemptive meaning to the currently hackneyed phrase: a "self-fulfilling" prophecy.

As she concludes 80r and begins 80v, we find a freshness and candor that is both radiant in expressing the clarity of her will, and also endearing in its anti-narratological resequencing of "natural" order: she does not proceed along the conventional narrative axes of "sought and saw, wanted and had," but rather **"And thus I sawe hym & sought hym and I had hym & wanted hym."**

80v. —**the clerenes of fynding**. "To seek and see and trust" is a reflection of the Pauline trinity of faith, love, and hope; it is itself a finding imbued with a special grace, and graced in turn with a special clarity.

81r. —**the sekyng is as good as beholdyng**. Julian herself offers a gloss for this phrase, which to modern ears may seem to require no glossing, appearing to us as already transparent. She writes: "it is god's will we seek into the beholding of him." The reason she felt the need for the gloss is that in ME, the word "beholding" was semantically far richer then than its modern shadow. As indicated earlier, ME "beholding" is an extended and intensified form of "holding." But something more is present when you add the prepositions "into" and "of":—**into** the beholding **of** him. The verb then loses its transitivity. The proactive sense of seeking moves into the more ritual, reactive sense of beholding, and passes further into senses that are even more static: senses of "holding onto," "enclosing," "possessing," and "retaining."

Julian democratizes the processes of signification; she is teaching all of her evencristen how, more than what, to see. It strikes me that the "thinness" of actual imagistic representation (relative to, say, Hildegard of Bingen) of things seen in her vision is offset, actually more than made up for, by verbal intensity. Her language reflects what happens to her in her head not only as the result of what she sees, but also the process by which she sees it.

Thus, as I have already suggested, her ludic use of words functions with a high seriousness—and helps us more to track the process and the progress of the pilgrimage toward meaning, than to judge any actual success of achieving meaning, a function that strikes us as always important, but somehow decreasingly crucial here.

81v. —**our sekyng of his yefte**. I have emended Sister Julia Holloway's transcription of **yeste** [act, geste] to **yefte** [gift]. The manuscript allows reasonable doubt, and Sister Julia herself in other locations transcribes what appears to be the same word as **yefte** as well, which to my ear much better accords with the range of meanings that Julian of Norwich seems to attribute to it. In the next section, Julian receives a vision of

God in a point of light: this leads to meditations on the presence of God in the schemes of creation.

God in the Creature: "That Yefte and that Mede" (82r-86v)

[82r (cont.). And after this **I saw God in a poynt**, that is to say in my understanding, by which sight I saw that he is all thing[s], I beheld with **a visement** [assistance], seeing & knowing in that sight, that he does all that is done, be it never so little. And I saw that no thing is done **by happe** [by chance], nor by **auenture** [luck], but

[82v] all by the **foreseeng of goddys wysedom** [the foresight constituent to God's wisdom, our foresight regarding God's wisdom]. And if it be happenstance or adventure in the sight of man, our blindness & our **unbeforesyght** [lack of foresight] is the cause. Wherefore well I know that in the sight of our lord God is no happenstance nor adventure. And therfor **me behouyd nedisly to graunt** [it became useful [and] needful for me to grant] that all thing that is done, it is well done, for our lord does all. For in this time the **wurkyng of creature** [working of creatures, creation] was not **shewed** but of our lord God **in creature** [in creation, in the created], for he is in the midpoint of all thing, and all he does. And I was sure that he does no sin. And

[83r] here I saw truly that **sin is no dede** [deed]. Also [I saw] among other **shewyngs** our good lord meaning thus: See I am God; See I am in all things; See I do all things. See **I leste neuer myne hande of** [never leave my hand off] my work, nor never shall without end. See I lead all things to the end that I ordained for them, from without beginning, **by the same myght wysedome and loue that I made it with**. How should then any thing be amiss? I saw full surely that he changes never his purpose in no manner of thing, nor never shall without end, for there was no thing unknown to him

[83v] in his rightful ordinance from without beginning. And therefore all things were set in order before anything was made, as it should without end. Also **in the ninth showing our lord God said to her thus: Art thou well payed** that I suffered for thee? And she said yea good lord, grant mercy: yea good lord, blessed must thou be. Then said Jesus, our good lord God, if thou be payed, I am payed. It is a joy, a bliss,

& an endless **lyking** [joy, resemblance to you] to me that I ever suffered passion for thee, and if I might suffer more, I would suffer more. And in these same

[84r] words if I might: I saw truly that **as often as he might die**, just so often he would, & love should never let him have rest till he had done it. And I beheld with great diligence for to know how [often] he would die if he might, and truly the number passed my understanding in my wit so far that my reason might not, nor could not, comprehend it, nor take it. And when he had so often died or should, yet he would set it at nought for love. For though the **swete** [sweet, savory, but also sweaty] manhood of Christ might suffer but once, **the goodness of him may**

[84v] **never cesse of profer** [never stop being offered], everyday the same if that might be. Also it is God's will that we have **trew lyking with him in oure salvacion** [true resemblance to him, affection for him, in and for our salvation], and therein he will that we be mightily comforted & strengthened, and thus will he, merely with his grace, that our soul be occupied, for we be his bliss, his **mede** [drink, reward, but also fee, even bribe] and his worship. And we be his crown. And this was a singular marvel & fully delectable beholding that we be his crown. This that I say is such great bliss to our lord Jesus, that he sets at nought all his travail & his hard pass

[85r] ion & his cruel & shameful death. The father is full pleased with the deeds that Jesus has done for our salvation. Wherefore we be not only his by his being, but also by the courteous **yefte** [gift, deeding] of his father, for we be his bliss and his **mede**, as it is said before, and **that yefte and that mede** [that gift and that reward] is so blissful to our lord Jesus that his father might have given him no meed that might have **lykyd** [pleased, resembled] him better. For **in us he lykyth** [takes pleasure in us, resembles and so signifies himself in us] without end, and so shall we within him, with his grace. All that he has done for us and does &

[85v] ever shall do, was **never a cost nor charge** to him, nor might be, but only what he **dedde** [did, deeded] to our manhood, beginning at the **swete** [sweet, sweaty] incarnation, and lasting till the blessed rising up on Easter day in the morning. So long **dured** [lasted, endured] the cost & the charge **aboute** [of, to] our redemption **in dede** [indeed], of which **dede** [act,

deeding, gift] he enjoys endlessly, as said before. Also Jesus will that we take **hede** [heed, mind, head], to this bliss that is in the trinity of our salvation, and that we desire to have as much spiritual **lykynge** [affection and desire for, resemblance to] his grace as is said before. That is to say, that the **lykynge of** [image of, desire for]

[86r] oure salvation **belyke** [bear resemblance, be drawn] to the joy that Christ has in our salvation that shall continue while we be here. All the blessed trinity wrought in the passion of Christ, **mynystryng** [administering, ministering] abundance of virtues & **plenty** [plenitude] of grace to us by him, but only the maiden's son suffered, whereas all the glorious trinity endlessly enjoys. And this was **shewed in this worde**: "**Art thou wel payed**?" By that other word that Christ said, "**Yf thou are payed, I am payed.**" As if he had said: it is joy & **lykyng I noughte me** [pleasure enough for me, for affection that, for resemblance (to you) that I emptied myself], and I ask nothing else of thee

[86v] for my **traueyle** [travail, labor, pain], but that I might **pay** thee. And it [is] this he brought to my mind, the **propertee** [property, character] of a glad giver. A glad giver taketh but little **hede** [heed, head] at the thing that he giveth, but his desire is in all his intent, to please him & solace him to whom he giveth it. And if the receiver take the gift gladly & thankfully, then the courteous giver setteth at nought all his cost & all his travail for joy and delight that he hath, for he hath so pleased & solaced him that he loveth. Plenteously & fully was this showed:

82r-86v. In her meditations on the roles God plays in the scheme of things, she uses a fair amount of word-play herself. She is particularly eager to explore the ironies inherent in situations when one compares the calculus of debt and justice across human and divine systems.

82r.—I saw God in a poynt. This is one of Dante's culminating images of God in the *Paradiso*, which Dante himself probably lifted from the *Summa* of Thomas Aquinas. Although unlikely that Julian read Dante's text, it is more than possible that she heard about this image in the *Paradiso* from any number of local and regional sources. The poem was a favorite among Italophiles in fourteenth-century London, where important northern Italian families were resident and played roles crucial to the City's fortunes in trade and commerce. The point captures the idea of God as fulfilling the function of Aristotle's primum mobile, the First and Unmoved Mover, and ordinating point of energy of the cosmos. One does best to think of the primum mobile as moving all that is not itself by the power of attraction it has for everything in the world, which in the Christian worldview—in which the primum mobile is God—is not only the source from which all light and love emanates, but to which, as the central gravitating point, all love returns.

82r. **ne happe ne aduenture**. As she sees God in the Point of Light, her meditations lead her into the doctrine of providence, and the notion that, in spite of appearances to the contrary, nothing occurs by hap or chance, that all is pre-ordained and foreknown in the Mind of God—seen here as the unmoved point drawing all to it in love.

83r. **sin is no dede**. "Sin is no deed." "And I was sure that he doth no sin. And here I saw truly that sin is no deed." To avoid the Manichaean trap, Julian must understand evil as nonbeing (i.e., not part of God) and particularly not as some nightmare of an Anti-god that participates in reality on God's ontological level. To award such a strong ontological validity to sin and evil would be to diminish divinity itself, whose prime attribute is being (I am that I am). But of course sin and evil do real and devastating work in the world. The task is, if evil is so powerful, yet has no real entity of its own, to find out what it really is. And Julian takes the via negativa: she begins with what it is not.

Thus for Julian, sin is envisioned, not as a positive entity in itself, but, in good orthodox fashion, as a kind of bad loving. Its reality lies not in the Creator, but in us the created. It is what we would now call a psychological reality: a direction of the will. Dante defined sin as false loving: excessive, defective, or misdirected. The great Hildegard scholar, Sister Adelgundis Führkoetter, says that Hildegard had a kind of romantic horror of the Devil as actual bogey-man, the *Durcheinanderwerfer* (the "thrower-apart-of-connected-things"). Though Hildegard does paint, in words as well as in pictorial images, terrifying visions of the Devil, I have my doubts that she thinks he exists in the same modality in and through which God exists. Julian surely does not. Julian is more ghostly, perhaps more Augustinian; but that is not to say that for Julian evil is some intellectual abstraction. As Augustine did, so Julian saves real evil for us by the very assertion that it lacks the status of "deed"—her denial returns it to our care and cure. It becomes ours again: *c'est notre métier*. To say "sin is no dede" is theologically correct in terms of heterodoxy, and is thus enough. She has no more to say about sin in W, but has some very interesting elaborations in S:

Ah, wretched sin! What art thou? for I saw that God is all thyngs; I saw not thee. And when I saw that God has made all things, I saw thee not. And thus I am sure that thou art not. And all that loves thee and is like thee and follows thee and wilfully ends in thee, I am sure they shall be brought to nought with thee.[5]

83r **—I leste neuer myne hande of my work**: "I never take my hand from my work." This phrase is part of a set that Christ strings together just after Julian reports figuring out that "sin is no deed." It also follows another haunting phrase spoken by Julian in the previous folio: **"me behoyd nedisly to graunt** [it behooved me, proved useful to me, to grant] **that all . . . is well done, for our lord does all**." These two phrases echo two of the most famous lines in Julian's work, lines that are not present in W: "Sin is behovely" and "All shall be well, and all manner of thing shall be well." To appropriate sin as our own does not mean that we cannot draw a certain comfort from the fact that God knows, and has foreknown all sin beyond time. In fact this is one of the main "justifications" by which humans can excuse God for allowing the presence of sin in the world, which is not the same as the "explanation" that its presence is a function of a disordered human will. Perhaps a more important justification, from the human point of view, is that God must allow its presence in order to allow humanity a credible degree of free will: if humanity is to be allowed to choose freedom, a real alternative must be there to choose from. But that aside, in the Julian logic, all manner of thing SHALL be well, because in the timeless, eternal Mind of God it has long been "foreseen," "seen," and dealt with in love and justice. That is what she means by having Christ say here that he never "leaves his hand from his work."

83v **in the ninth showing our lord God said to her thus**. This is the only hard evidence I can find that W has been lifted from other sources. The "ninth showing" reflects the strategies of L, which moves from numbered shewing to shewing.

But even more intriguing here is Julian's sudden reference to herself in the grammar of the third person pronoun. Such reference, which this singular instance in W also happens to share with other versions, has been seen by some critics as evidence that at least at some stage, Julian had used a male scribe to transcribe her visions onto parchment. And though I finally stand on the other side of that issue, and believe

---

5. Quoted by Watson from F. Beer ed. of S (75.27–38), in his *Speculum* article, "Composition," 668–69.

that she learned early on to write down her own brilliant English by herself, and then did so, I am struck by a third possibility argued recently by Lynn Staley Johnson, that Julian has incorporated the **idea** or image of a scribe into her text as a trope. Johnson argues that by using the image of a male inscribing the visions of a woman (by now quite a tradition has developed since the pioneering of Hildegard), she was bootlegging into the text the additional status and sense of legitimacy men paid to a woman who had had her work "vetted" by a man.[6] As a critical hunch, it is interesting enough, but not overwhelmingly compelling.

83v–86r. **art thou well payed.** This sudden question introduces the great theme of mercantile exchange, inserted paradoxically amidst the grace of Christ's kenosis, that runs over the next six folios. It is another extended concatenation involving words, most emphatically the words "pay," "cost," "meed" (reward), "gift," and "deed." Julian plays all the money talk against the mystery of grace, and thus represents the difficulty of playing human frames of reference against those of divine will. One of the master moments where all this came together for the medieval imagination, of course, was the book of Job, where the point of examining minutely the logic of Job's suffering against the works of his life seemed to fall so radically short. In the case of such "undeserved" suffering on the part of the suppliant who calls "if thou art indeed just, Lord," the very question of "justice according to whom" forces itself into the open. And, of course, it is the point of the biblical narrative to reveal that human schemes and understanding of human logic and justice have precisely *nothing* to do with whatever it is that is in the Mind of God. Job's demand for logical justification is met with the sudden and violent voice speaking from the Whirlwind that answers his question with a far more enormous question: "Where were you when I laid the foundation of the earth?" There is no answer that human logic can counter to that, so Job quite appropriately remains silent and sifts dung and dust over his head; his "answer" seems finally not only eloquent, but deeply "just" in its own way.

Here in Julian's *Shewings*, the interrogator is Christ himself, and he puts the question in human terms, which is appropriate insofar as in one of his aspects he is surely human. The situational irony of course resides in the fact that within him dwells as well the divine logos, whose logic is immeasurably other and beyond the kind of logic the human voice of Christ is putting to Julian—and to us. Here it is Christ, not

---

6. See "The Trope of the Scribe and the Question of Literary Authority in the works of Julian of Norwich and Margery Kempe, *Speculum* 66 (1991), 820–38.

bone-brained Job-as-us asking questions about the logic of works: of fair dealing, of tit for tat, etc. And, of course, asking the question in terms of its most elevated level of conception: justice itself.

The folios proceed to present a colloquy in which Christ asks and speaks, leaving the answering to be done in the silence of Julian's head—which she lets us share as our own reception room for receiving and dealing with the words of God.

Have we been well payed? Was his death on the cross "enough" for us, in terms of buying our redemption? Julian uses the multiple meanings of her words to good advantage: they allow Christ to reveal his double nature as he uses them. For example in 83v, he says "if thou be payed, I am payed. It is a joy, a bliss, & and endless **lyking** to me that I ever suffered passion for thee." The word at issue is **lyking**. In one of its senses, it accords with the other two nouns with which we find it: joy and bliss: so, **lyking** should be read as "taking pleasure in." But as we know of the centrality of the *imago Dei* relation by which we are "like" Christ, and he is "like" us, then his suffering on the cross is also the "like" of similitude: from the beginning of the world, being outside the constraints of human time, he has always already suffered his kenosis in the preordained mystery of the incarnation. He has always taken a **lyking**, or a similarity to us as he "ever suffered passion for" us.

The way in which the "economy" of mercy surpasses and renders dull the "economy" of justice continues in 84r—where the paradox inherent in Christ's double nature is raised again and again in terms of suffering—only this time even more pointedly in that radical suffering which is death itself. As human, he can die but once; as God he can never die, but as he chooses to do so in one of his aspects, he dies once infinitely. It is this very illogicality that blows apart the quid-pro-quos of the human enterprise of hair-splitting and that most spectacularly reveals the higher, "unparceable" modalities of divine grace. The "manhood of Christ might suffer but once, the goodness of him may never cease of proffer." Julian chooses the word "proffer" because it is first and foremost a business term, and only secondarily, upon further consideration, can it be seen as a term appropriate in the give and take of grace.

Our sense of three other words needs to be enriched with the fuller medieval range of meaning: **mede, yefte,** and **dedde**. Each has a double set of semantic charges. **Mede,** because of the lack of stringency of vernacular spelling conventions in the Middle Ages, can refer to the drink "mead" (a rich hops beverage) or to "meed": a sum of value, usually in hard cash or goods that can interchangeably act as a payment, reward, or bribe. **Yefte** has in itself no double sense: it means "gift." But in written form it is often, because of the ways one wrote the letters s and f, often indistinguishable from **Yeste** which means action, or accomplishment (from Lat. *gestus*—attitude, gesture, deed, and OF geste, ditto). The odd thing is that over half the time one sees this word in W, one feels that the context could allow either reading. I have chosen to read it consistently as **Yefte** or "gift", first because of the specific repetition of the word in collocation with **mede** in 85r; secondly, because of the large amount of giving and taking going on around the appearance of the word in the surrounding folios, and finally because the sense of "gift" always works here and the sense of "gesture" or "deed" does not. **Dedde** usually means "deed" in a legal sense of estate transactions, though it can also be spelled that way as a past participle of "dead." That said, the reader can then "turn on" the additional semantic resonance of these three words and read the folios with a richer and fuller sense of appropriate semantic tonality. All of the word-play sustains the basic paradox: the non-match of systems, and the really rather witty and amusing way in which the words that work so well for one system (business and trade) work so poorly in the other (ethics, morality, and theology). W's great *visio* of Christ on the Cross now comes to Julian.

A Shewing: *Our Lord loked into his syde*
& beheld, enioyenge (86v–88v)

[86v (cont.)] Plenteously & fully was this showed: **Also with glad chere** [thus with bright visage, flesh, and happy look and face], **our**

[87r] **lord looked into his side & beheld, enjoying**, and with his **swete** [sweet, sweaty] looking he led further the understanding of his creatures by the same wound into his side within. And there he **shewed** a fair delectable place & large enough for all mankind that shall be safe to rest in peace and love. And therewith he brought to mind his **dereworthy** [beloved, prized] blood & his precious water, **whyche he lett poure all out for loue.** And with that **swete** [sweet, sweaty] **beholding** [beholding, enclosing] he **shewed** [put on show, revealed] his blessed heart even cloven in two. And with this **swete** enjoying he **shewed** in understanding in

[87v] part the blessed godhead, **as ferforth as** [to the degree that] he would at that time, strengthening the poor soul for to understand as it may be said, that is **to meane** [intend, signify, mediate, transact, transfer] the endless love that was without beginning, & is and ever shall be. And with this our lord God

said, full blessedly, Look how I love thee, as if he had said, My darling, behold & see thine own brother, thy sovereign; My child behold & see thy lord God, thy maker & thy endless joy, see what **lykyng** (liking, pleasure, resemblance] & bliss I have in thy salvation. And for my love enjoy with me. Also to more

[88r] understanding his blessed word was said: **Loo how I loue the**, as if he had said, Beholde & see that I loved thee so much, that I died for thee, that I would die for thee, and now I have died for thee & suffered willingly whatever pain I may, and now is all my bitter pain, & all my travail turned to endless joy & bliss both to me & to thee. How should it now be that thou **shuldiste** [wish for] anything through me that **lykyth** [pleasures, resembles] me but that I should full gladly grant it thee, for my **lykyng** [affection, resemblance to you] is thy holiness & thy endless joy & bliss with

[88v] me. This is the simple understanding that I can say of this blessed **word** [word, sentence]: **Loo how I love thee**. All this **shewed** our lord God to make us glad and merry.

86v–87r. At the heart of this vision are two images: one of pictures, the other of words. The first figures Christ looking into the spear-wound in his side, and viewing therein the company of the elect. Christ "glosses" this vision by saying: "**Loo how I loue the**." As he speaks to Julian, she stands at the foot of the cross. Julian then turns to us and attempts her own gloss on the "word" of Christ.

87r. our lord loked into his syde & beheld, enioyenge. This is the vision promised at the end of 86v, in which all is "plenteously & fully shewed." It is quiet and terrifying. Christ on the cross looks into the wound in his crucified side: his mode of looking is **swete**, both sweet and sweaty; blood and water pour out of his self-emptying, self-noughting side; inside it teems with the entire company of the elect. Julian, looking with us peering over her shoulder sees that it is a bloody, sweaty, sweet, and delectably good place in there: big enough for all mankind to rest within. The syntax of the language reporting this looking is also a minor miracle: "and with his **swete** [sweet, sweaty] looking he led further the understanding of his creatures by the same wound into his side within." There is simply no getting around the way Julian sinuously sets us up to "see" this wound "as" a fore-imago of the New Jerusalem. Later on this same wound of entry will be "seen as" a nipple of sustenance (cf. "may he lead us to his blessed breast by his sweet open side . . . ," 96r below); here we are forced to see the wound as a womb of gestation, with the fetal myriad awaiting birth. Anticipating the great maternal imagery with which W closes, the crucified Christ looks into his wound/womb as a Mother would look speculatively into her own womb, and as we look with him into his vaginal mandorla, we can see all of the once struggling but now born-again members of Christ's body who, through the redemptive death of Christ, have always already been reborn and are now imaged forth as at rest in the New Jerusalem: "and there he **shewed** a fair delectable place & large enough for all mankind that shall be safe to rest in peace and love."

88r. —**Loo how I loue the.** Christ's own "interpretation" of the imago of his kenosis is the Verbum of his reaction to seeing this wound: "Look how I love you." In his hypostasis, the Logos/Verbum and the Pictura/Caro are One. Julian of course is not as absolutely privileged as the God in whose image she was made: she must use human words to elaborate the meaning of the Divine Word. And so she engages in a moving gloss of **Loo how I loue the**, during which, by modes of repetition, she gives the finish of a pictura to a phrase that never ceases speaking.

87v. —**see what lyking & blisse I haue in thi salvacion.** She also concatenates the word **lyking** so that its double meanings of pleasure and similitude come again to the fore, saying about Christ's kenosis, "his blood & his precious water, **whyche he lett poure all out for loue.**" She then has Christ himself say that it is a "**lyking & blisse**" and ask Julian (and us) to enjoy it "**for my loue.**"

88r. —**for my lykyng is thi holynes and thi endeles ioye & blysse with me.** Here the *imago Dei* relationship associated as a subtext of the word **lykyng** rises completely to the surface of the discourse in full parity with the word's more quotidian senses of pleasure and joy.
  —**behold and see.** Julian here uses the formula most famously embedded in the Lamentations of Jeremiah, and used, *in figura*, as the motto of Mary in the pietà posture in which she held the dead Christ after the descent from the cross: "behold and see [*attendite et videte*], if there be any sorrow like unto my sorrow." The reversal here is breathtaking: as Mary is imagined to have spoken these words of Ur-sorrow upon viewing, like the City Desolate, her dead son in the traditional pietà iconography, Julian interprets Christ's words "Loo how I loue you" AS IF he were saying in joy the same thing, but in these words: "**Beholde & see** that I louyd the so meche [that] I dyed for the, that I wolde dye for the, and now I have dyed for thee." The trinitarian

concatenation of time past, present, and future manages to view the moment both from the temporal perspective of Christ's human nature and the eternal perspective of his divinity. From the perspective of his hypostasy the pain is the joy, the sorrow is the bliss.

Julian's next shewing is also a verbal, rather than a pictorial image: **I am ground of thi besekyng,** and she devotes eleven folios to her gloss on this verbal image spoken by the mouth of Christ.

The Verbal Icon: **He shewed thees wordis: I am ground of thi beseking** (88v–94r)

[88v (cont.)] Also I understand truly that all manner [of] thing is made ready to us by the great goodness of God. In so far as the time we ourself be in peace & in charity we be verily safe. But for that, **we may not haue this in fullness while we ben here.** Therefore it befalleth us ever more to live in sweet prayer, and in lovely **longing** [belonging to, longing for] our lord

[89r] Jesus. Also our lord **shewed for prayer** [revealed (the requisites) of prayer], in which **shewyng** I saw two conditions in/of our lord's **meanyng** [meaning, mediation, agency]. One is rightful prayer, and the other is sure trust. But yet ofttimes our trust is not full. For we be not sure that God hears us, as we think, for our unworthiness, & for that we feel no thing. For we be as barren & as dry oft times after our prayer as we were before, and thus in our feeling. Our folly is cause of our weakness. For thus I have felt in myself. And all thus brought

[89v] our lord suddenly to my mind and **shewed thees wordis** [revealed these words] and said: **I am grounde of thi besekyng** [I am both the reason for and the object of thy seeking and entreaty]. First it is my will that thou have it, and I make thee to will it. **How shulde it than be** that thou shouldst not have thy **beseyking it** [beseeching it] since I make thee to **besekyng** [be seeking it], and **thou besekyst it.** And thus in the first reason of the three that followeth, our lord God **shewyth** a mighty comfort as may be **seying** [seeing, saying] in the same words in the first reason. where he says **and thou besekyst it** there he **shewyth** full great pleasure and endless **mede** [mead, meed] that he

[90r] will give us for our beseeching. And in the sixth reason there he says: **How shulde it than be.** This was said as an

unpossible [impossibility]. For it is the most impossible that may be that we should beseech mercy & grace, and not have it. For of all thing that [is what] our lord makes us to beseech. [He] himself hath ordained it to us from without beginning. Here may we [know] then that our beseeching is not cause of the goodness & grace that he does unto us, but his own proper goodness. & that **shewyth he sothfastly in all these swette words** where he says:

[90v] **I am ground of thi prayer & of thi besekyng.** And our lord will that this **beknowen of** [be known to, be known among] all his lovers on earth. And the more that we know it, the more should we beseech it, if it be wisely taken, and so is our lord's **menyng** (meaning, mediation, agency]. Wise seeking is a true, gracious, lasting will of the soul, united & fastened into the will of our lord God himself. He is the first receiver of our prayer, as to my sight, and he takes it right thankfully and highly enjoys [it]. He sends it up above & sets it in treasury where it shall never perish. It is

[91r] there before God with all his holy company continually received ever speeding our needs. And when we shall **underfong** [undertake, take up] our bliss, it shall be granted us for a degree of joy with endless worshipful thanking of him. Full glad & merry is our lord God of our prayer. He looketh after it, and he would have it, for with his grace it makes us like unto himself **in condicion** [by condition], [even] as we be **in kynde** [by nature]. Also he saith pray though thou think it **savour thee not** [saves you not, is not to your taste]. Also to prayer: [it] **langith thankyng** [it extends thanking, belongs to thanks]. Thanking is a true inward knowing with

[91v] great reverence & lovely dread turning our self with all our might into the working that our lord God stirred us to, enjoying & thanking him inwardly, and some time with plenteousness it breaks out with voice, and says good lord grant mercy, blessed must thou be, and some time when thy heart is dry & feels not, or else by temptation of our enemy, then it is driven by reason & by grace to cry up on our lord with voice rehearsing his blessed passion & his great goodness. And so the virtue

[92r] of our lord's word turns into the soul & quickens the heart & enters in by his grace into true working, and makes it to pray full blessedly, to enjoy in our lord God. It is a lovely

thanking in his sight. Our lord will that we have true understanding, and namely in three things that belongeth to our
prayer. The first is **by whom** and **how that** our prayer **spryn-
gith** [springs up], **by whom** he **shewed** when he said: **I am
ground**. And **how by**, his goodness, for he saith, first, **It is my
wyll**, and for the second, in what manner & how

[92v] we should pray, so that our will be turned into the will
of our lord God enjoying. And so **meaneth he** [he means,
intends, makes happen] when he says: **I make the to will yt**.
For the third, that we know the fruit & the end of our prayer.
That is to be **oned** [united, unified, made one with] and like
unto our lord in all things. And to this **menyng** [meaning,
mediation, means of union] & for this **ende** [end, goal, closure]
was all this lovely lesson showed. And he will help us, & he
shall make it so as [if] he says himself: blessed must he be. For
this is our lord's will. That our prayer & our trust be both
alike large. For if we trust

[93r] not as much as we pray, we do not full worship to our
lord in our prayer, and also we tarry & hurt ourself. And the
cause is, as I believe, for we know not truly that our lord God
is ground himself **of** [of, from and to] whom our prayer
springs. And also that we know not that it is given us by his
grace of his great and tender love. For if we knew this, it
should make us trust to have our lord's gift [be] all that we
desire. For I am sure that no man that asks mercy & grace with
true **menynge**, but mercy & grace be **fyrst** [first, at once] given

[93v] unto him. But sometimes it comes to our mind that we
have prayed [a] long time & yet we think that we have not our
asking. But for this we should not be heavy. For I am sure by
our lord's **menyng** [intention, meaning, mediation, agency]
that either we **abyde** [are to await] a better time, or more grace,
or else a better gift. He will that we have true knowing in and
of himself, that he is **being** [alive, and also *ens*, being itself].
And in this knowing he will that our understanding be
grounded [impelled, fortified] with all our **myghtis** [powers,
capacities, possibilities], all our **entent** [intent, attending], & all
our **meanyng** [meaning, mediations, transaction, enactment].
And **in this ground** [on this basis, for this reason] he will that
we take our

[94r] **stede & our wonyng** [place, stand, or homestead, and
our living, or place of habitation]

88v–94r. As the previous section elaborated understanding of a visual image, the next unpacks a verbal articulation AS an image. Appropriately the speaker of this sentence, "I am the ground of thy **besekyng**" is Christ, the Way and the Word. Julian again returns to the issues surrounding prayer, and this time begins her meditation by splitting the activity of prayer into two aspects or conditions: Prayer and Trust. She begins with our need (and we recall that "he comes down to the lowest part of our need") and then she takes the key word of Christ's saying, "**beseking**," and splits it into two constituent meanings that match and answer the two conditions of prayer and trust. The prayer is the asking, the trust is faith in the answering. She then turns to the aspect of answering, and finds two meanings in Christ's reponse of "endless *mede*" which answer the two conditions of need. The section closes with a recapitulation of the meanings of the word *ground*, and the promise that the answer now/nunc is in the Eucharist; the answer then/tunc, will be in the union with the body of Christ after the resurrection.

89v, 90r. —**shewed thees wordis; shewyth he sothfastly in all these swette words where he saith: I am the ground, etc.** It is in the words AS images that we see things here. Julian's point is that the imago we need to understand is to be found in the coalescence of pictura and verbum together, and that we can recuperate the same essential referential integrity for a sentence made of words, as we more automatically grant a picture made of images. And as both modes have their own integrity of being and function, both modes require elaboration in the quest for meaning. As we would expect, Julian sees this issue simultaneously in theological and exegetical terms. So her formulae "shewed these wordis," "shewyth in all these sweet words" do double duty. First, they emphasise the Verbum as well as the Pictura, and as the Pictura of Christ in his traditional imagery on the cross melds with the showing of Christ in his Words ("I am the ground of thy **besekyng**), we feel as well as see Verbum and Pictura coalesce into the hypostatic Imago of Christ: and we see again and feel afresh the promised truth of both the Johannine identification of Word and Flesh: et Verbum caro factus est: (John 1), and that spoken by Christ himself: I am the Word and the Way (John 14). Julian takes the sentence (or **word**, the ME singular form of "this word" is often used as a collective plural when identifying a phrase or a sentence) of Christ: "I am the ground of thy **besekyng**," and provides a rich and impressive gloss on it over the next eleven folios. She proceeds in the strategies of an act of prayer, in its dual aspects of asking and of answering. For purposes of easier reference in our commentary, we will break this section down into these subsections:

88v–90v: the askings (i.e., two meanings of **besekyng, mede,** etc); and 90v–94r: the answerings (the granting: 90v; thanksgiving: 91r-92r; efficacy: 92v; exposition of *"ground"*: 93r-94r). As for the askings:

88v. **—we may not haue this in fullness while we ben here.** Julian begins her exposition on Christ's word with a reminder of our essential situation, anticipating the Corinthian nunc/tunc articulation of Paul on which she will dwell extensively later on: "Now we see through a glass darkly, then face to face." Her point is that as isolated as we are, we can use prayer to bridge the gap between our desire now and its requital then. But Christ's word for this is not "prayer" itself, but the word **besekyng.**

89r. **—I am ground of thy besekyng.** In modern English, **besekyng** has one essential meaning: "beseeching." In Middle English, however, it is a homophonic pun, or amalgam of two of our modern words: "beseeching" and "be seeking." Julian plays with this double semantic thrust to great advantage. First she divides "prayer" into two necessary **condicions,** into which have been enfolded both the asking and the answering: Prayer and Trust. We then discover, by her playful stretching of the inherent diversity of meaning in **beseking,** that we "seek" as we "pray" insofar as we are not yet one with our desire; we "beseech" in our prayers insofar as we "trust" they will be answered. "How should it then be that thou shouldst not have thy **beseyking** it since I make thee to **besekyng** it?" And Christ himself stipulates here that he must himself somehow be understood as fulfilling the justifying "ground" of both aspects of prayer: the asking and the answering. The promised response is also couched in yet another homophonic pun: Julian says that in the very act of saying these words, Christ "**sheweth** full great pleasure and endless **mede.**" Mede is both a drink and a reward: now/ nunc a figure of the eucharistic wine-as-body-of Christ, a living sign this side of death of the then/tunc "reward" which will be the mystical union with Christ after the resurrection of the body. As she says, the **mede** is endless.

92r. **—it is a louely thankyng in his syght.** The second half (91r-93v) of Julian's disquisition concentrates on the aspect of answering over that of asking. Central to her emphasis is the reciprocity of thanksgiving she sees at the heart of the conversation between God and humanity which she imagines prayer in fact to be. And the trust we have in the process is grounded in our understanding in the efficacy of prayer: it is a matter of **our** trust in **Christ's** efficacy.

92v. —**So meneth he when he says: I make the to will yt.** Prayer works because it is circular, it loops around in an embrace of the petitioner and the solicited. Julian captures here, in a refreshing and surprisingly elastic manner, a way of reconciling, at least momentarily, the irreconcilables of predestination (**I make the**) and free will (**to will yt**). And Julian anchors that verbal reconciliation by once again taking advantage of the multiple meanings available to her in the word **menyng**: as embodying both will and intention, and as embodying the mediation and realization of such intention, by "means" of action, into hard reality. "And to this **menyng** & for this **ende** was all this lovely lesson shewed." It is God's proven capacity to convert will into reality, demonstrated since the opening salvo of Genesis ("let there be light—and there was light") that is the "ground" of our "trust" and "beseeching."

93v. —**in this ground.** Julian closes this period of meditation on the meaning of "I am ground of thy **besekyng**" with this culminating concatenation of power words: "He will . . . that we have true knowing . . . that he is **being**. And in this knowing he will that our understanding be **grounded** with all our **myghtis**, all our **entent**, & all our **menyng**; And **in this ground** he will that we take our **stede and wonyng** (stand and habitation)."

In the next thematic "surge" of concern, which itself is made up of two curves of emphasis, Julian moves from the mediation of prayer which seeks unification, to the direct ground of that unification, which is loving itself—and in very certain Pauline terms: loving now (nunc), and loving then (tunc).

Nunc, or Loving Now: "to be all onyd [unified] into him and entende to his wooing" (94r-96r)

[94r] And by the gracious light of himself he will that we have understanding of three things. The first is the noble & excellent **makyng** [making, conception, genesis, beginning]. The second is, the precious & loveworthy **ayen byeng** [everbeing, becoming again]. The third is, that all thing that he hath made beneath us, to serve us, **he for oure loue kepith it** [he sustains it for love of us]. Then **menyth** he thus, as if he said: Behold & see that I have done all this before thy prayer, and now thou art & [thou] prayest me. And this our lord God **meanyth**, that it **longith us** [it belongs to us, we long] to know that the greatest

[94v] dedes be done, as holy church teaches. And in thee [thy]-

self we have what we desire for our souls, and then we see not for the time what we should more pray [for], but all our **entent** [intent, attending] with all our might is set wholi **into the beholdyng of hym** [in looking at him, holding onto him, being in his debt], And this is a high & **unparceable** [indivisible, unparsable] prayer, as to my sight. For all the cause wherefore we pray, is **onyd** [united, unifying] into the sight and the beholding of him to whom we pray marvelously enjoying with reverent dread and so great sweetness & delight in him that we cannot pray

[95r] anything but as he **sterrith** [steers, stirs up in] us for the time. And well I know, the more the soul seeth of God, the more it desireth him by grace. But when we see him not so, then feel we need & cause to pray, because of our failing, and for enabling ourselves to our lord Jesus. For when a soul is tempested & troubled, and left to itself, then is time to pray, to make him[self] **souple and buxum** [pliant and submissive (and thus comely)] to God. But he, by no manner of prayer maketh God supple to him, for he is ever alike in love. And thus I saw what in time

[95v] our need is, why we pray; then our lord God followeth us helping our desire. And when we of his special grace plainly behold him, seeing no other needs, then we follow him & **he draws us into him[self] by love**. For I saw & felt that his marvelous & his fulsome goodness fulfills all other mights, and therewith I saw that his continuing working in all manner thing is done so **godly** [in goodly, in godly fashion], so wisely, & so mightily that **it pleases all our ymagyining** [powers of imaging forth, desires, imagining], and all that we can **meane** & think. And then

[96r] we can do no more but behold him & **enjoying with a mighty desire to be all onyd** [united, unified] **into him and entende** [attend, listen, tend] **to his wooing**, and enjoying in his love and delight in his goodness. And thus by his sweet grace shall we in our own meek continuing prayer communing unto him **now in this life by many privy touching** of sweet ghostly sights & feeling measured to us as our simpleness may bear it. And this is wrought & shall be by the grace of the holy ghost, so long till we shall die in **longyng for** [longing for, belonging to] love.

94r-96r. This section shows with special clarity the arbitrary effect of my editorial decision to divide W into sections in the first place. We do better to think of these folios as constituting one wave or surge of thematic concern that in turn helps lift the next wave up even higher. Here she examines the quality of love this side of death, and firmly places the source of our enjoyment **now** in our as yet to be fulfilled desire **then**. Her basic strategy is to set up a direct colloquy with St. Paul's famous mirror formulation in 1 Corinthians, by suggesting the pleasure to be found in the hints we have now of the deep joy we shall have then when we see him face to face, and know him then as he knows us now.

94r. —makyng . . . ayen being . . . he kepith it. Again Julian frames our sense of time past, present, and future in the trinitarian, biblical/ cosmic terms of Genesis, in the Incarnation as a fact of human history, and in the New Jerusalem of the world to come as John fortells it in Revelation. The diction also echoes back to the beginning of Julian's own text of *Shewings*, with the word play on *makyng* which she incorporated into her vision of the Virgin at the very beginning, and the three-part enclosing of love that she envisioned Christ as Maker having for the "lytil thyng" the size of a hazelnut of which he was the Maker, the Lover, and the Keeper.

94v–94r. —all our entente . . . is set wholi into the beholdyng of hym. The folio begins with "in thee we have what we desire." But it is of course the desire now for fulfilment then. As she begins her concatenation of desire, she uses the root verbs of "longing" (in "belonging") and "holding" (in "beholding") in such a way as to make the prefixes act more as emphatics, than as markers of semantic difference. At the end of 94r she writes "**it longith us to**," which means both "we long to" as well as "it is our duty and right to—it belongs to us to . . ." This helps prepare for a special emphasis on "holding" that is latent in the key phrase in 94v, in which our entire **entente** (which has in it the future sense of "attending to" as well as the present sense of "intending to") is vested wholly in "**the beholdyng of hym**" which means the promised future of "holding" as well as "beholding of" Christ in Glory.

95v. —God followeth us helping our desire. Once we feel desire for him, he knows it, and then "our lord God followeth us helping our desire. . . . then we follow him and he draws us into him[self] by love."

96r. —with a mighty desire to be all onyd into him and entende to his wooing. **Onyd** = made one with him, but more forceful when put, as here, in the accusative sense of being "united **into** him." **Entende** repeats the French form of the word "intend," which brings the sense of "attending" and "listening" to the fore, as well as "intending" and "willing." All of this enjoyment now is anticipatory of then, although we will be tickled in our growing anticipation by **many [a] privy touching** of sweet ghostly sights & feeling measured to us as our simpleness may bear it, until "we die in **longyng for loue**." Julian's trick here is to enhance our sense of the delicious "reality" of the paradise to come by spicing our **ymagyning** it with the "privy touches" of the best of here and now. God will send us the kinds of anticipations we most wish to receive in those touchings: but they will be only what we can bear, for as Eliot put it in "Little Gidding," humankind cannot bear very much reality.

And then Julian moves from *nunc* to *tunc* and St. Paul.

Tunc, or Loving Then: "this dereworthy soule
was preciously knytt to him in the makyng" (96v–99r)

[96v] And then shall we all come in to our lord God our selves clearly knowing, and God fulsomely having, and we endlessly be had all in God, him verily seeing & fulsomely feeling, & him ghostly feeling & him ghostly hearing & delightably smelling, and sweetly swallowing, **and thus shall we see God face to face,** most nearly & fulsomely. The creature that is made shall see and endlessly behold God that is the maker. For thus may no man see God and live after, that is to say in this **dedly** [mortal, with echoes of deeds, the active] life. But when he of his special

[97r] grace will **shew hym here** [reveal himself here], **he strengthens the creature above the self**, and he measureth the doing after his own will, as it is most profitable for the time. Truth sees God, & wisdom beholds God, and of these two comes the third: and that is a marvelous **holidelyte** [holy delight] in God, which is love. Where truth & wisdom is, verily there is love & verily communing of them both, and all of God's making, for God is endless sovereign truth, endless sovereign wisdom, endless sovereign love **un**

[97v] **made** [uncreated]. And man's soul is a creature in God, who has made [in it] his own **propertees**, and ever more it does what it was made for. It sees God and it **beholdyth** [beholds, holds onto] God, and **it loves God so that God enjoys in the creature, and the creature enjoys in God: endless mar-**

veling. In which marveling he sees his God, his lord, his maker so high, so great & so good in reward of him that is made that scarcely the creature seems [to be] anything in and of himself. But the clearness & cleanness of truth & wisdom makes

[98r] him to see & to be known that he is made for love, in which love God endlessly keeps him. Also he will that we know that our soul is a life, which life of his goodness & grace shall **lefte in** [lifted into, left alive, remain in] heaven without end, him loving, him thanking, and him praising. Also he will that we know that the noblest thing that ever he made is mankind, and the fullest substance, and the highest virtue is the blessed soul of Christ. And furthermore he will that we know that this loveworthy soul was preciously knit to him in the ma

[98v] king, which **knat** [knot, knitting] is so subtle and so powerful, that it is united into God, in which union it is made endlessly **holy** [holy, but also a fore-echo of holey]. Furthermore he will that we know & understand that all the souls that shall be saved in heaven without end be knit in this knot, and joined in this union, and made holy in this holiness. And for great endless love that God hath to all mankind, he maketh no departing in love between the blessed soul of Christ, and the least soul that shall be saved. For it is well easy to **lyve** [believe] & to **trowe** [trust] that the dwelling of the

[99r] blessed soul of Christ is full high in the glorious godhead, and truly as I understand in our lord's **menyng** [meaning, gathering]: where the blessed soul of Christ is, there is the substance of all the souls that shall be saved by Christ. Highly ought we to enjoy that God dwelleth in our soul, and much more highly we ought to enjoy that our soul dwelleth in God. Our soul is made to be God's dwelling place, and the dwelling place of our soul is in God, who is unmade.

96v–99r. Julian surges ahead to her own imaginative "shewing" of the joy of paradise, which she depicts as fully sensual.

96v. —and thus shall we see God face to face. As we will later see, in Paul's terms, "God face to face" it will be marked by sensual orchestrations of "ghostly" feeling, hearing, delightably smelling, and sweetly swallowing. And however these terms are qualified by the word "ghostly," we remain struck by the power of physicality in the diction. But almost as soon as we have begun to enjoy that momentary, fleeting imaginative fore-sense of pleasure that awaits us in the *tunc* of Paul, she returns us to the *nunc* of our Exodus, reminding us that here, "in this **dedly** life," we cannot see God and live. . . . This dictum holds true for all with only one exception: if and when we are awarded the "special grace of revelation," which will "**shew hym here.**"

98v. —**knit in this knot**. This weaving or knitting imagery is more than a woman writer's traditional occupational hazard; it images forth an extremely central aspect of the feminine poetics of revelation. The relation of weaving cloth and weaving text is an association going back past the image of Helen weaving the narrative of the Trojan War when we first discover her in *Iliad* 3. It is later deeply linked in the Latin word *textus*, which meant both "woven fabric" and "literary text." Julian's image of the weaving of natures in the special case of Christ's hypostasy, and in the general case of our *imago Dei* relation to the Creator, is of course mediated by her weaving together holy texts of the Bible. Weaving is also, in a more abstract sense, a winding of something around a nothing, and this capacity of God as weaver has from the beginning been anticipated by one of Julian's early, opening images of Christ: "He is oure clothyng" (73v).

Julian now moves into higher philosophical gear, as she further explores the implications of the hypostatic union of divine and human nature in the historical person of Christ: she brings us to a "higher Understanding" of the relationship obtaining between substance and "sensualyte."

A Higher Understanding: "he is mene that keeps
the substance & and sensualyte together" (99r-102r)

[99r (Cont.)] A high understanding it is inwardly to see & to know that God which

[99v] is our maker, dwelleth in our soul. And a higher understanding it is and more inwardly to see & to know our soul that is made dwelleth in God **in substance** [physical stuff, but also incorporeal basis of being, essence, quintessence, divine essence], of which substance by God, we be what we be. Also the almighty truth of the trinity is our father, for he made us & keepeth us in him. **And the deepe wysedom of the trinity is our moder** [mother], in whom we all be **enclosed**, and the high goodness of the trinity is our lord, and in him we are **closed** [delivered to our end and goal], and he is in us, all power, all wisdom and all goodness, one God, one

[100r] lord, and one goodness. Also I saw that Christ, having us all in him who shall be saved by him, worshipfully presenteth his father in heaven with us which [are] present. Well thankfully his father receives, & courteously gives it to his son, Jesus Christ. Which gift & working is joy to the father, and bliss to the son, & **lykyng** [relish, delight, and resemblance] to the holy ghost. And of all thing that **to us longyth** [belongs to us, reaches out to us, we long for], it is most liking to our lord that we enjoy in this joy, which is in the blessed trinity of our salvation. Also I saw ful surely that [it]

[100v] is readier to us, and more easy to come to the knowing of God, than to knowing of our own soul. For our soul is so deeply grounded in God, and so endlessly treasured, that we may not come to the knowing thereof till we have first knowing of God which is the maker, to whom it is joined. But not withstanding, I saw that we have **kindely of fulnes** [by nature the full capacity] to desire wisely, & truly to know our own soul. Whereby we are taught to seek it where it is, and that is in God, and thus by the gracious leading of the holy

[101r] ghost, we should know them both in one, whether we be stirred to know God, or our own soul, it are both good & true. God is nearer to us than our own soul, for he is [the] ground **in** [in, on] whom our soul stands, and he is **mene** [the means] that keeps the substance & and **sensualyte** [sensing capacity, appetite, desire, lust] together so that it shall never **depart** [be parted]. For our soul sits in God in very rest, and our soul stands in God in sure strength, & our soul is rooted by nature in God in endless love, and therefore if we will have knowing of our soul, & communing & dal

[101v] liance therewith, it is to our well being to seek into our lord God in whom it is enclosed. And **annentis** [with regard to] our substance it may rightfully be called our soul, and anent our sensuality it may rightfully be called our soul, and that is by the joining that it hath in God, that worshipful **cite** [site, city] that our lord Jesus sits in. It is our sensuality in which he is enclosed, and our **kyndely** [natural] substance is **beclosed** [beclosed, wrapped up] in Jesus Christ, with the blessed soul of Christ sitting in rest in the godhead. And I saw full surely that it **behouyth nedis** [benefits our needs]

[102r] that we shall be in longing and in penance, **into** [until, into] the time that we be led so deeply into God that we may

verily & truly know our own soul. And truly I saw that into this **high depenes** [high deepness] our lord himself leads us in the same love in which he made us, **in** [by/in/into] the same love by which he bought us by his mercy & grace through virtue of his blessed passion.

99r-102r. In further meditation on the mystery of the trinity, Julian probes two dualities that will begin to converge in the vision of the incarnation embedded in the following final great vision of Jesus as Mother (102r-111v). Here we have a culmination of what has gone before, illuminating on its own terms, but all of which also functions as a set-up for the spectacular finish to come. Julian figures here in this section the way Christ reconciles the "sensuality" of his human nature with the "substaunce" of his divinity in his hypostasy; and, by drawing on the female figures central to sapiential literature, she begins the extremely tricky task of figuring Christ as the ultimate reconciler of gender. She figures him forth as the male aspect of his Father and the female aspect of his Mother in a culminating figure of mystic androgyny—a function already prefigured in the haunting **shewing** of folio 87r, in which she pictures Christ as gazing into the vaginal mandorla of his own wound. These and the coming folios are filled with fore-figuring, and increasingly intense feminine images of fullness, linking, kindlyness, and/or naturalness and enclosing.

99v. —and the deepe wysedom of the trinity is our moder. This is Julian's first use of the mother image to begin her storming of the male battlement of received notions of the trinity. The female figures in wisdom literature (i.e., Sapientia, Ecclesia, Prudentia, etc.) are traditional figures of the mediatrix in medieval theology, and of course are centrally fulfilled by Mary herself in the Christological narrative. But to couch such a normally literary figure as sharing in the intimacy of "our mother" is to signal a potentially new direction, however safe a move this may be here for starters. Julian will very soon take far greater risks.

101r. —he is mene that kepith the substance and the sensualyte togeder so that it shall neuer depart. This echoes the traditional (and interminable) scholastic arguments concerning realism. Julian's position, as we can now predict, is not the analytic one of choosing one side or the other, but the synthetic one of mystic reconciliation of substance as divine nature and sensuality as human nature in the hypostasy of Christ. Julian is now ready for her final triumph of the *Shewings*: her astonishing meditation on Jesus as Mother. Because of the length of this final surge of discourse, I risk even greater marring of its grand rhetorical effect by further subdivision into three thematic concentrations, interrupting twice for intermediate commentary.

God is Our Mother:
"I it am that is to say I it am" (102r-111v)

[subsection 1. Feminizing the Trinity: God as Family]

[102r continued] And not withstanding all this we may never come to the full knowing of God till we first know clearly our own soul. For into the time that it be in the

[102v] full power we may not be all fully holy. And that is that our sensuality, by the virtue of Christ's passion be brought up into the substance with all the profits of our tribulation that our lord shall make us to get by mercy & grace. Also, as verily as God is our father, so as verily God is our mother. And that shewyth he in all & namely in these **fiue te** [finity of, very few] words there where he saith: **I it am that is to say I it am** [I am that I am, Yahweh Yahweh] **the power & goodness of fatherhood. I it am**, the **wisdom & the kyndenes** [kindness, naturalness, of the nature] **of motherhood. I it am**, the **light & the grace, that**

[103r] **is all blessed love. I it am the trinity. I it am**, the unity. **I it am**, the high sovereign goodness of all manner [of] thing. **I it am**, that **makith thee to loue. I it am**, that **makith the to longe** [made you to belong, made thee for longing, made thee to desire], the endless fullness of all true desires. For where the soul is highest, noblest, & worthiest. there it is lowest, meekest and mildest. And of this substantial ground we have all our virtues in our sensuality by right of **kynde** [nature], and by helping & spreading of mercy & grace without the which we may not profit. Also Jesus, the second person in trinity

[103v] in whom is the father and the holy ghost, **he is verily our mother in kynde of** [by the nature, type of, in his kindness in] **our first making**, and **he is our very mother in grace, by taking of our kynde made** [by taking on our created nature, with strong echoes of choosing our kind, natural maiden]. I understand three ways of **beholding of** [beholding the presence of, divine appropriation of] motherhood in God. The first is [the] ground of our **kynde making** [the sort or type of

our creation]. The second is **takyng of oure kynde** [his taking on of our nature], and there begins the motherhood of grace. The third is motherhood of **werking** [working, (natal) labor] and therein is a further forth-spreading by the same grace of length and breadth, of height and of deepness without end,

[104r] and all is one love.

102v. —**I it am that is to say I it am**. Julian, in her search for a platform from which to launch her new vision of motherhood in the Godhead, chooses unerringly one of the most patriarchal moments in the Old Testament: the answer of God to Moses questioning on Sinai: "Yahweh Yahweh." As the notes in the Oxford Bible tell us, God speaks of himself as a third person grammatical construction even as he asserts his primal ontological attribute of universal BEING. Perhaps an acceptable, if primitive equivalent to the linguistic situation in Hebrew might be this: "And God Said: AMING. "Aming," a clumsy second choice would be the ridiculously sounding: "I be He be." In any case the grammatical situation is a blinding blaze of reflexivity: the first word for being is fulfilled in the second word for being which, in the radical situation where God enters into human discourse to tell us who HE is, must somehow also be the same word. Julian does her own best by isolating the two assertions of divine identity by intruding the explanatory "that is to say" between them: "'I Am' that is to say, 'I Am.'" However one slices it, no way I know works in English, and colleagues assure me the same kind of irreducible difficulty resides at the center of the "ur-articulation" in the original Hebrew. The important thing to keep in mind is probably this: that this is a paradigmatic case of linguistic overthrust: this is what happens at the extreme edge of human discourse where we discover its nature and limitation even as we watch it begin to fall apart in the presence of the numinous.

—**I it am the wysedome and the kyndenes of moderhed**. As Julian begins her implied inventory of repeated alternatives of reference to the opening phrase "I it am," she begins appropriately with the trinity, and asserts up front that the trinity consists of the power of the Father-hood, the wisdom of Motherhood, and the grace of Love. How are we to "interpret" this overlay over the traditional trinitarian formula of Father, Son, and Holy Ghost? Who gets to be the mother? The answer is as it must be: they all do. And that is because the gender identifications between Julian's new taxonomy and the old formulations are mediated by the attributes she supplies of their respective virtues: the power and goodness (of the Father), the wisdom and kindness (of the Mother), the light and the grace (of the Love). The minor miracle is how she keeps the potentially explosive dynamics of the trinity as a kind of cosmic mom-and-pop shop both appropriately elevated and in creative balance.

[Subsection 2. Jesus in the Service of the Mother:]

[104r, continued] But now **me behouyth** [it seems useful, benefits me] to say a little more about this **furthe spredyng** [spreading forth, ranging further]. As I understand, in the **menynge** of our lord, how that we be brought again by the motherhood of mercy & grace into our **kyndely stede** [natural state, condition, place of habitat], where we were made by the motherhood of **kynde loue** [kindly, natural love], which **kynde loue** never leaves us, our **kynde moder**, our gracious mother, for he would all wholly become our mother in all things. He took the **grounde of his werke** [grounding, reason for his work, of his (natal) labor] full lowly & full mildly in the maiden's womb, **takyng fleshe of** [taking flesh from, taking on flesh in] her, ready in

[104v] our poor flesh himself to do the service and the office of motherhood in all things. The mother's service is nearest, readiest and surest. It is nearest, for it is **of kynde** [is natural, comes by nature]. Readiest, for it is most of love. And surest, for it is of truth. This office no power could ever do the fullest, but Christ Jesus God and man **alone** [all one, alone]. We know well that all our mothers bear us with pain & **to deyeng** [to the point of death, into death and dying]. but our true mother Jesus, he alone beareth us to joy & to bliss, and endless living, blessed must he be. Thus he sustains

[105r] us within him in love, and **traveyled in to** [labored into] the **full tyme** [full term, the fullness of time] so that he would suffer the sharpest throes, and the most grievous pains that ever were or ever shall be, and died at the last. And when he had done & so **borne** [bore, gave birth to] us into bliss, yet all this might not **make a sythe to** [complete a moment of, complete the journey of] his marvelous love. And that shewed he in these high overpassing words of love: **Yf I might suffer more, I wulde suffer more.** He might no more die, but he would not **stynt of workyng** [stop working, cease in his (childbearing) labor] as long as he needed to feed us,

[105v] for the precious love of motherhood had made him debtor to us. The mother may give her child to suck her milk,

but our precious mother Jesus, he may feed us with himself, and does so ful courteously & full tenderly with the blessed sacrament of his body & blood that is precious food of very life. And with all the sweet sacraments he sustains us well mercifully & graciously. And so meant he in these gracious words, where he said: **I it am**, that holy church preaches thee and teaches thee. That is to say,

[106r] all the health & the life of sacraments, all the virtue & the grace of my word, all the goodness that is ordained in holy church to thee: **I it am**. The mother may lay her child tenderly to her breast, but our tender lord Jesus he may closely lead us to his blessed breast by his **swete** [sweet, sweaty] open side, and show us therein part of his godhead, and the joys of heaven with ghostly sureness of endless bliss. That shewed he in these **swete** words, where I said: **Loo, how I love the**, beholding into his side, enjoying this fair lovely word, mother;

[106v] it is so sweet & so **kynde** [natural, kindly] in itself: but it may not truly be said of anyone nor to anyone, but to him and of him that is very mother of life & all. To the **properte** [property, propriety, characteristics of motherhood] **belongyth** [longs to, belongs] **kynde love wysedom & knowing** [nature, natural and kindly love, wisdom, & knowing] and it is God. For though it be so that our bodily forthbringing be but little, low & simple in reward for our ghostly forthbringer, yet it is he that doth it in the creature by whom that it is done. The **kynde** loving mother that thinks and knows the need of her child, she keeps it full tenderly as

[107r] the **kynde** [type and nature] & condition of motherhood will. And ever as it waxes in age & in stature, so she changes her working, but not her love. And when it is waxen of greater age, she suffers it to be chastised in breaking down of vices to make the child to receive virtues & grace. This working with all others that the good our lord doth in them by whom it is done, thus he is our mother in **kynde** by the working of grace in us, lower parts for love of the higher. And he wishes that we know it, for he would

[107v] have all our love fastened to him.

104r-107r. The first surge of this final concatenation on Jesus as Mother (102r-103v) focused on the Mother more as an abstract role in an imaginable schema of Godhead than as a living woman. In this next section, Julian moves to garner an inventory of more familar, personal images of motherly "services" that we all recognize from experience in order to provide an array or backdrop for her positioning Christ, in *his* service, against them as an imaginable woman. The resonance of the match or fit will be of primary strategic value to her larger quest, as she demonstrates, rather than simply declares, the ways in which it is indeed appropriate to think of Christ as a "real" Mother. Slowly but surely, then, the focus of attention shifts from the abstract idea of motherhood to a focus on Christ, and his capacities to embody a credible version of motherhood. But Julian's orthodoxy is still strong, the resulting image of Christ as Mother is intensely perceived and powerfully depicted, yet never as an aspect dominating his hypostasy, that "dualistic" unitary fact of his being.

104r-102v. —**he took the grounde of his werke . . . in the maydens wombe takyng fleshe of our poor fleshe hym selfe to do the seruice and the office of moderhed in all thyng.** All the richly elaborated services and offices of the mother are then gathered and played against the services of Christ: and of course the differences are as telling as the similarities:

105v. —**The mother may give her child to suck her milk, but our prescious mother Jesus, he may feed us with himself.** The image of Christ suckling the child is at first rendered less radical by the way Julian supplies her image of the sacrament of the eucharist as the modality of imagined lactate transfer. But Julian obviously recalls her vision of Christ in 87v when she shortly returns to the image of the infant at the breast:

106r. —**The mother may lay her child tenderly to her breast, but our tender lord Jesus he may closely lead us to his blessed breast by his swete open side, and show us therein part of his godhead . . .** The radical crossing of normal gender barriers can no longer be denied or ignored. The logic of the lactating analog between the wound of the crucifixion, the vagina of birth, and the nipple of nurture, and the eating of the Corpus Christi in the sacrament of the eucharist is intrinsically linked and inviolable. We must face the fact that at least for the moment we are in the liminal domain of that revelatory territory that the two genders have shared in western tradition during many moments of apocalyptic encounter. Not the least of these was the dream of Perpetua as she envisioned her own martyrdom, when she dreamed she was suddenly transformed into a male body, or those moments of extreme love in Hildegard's correspondence when she linked genders in her modes of depicting her relations with the nun Richardis and her mother the marchioness. It is precisely on this shared playing field that embraces the marginal limits of both sexes that a central revelatory power resides. That was surely intuited in the creation formula in Genesis, where the first half of the verse guarantees we were made in God's image, and the second that as imago Dei we were created male and female together. The image of separate genders coalesces in the image radiating from that text, and it melts down into the implied androgony of God, the original of those doubly reflecting images: YHWH YHWH: Aming Aming.

[Subsection 3. The Grace of the Jesus Mother; we the children:]

[107v, continued] And in this I saw that all our debt that we owe by God's bidding, it is to fatherhood and motherhood, as fulfilled in true loving of God. Which blessed love Christ works in us, and this was **shewed** in all. & namely in the high plenteousness [of] words where he said: **I it am that thou louyst**. And in our ghostly forthbringing he uses more tenderness in keeping without comparison by as much as our soul is of more price in his sight. He **ken** [knows how to, can] delight our understanding, he

[108r] **addith** [adds to, aids] our ways. He eases our conscience, he comforts our soul, he lightens our heart, & **penyth in** [takes pains in, works by] partial knowing, and [by] loving in his blessed godhead, with gracious mind in his manhood & his blessed passion, with courteous marveling in his high overpassing goodness. And [he] maketh us to love all that he loves, **for** [on account of] his love, and to be payed with him & with all that he does & in all his work, and when we fall hastily, he raises us by his lovely **beclepping** [calling] & his gracious touching, and when we be strengthened by his

[108v] **swete wurkyng** [sweet, savory, sweaty working] then we will fully choose him by his grace to be his servants & his lovers lastingly without end. And yet after this he suffers some of us to fall more grievously and more hard than ever we did before, as we think. And then we think we be not those which [are] all wise, that **all were nought** [was brought to nothing] that we have begun, but that is not so, for we need to fall, and we need to know it & to see it. For if we fall not, we should

not know how feeble and how wretched we be of our self. And also we need to see our

[109r] falling. For if we see it not, though we fall, it should not profit us. & commonly first we fall, and after we see it, and through that sight by the mercy of God we be low and meek. The mother may suffer her child to perish; but our heavenly mother Jesus Christ will never suffer us that be his children to perish, for he is all power, all wisdom and all love, and so is no one but he, blessed must he be. Also often times when our falling & our wretchedness is **shewed** us, we be so sore adread & so greatly ashamed of

[109v] our selves, that we scarcely know where we may **holde** [hold, hide] ourselves. But then our courteous mother will not that we flee away, for to him there were **no thing lother** [nothing worse], but he will then that we use the condition of a child, for when it is diseased or adread, then it runs hastily to the mother, and if [it] may do no more, it cries on the mother for help with all its might. So will our lord that we do as a meek child, saying thus: My **kynde** mother, my gracious mother, my loveworthy mother, have mercy on me. I have made

[110r] [my]self foul & **unlyke to the** [unlike thee, not to your liking], and I neither may nor can amend it, but with thy help & grace. And if we feel us not eased then soon, then be we sure that he uses the condition of a wise mother. For if he see that it be more profit to us for to weep & mourn, then he will suffer it with ruth & pity into the best time for love. And he will then that we use the property of a child that evermore **kyndly** trusts to the love of the mother in weal and in woe. And our lord God will that we take us mightily to the faith of holy

[110v] church, and find there our love-worthy mother in solace of true understanding with all the blessed **commoun** [community, communion]. For one singular person may oftentimes be broken as it seems to the self, but the whole body of holy church was never broken, nor never shall without end. And therefore a sure thing it is, and a good & gracious to will meekly, and mightily fastened & and joined to our mother holy church that is Christ Jesus, for the flood of mercy that is his love-worthy blood & precious water: it is plenteous to make us fair and clean. The blessed

[111r] wounds of our savior are open and enjoy to heal us.

The sweet gracious hands of our mother are ready & diligent about us. For he in all this working uses the very office of a **kynde** nurse that hath nothing else to do but to attend about the salvation of her child. It is the office of our lord Jesus Christ to save us. It is his worship to do it, and it is his will we know it. For he will that we love him sweetly, and trust on him meekly & mightily, and this he showed in these gracious words: **I kepe thee full surely** [safely, surely].

[111v] Furthermore a **kyndely** child despairs not of the mother's love, and **kyndely** the child presumes not of it self. **Kyndely** the child loves the mother, and each of them both the other.

107v–111v. In this extroardinary Jesus-as-Mother sequence, we have moved from the universal idea and role of the mother, to Christ and his various appropriations of that role, to the emphasis here in the final section on ourselves as the inheritors of that radical form of motherhood: on our humanity as the children. This is the underlying strategic movement of the entire sequence: the trinity of address that runs from the Mother, to Christ-as-Mother, to us as having Christ for a Mother.

107v. **—when we fall hastily, he raises us by his lovely beclepping** [calling] & his gracious touching. There is something haunting about Julian's likening the mother's calling of the child to "the voice of his calling" to us, and we begin to see, as she closes this tribute to the feminine aspects of divinity, that she has indeed fully integrated the imagery, the role-playing, the whole range of maternal associations lurking in our horizons of experience into her new vision of Jesus. The sequence closes with a firm focus on us, and whether we have the grace to accept all this as "natural" children:

111v. **—Furthermore a kindely child despairs not of the mother's love, and kyndely the child presumes not of itself. Kyndely the child loves the mother, and each of them both the other.** Here the very absence of any specific verbal reference to Christ is a sure index, in the current context, of his fully integrated presence in the natural and compassionate, **kyndely** world of contiguity figured in general by mothers and children, and in particular by her opening vision of the *Shewings*, by the mother Mary as she gazed in quiet on her son Jesus.

Explicit: "Suddenly thou shalt be taken." (111v–112v)

[111v (cont.) Also I had great desire & longing for God's gift to be delivered of this world & of this life. For oftentimes I beheld the woe that is here in this life, and the weal & the blessed being that is in heaven. And methought sometimes though there had been no pain in this life but the absence of our lord God, it was more than I might bear. And this made

[112] me to mourn & busily to long. And also my own wretchedness, sloth & irkness helped there too, so I liked not to live & to travail as it fell to me to do. And to all our courteous lord God answered for comfort & patience, and said these words: **Suddenly thou shalt be taken** from all thy pain, & from all thy sickness, from all thy disease, and from all thy woe, and thou shalt come up above, and thou shalt have me to thy meed & reward, and thou shalt be **fulfilled of** [filled full of, fulfilled with] joy & bliss, and thou shalt never more have no manner of pain,

[112v] neither no manner of sickness, no manner of misliking, nor no wanting of will, but ever [be] in joy & bliss without end. What should it then grieve thee to suffer a while, since it is my will & my worship. It is God's will that we set the point of our thought in this blessed beholding as often as we may, & as long.

111v–112v. As flowing, sinuous, and lush as the forwarding of the discourse has been throughout the W version of the *Shewings*, the end comes, as always, suddenly. The deliverance of birth, so intrinsic in the opening image of Mary, and so central to the closing Jesus-as-Mother sequence, now takes on more embracing meanings: "And I had great desire & longing for God's gift to be delivered of this world & of this life." In very short shrift, Christ answers her moment of weakness: "Suddenly thou shalt be taken, and thou shalt have me to thy meed and reward." The final sentence that we are given is a minor miracle of closure; so suddenly distanced in tone and timbre that it is more than merely conceivable that Julian has left and we are hearing the scribe. What is more likely, given Julian's affection for the trope of the scribe, that she wrote it so that we can imagine herself as seer speaking it, even as we can also imagine her as scribal revisionist recollecting it:

"It is God's will that we set the point of our thought in this blessed beholding as often as we may, & as long."

The last phrase of the *Shewings*, in the undeniable position of closure, does not signal closure. It is an adverbial of time, of indefinite continuance. Nothing is over. We have not been released from the project; on the contrary. The words that inexorably follow "as long" need neither be said nor written: their necessity is absolute in the quivering air. It is generated by the adverbial phrasing itself; "& as long" invites us into a kind of mystical, almost nuptial relationship with Julian as she signals that she is about to vanish into silence. Her words are a firm assertion that her silence means nothing more than a shift in mode. As we complete the reading of her words, we are exhorted to join her continuing meditation in silence on the kenosis of Christ, his self-emptying into Glory, as often as we can, and for as long as we all shall live.

Afterword:
Conclusions, Contexts,
Open Questions

Perhaps the first two questions to ask here at closure are: What
have we done? What have we found out?

After a preliminary glance at the *Passio* of Vibia Perpetua, we have
read rather closely in the work of two women writers, one who began
the rich epoch of European women's medieval visionary literature, and
one who for all intents and purposes ended it. I have left it pretty
much up to readers to make their own running comparisons with Hildegard as we worked on Julian's *Shewings*. Why? Largely because of
the nature of this sort of inquiry; it is necessary to get one's first fix
on these texts in and on the writer's own terms.

What have we found out? That Hildegard and Julian were first of
all profoundly different intelligences, residing in profoundly different
sensibilities, speaking out of profoundly different personal histories
and cultures. We also found that at the core, their intelligences were
faced with essentially the same challenge. Each was visited by an over-
powering sense of the presence of God, who in paranormal ways
brought to them extraordinary visions to the eye and ear. Each woman
was simultaneously burdened with what she felt was a divine imperative
to convert her unique visionary experiences into a form shareable with
her fellows.

I have resisted any inclination to discuss their strategies in terms of
possible models, except to mention along the way some obvious facts.
Hildegard, in the forefront of this medieval company of woman visionaries, had no textual models for understanding her experience other
than her own reading and hearing of Paul and the prophets of the
Old Testament. Julian, at the end of that curve of women nearest to
us in time, had at least theoretical access to a growing and rich tradition

of women's visionary literature. At the very minimum, she must have heard about Clare of Assisi, Bridget of Sweden, and most probably Catherine of Siena, and very possibly many others. And it is fairly certain that Margery Kempe tells us the truth about visiting Julian and conversing with her extensively on one of her many trips. But with all this in mind, close reading of their texts confirms they both worked essentially alone; many minor details and strategies may reveal a passing awareness of earlier models; but at the core, each of their works are inimitable, and were in no central, non-trivial way modeled on extant texts. But even as we grow to appreciate that hard and shining fact, we also sense some deep commonalities of strategy that they shared.

As we observed with some care the work of these two women, along with that of Vibia Perpetua, we found a number of strategies that each woman discovered for herself, but that they nonetheless also pursued in common, strategies which taken together constitute a style, which shapes what I call, at least tentatively, a feminine poetics of revelation. It is a fluid, enumerative, and ultimately synthetic style, full of enormous energy and extraordinary intelligence. It runs against the scholastic grain. It is curvilinear, phasic, and repetitive. It avoids analytics based on dividing our sense of the things of this world into the clear domination and subordination of established hierarchies. It also avoids common signals announcing impending closure, and invents lexical, grammatical, and rhetorical strategies for enhancing our expectation and pleasure in continuance. It is personal and provocative: it invites us to imagine what it is like to be visited by unmediated divine address.

For most readers, the legacy of text left by these women is substantial, interesting, and impressive in affective power. Yet the feminine style that they employed in the service of mediating the presence of God can (and should) leave traditional readers and critics with a very big question: where is the authority located for readers when it comes to determining value? How can we test and weigh the kinds and degrees of reliability, truth, and beauty that most of us find here? Unless personally privileged and burdened with direct access to the mind of God, none of us can really judge how accurately these women reported God's word. Or perhaps there was a hidden cabal, a kind of female order of Ladies Templar? And a corresponding conspiracy of intrusive female prophesying, rather than the more comfortable, "male" stoicisms of silence? Or perhaps we are really witnessing a kind of mass female hysteria between the twelfth and the fifteenth centuries, perhaps there was too much lead in the water that these women drank? Or perhaps the details have gone missing of a shared pathology, as some more recent, serious, and undeniably interesting proponents of a theory of migraine propose? The inescapable fact of the matter is that if we cannot place with confidence our authority as competent readers of this discourse in our knowledge of God, or in the historical record, or in our own personal visionary experiences, or in our literature, or in our professors—and I feel certain we cannot find the authority we seek in any of these precincts—then our last recourse is to seek the authority we require in ourselves: in our own vulnerable, and very mixed bag of learning and opinion, of memory and desire. That decision, even if made with a rarely felt confidence of mind and heart, does not mean we can afford to ignore all available supporting information, in confirmation or in challenge.

For one thing, these women were not exactly writing in a literary vacuum—though the vexed question of the kind and degree of access they had as women to what should have been their own literary tradition will not go away. That aside, the literary context of their writings I have barely touched on, and for what I hope are good reasons. I have already argued that the first tests of these visionary works should be grounded in and on their own terms. But in any inquiry probing further into the work of these women, we would of course need to examine not one, but several traditions in order to construct a more historicised sense of context for their texts. We can begin such an enumeration by speaking very generally about two of them.

First, there is the dominant male tradition of the Middle Ages, and here I *do* mean "male" in terms of biologically determined men. That male tradition itself has two sometimes quite intertwining branches. There are the men, who like our women, report vision. We first reach back in our minds to Old Testament prophets such as Ezekiel and Daniel, then to the later Hellenistic and Roman fall-out of Plato's *Phaedrus* and *Timaeus*, and, finally, and most powerfully of all for these women, St. Paul on his way to Damascus. Then we move forward in time to figures such as Bonaventure, Bernard of Sylvester, Alan of Lille, Langland, and the Pearl Poet. And there are the more consciously secular literary men, ranging from such early writers as Prudentius and Boethius, to such later writers as Guillaume de Lorris, Jean de Meun, John Gower, and Geoffrey Chaucer, men who had already discovered the value of using the genre of the "visio" as a useful literary tool. Dante sits firmly and somehow at ease in the middle. And all of the important texts of these men have long been available in carefully edited editions.

One cannot say the same about the texts of that second great tradition, the tradition of medieval women's visionary writing, more or less framed by our two subjects Hildegard of Bingen and Julian of Norwich. In fact one of the major contributions of the feminist "revolution" has been to provide the focus, energy, and intellectual sophistication required to fill in much of the lamentable gap of missing texts authored by women writers that has long been a fact of a medieval scholar's life—whether for woe or joy it sometimes seems hard to tell. The past ten years have seen a specially remarkable and gratifying surge of activity that has already gone a great distance in rectifying this problem.

To backtrack a bit, the greatest contributions of the post-War years on Hildegard were made by Germans, most of them women, many of them associated with the religious orders that provided original refuge for the medieval visionaries whose texts they have edited and published. Julian scholarship has more recently been vitally recharged by the activities of a group of British and Canadian specialists in fourteenth-century mysticism. The five volumes now available recording the Exeter Symposia, and edited by Marion Glasscoe, comprise an indispensable library of enormous value to students and scholars of medieval culture.

But most of the most important work done in the last decade in terms of publishing unavailable texts has been the work of women working in and out of the American medieval community, perhaps more energetically reflected in the annual convention at Kalamazoo, Michigan (affectionately known to its participants as the "Zoo") than on the staid banks of the Charles River where the establishment of the Medieval Academy of America engages in its magisterial rituals. Still, it must be said that one of the Academy's standing committees, CARA, the Committee on Centers and Regional Associations, has been a valiant and effective emissary of the Academy to the various frontiers of medieval culture situated west of the Charles. And the extraordinary publishing effort at SUNY Binghamton, brilliantly directed by the efforts of Mario di Cesare and Paul Szarmach, has made an enormously rich contribution to our stock of texts in the publishing program known as MRTS: Medieval and Renaissance Texts and Studies. The Select Bibliography at the back of this book lists some of the texts readers will find useful for further pursuing the many large and open questions that have been raised here, and that remain to be further considered.

Nevertheless, even though we now have a much broader and richer inventory of primary texts to deal with, these are still very early days indeed in terms of gathering a sufficient inventory of reliable critical, historical, and theoretical secondary writing with which we can enhance our interests in and capacities for reading the primary visionary texts of the Middle Ages. I believe that fact is not purely a matter of historical accident or gender politics; it has deeply to do with the general but nevertheless central question regarding the location of readerly authority that I just raised.

Reliable scholars are loathe to enter into the domain of critical battle if there is no set of "objective" criteria available against which they can test the validity of their own findings, as well as those of others. And as we have seen, there is no obvious set of criteria of corrigibility available for texts written by people who want to tell us what it meant to have been addressed directly by God. After we summon up as much historical information and theoretical speculation as we can gather together in our attempt to encounter these texts wisely, we are on our own.

As I have tried to demonstrate as well as argue in this study, we do ourselves and the writers we are trying to read a real and important service when we temper the optimistic enthusiasm we naturally bring to any worthwhile effort with a clear and steady realization that we are very unlikely to wind up with any unequivocal observations, verifiable hypotheses, or, much less likely, any persuasive conclusions. We must be willing to deal in the dark. We must bring all of our historical knowledge as well as our native intelligence, lucidity, and realism to bear on the project. We will also require, for any sense of gratification at the point of ending, as much good will, humor, and hope regarding the human condition as we can muster. We must use the full range of our experience in the fellowship of humanity as the source of our final authority. May it be adequate. We really have no other choice.

Boulder, Colorado—Palm Sunday, 1994

Select Bibliography
with Notes

WORKS CITED AND SUGGESTIONS
FOR FURTHER READING

HILDEGARD VON BINGEN

Texts:

Epistolarium, ed. Lieven Van Acker. *Corpus Christianorum Continuatio Medievalis*, Turnhout: Brepols, 1991. There is no English translation of the letters as a whole, but some key letters have been edited and translated by Dronke in *Women Writers*. There is an important German translation of many of the letters edited, with excellent commentary, by Adelgundis Fuehrkoetter, *Briefwechsel*, Revised Edition, Salzburg: Otto Mueller, 1990. On the Letter to the Prelates of Mainz: See *Briefwechsel*, 235–41, for a German translation of the letter in the form edited by Van Acker, with a useful historical note. An important fragment of the letter has been edited from the Berlin manuscript by Dronke for his *Women Writers*, 313–315, with translation and penetrating commentary, 196–99.

Liber Divinorum Operum (De operatione Dei). J.-P Migne, ed. *Patrologia Latina*, 197, 739–1038. The only modern translation is in German: Heinrich Schipperges, *Welt und Mensch*, Salzburg: Otto Mueller, 1965.

Liber Vitae Meritorum. J.-P. Pitra, ed. *Analecta Sanctae Hildegardis*. Monte Cassino: 1882, 1–244. There is an English translation by Bruce W. Hozeski, *Hildegard of Bingen: The Book of the Rewards of Life*, New York and London: Garland, 1994.

Scivias, ed. A. Fuehrkoetter, with Angela Carlevaris, in series *Corpus Christianorum Continuatio Medievalis*, 63 and 63a. Turnhout: Brepols, 1978. Cf. Migne, ed., *Patrologia Latina* 197, 383–738. The most reliable English version is *Hildegard of Bingen: Scivias*, translated by Columba Hart and Jane Bishop, with preface by Caroline Walker Bynum and introduction by Barbara Newman (New York: Paulist Press, 1990).

Vita Sanctae Hildegardis [The Life of Saint Hildegard]. J.-P. Migne, *Patrologia Latina* 197, 91–130. The *Vita* is an indispensable tool in any work on Hildegard, but using it in its current state of accessibility presents some irresolvable difficulties. There is no complete English translation: there is a fairly reliable German translation. The *Vita* itself survives in several manuscripts which differ from one another in often significant details, and there is no variorium edition that collates and embodies the entire manuscript tradition. Dronke has made his own collation of all relevant manuscripts and printed major sections of his "best" version of the Latin in *Women Writers*, 231–241, as well as offering some English translation (ibid, 145–46, 150–51, 153). Thus if one is doing close work on the *Vita* as a whole, and cannot consult the original manuscripts, one must work with the printed edition available in *PL*, the sections printed by Dronke, and *Das Leben der heiligen Hildegard von Bingen* (Duesseldorf: Patmos, 1968), and the German translation of the whole by Adelgundis Fuehrkoetter. Fuehrkoetter collated her edition for her translation from the major sources, but did not print any Latin text. Using the *Vita* is further complicated by the fact that both Gottfried, who wrote the first book before his death in 1175 and Theoderic, who wrote Books 2 and 3 after Hildegard herself had died in 1180, quoted liberally from Hildegard's own writings and letters. Many of these passages we can check against other manuscripts, others not. I assume that Gottfried also used additional notes gathered directly from Hildegard during the few years he acted as her provost before he died, and that these were available to Theoderic as he put it all together when fulfilling his abbatial commission, but they are no longer available to us. In any case, in this study I only use passages from the *Vita* that appear in her own voice, and indicate when I am using the *Patrologia*, and when I am using Dronke.

Special Studies:

Liebeschuetz, Hans. *Das Allegorische Weltbild der heiligen Hildegard von Bingen.* Darmstadt: Wissenschaftliche Buchgesellschaft, 1964.

Newman, Barbara. *Sister of Wisdom: St. Hildegard's Theology of the Feminine.* Berkeley: University of California Press, 1987.

Schrader, Marianna and Adelgundis Fuehrkoetter. *Die Echtheit des Schriftums der heiligen Hildegard von Bingen.* Cologne/Graz: Boehlau, 1956. Indispensable study; includes much previously unedited documentation.

JULIAN OF NORWICH:

Texts:

The standard editions of Julian are: Short-text: *Julian of Norwich's "Revelations of Divine Love": The Shorter Version Edited from B.L. Add. MS 37790*, by Frances Beer, *Middle English Texts* 8, (Heidelberg, 1978) and *A Book of Showings to the Anchoress Julian of Norwich*, Part I, edited by Edmund Colledge and James Walsh (Toronto: Pontifical Institute of Medieval Studies, 1978); Long text: *Julian of Norwich: A Revelation of Love*, edited by Marion Glasscoe [from LS1, with ref to LS2], 2nd edition (Exeter: University of Exeter, 1986) and *A Book of Showings to the Anchoress Julian of Norwich*, Part II, edited from LP by Edmund Colledge and James Walsh (Toronto: Pontifical Institute of Medieval Studies, 1978). My summary of the manuscript tradition is drawn from Nicholas Watson, "The Composition of Julian of Norwich's *Revelation of Love,*" *Speculum* 68 (July, 1993), 638 n2. In this indispensable article, Watson takes the lead in arguing for a much wider time-frame than currently held likely in which Julian composed her lifework. See also the discussion of the manuscript tradition in Colledge and Walsh's edition of *A Book of Showings* (Part I) and important supplements and corrections provided by Marion Glasscoe in "Visions and Revisions: A Further Look at the Manuscripts of Julian of Norwich," *Studies in Bibliography* 42 (1989), 103–20. For the earlier traditional view, see Paul Molinari, *Julian of Norwich: The Teaching of a 14th Century English Mystic* (London: Longmans, Green, 1958, 1).

Other Texts and Studies related to Julian:
Cloud of Unknowing, edited (and translated) by James Walsh. New York: Paulist Press, 1981.

Deonise Hid Divinite, Phyllis Hodgson, ed. EETS, OS, 231 (London, 1955 for 1949).

Ellis, Roger. "Flores ad Fabricandum . . . : Investigation of the Uses of the Revelations of Bridget of Sweden in 15th C England." *Medium Aevum* 51(1982), 163–86.

Gillespie, Vincent. "Lukynge in haly bukes: Lectio in some Late Medieval spiritual Miscellanies," in *Spaetmittelalterlich Geistliche Literatur in der Nationalsprache, 2. Analecta Cortusiana*, 106 (1984), 1–27.

Glasscoe, Marion. "An Approach to Reading Julian of Norwich," *Analecta Cartusiana*, 106 (1984), 155–77.

Hilton, Walter. *Scale of Perfection*. Evelyn Underhill, ed. London: J.M. Watkins, 1948.

Liber Celestis of St. Bridget of Sweden., ed. R. Ellis, EETS OS 291 (1988). Useful introduction to Middle English translation.

Maisonneuve, John. The Visionary Universe of Julian of Norwich, in M. Glasscoe, ed. *The Medieval Mystical Tradition in England, 1.* Exeter, 1980.

Pallphrey, Brant. *Love Was His Meaning: The Theology and Mysticism of Julian of Norwich.* Salzburg Studies in English Literature, 94:4, Salzburg, 1982.

(Ward), Sister Benedicta. "Julian the Solitary," in *Julian Reconsidered*, Oxford, 1988.

Windeatt, Barry. "Julian of Norwich and Her Audience," *Review of English Studies* NS, 28 (1977), 1–17.

———. "The Art of Mystical Loving: Julian of Norwich," in Glasscoe, *Medieval Mystical Tradition*, 1 (1980), 55–71.

VIBIA PERPETUA
The following editions, translations and discussions provide indispensable assistance in reading this early martyrology: E. C. E. Owen, *Some Authentic Acts of the Early Martyrs* (London: Clarendon Press, 1927), 76–92; C. I. M. I. van Beek (ed), *Passio Sanctarum Perpetuae et Felicitatis* (Nijmegen, 1936) and *Passio Sanctarum Perpetuae et Felicitatis, Latine et Graece* (Bonn: Florilegium Patristicum XLIII, 1938); Erich Auerbach, *Literary Language and Its Public in Late Latin Antiquity and in the Middle Ages* (New York: Bollingen Foundation, 1965), 60–65;

E. R. Dodds, *Pagan and Christian in an Age of Anxiety* (Cambridge: Cambridge University Press, 1965), 47–53; H. J. Musurillo, *The Acts of the Christian Martyrs* (Oxford: Oxford University Press, 1972) and Peter Dronke, *Women Writers of the Middle Ages* (Cambridge: Cambridge University Press, 1984), 1–17. See also Peter Habermehl, *Perpetua und der Aegypter*, Berlin: Akademie Verlag, 1992.

Other Useful Texts and Studies:

Blumenfeld-Kosinski Renate and Timea Szell, eds. *Images of Sainthood in Medieval Europe*. Ithaca: Cornell University Press, 1991.

Brown, Peter. *The Cult of the Saints: Its Rise and Function in Latin Christianity.* Chicago: University of Chicago Press, 1981.

Bynum, Caroline Walker. *Jesus as Mother: Studies in the Spirituality of the High Middle Ages*, London, 1982.

———, *Holy Feast and Holy Fast: The Religious Significance of Food to Medieval Women*. Berkeley: University of California Press, 1987.

Dronke, Peter. *Poetic Individuality in the Middle Ages*. Oxford: Oxford University Press, 1970.

Minnis, A.J. *Medieval Theory of Authorship: Scholastic Literary Attitudes in the Later Middle Ages*. London: Scolar Press, 1984.

———, and A.B. Scott. *Medieval Literary Theory and Criticism, ca. 100-ca. 1375: The Commentary-Tradition*. Oxford: Clarendon Press, 1988.

Kurath, Hans, et al. *Middle English Dictionary*, Ann Arbor, 1954—

Lewis, C.S. *The Discarded Image*. Cambridge: Cambridge University Press, 1964.

Nolan, Edward Peter. *Now through a Glass Darkly: Specular Images of Being and Knowing from Virgil to Chaucer*. Ann Arbor: University of Michigan Press, 1990.

Petroff, Elizabeth Alvilda. *Medieval Women's Visionary Literature*. Oxford: Oxford University Press, 1986.

Robertson, Elizabeth. *Early English Devotional Prose and the Female Audience*. Knoxville: University of Tennessee Press, 1990.

Smalley, Beryl. *The Study of the Bible in the Middle Ages*. 3rd rev. ed. Oxford: Clarendon Press, 1983.

Stock, Brian. *The Implications of Literacy: Written Language and Models of Interpretation in the Eleventh and Twelfth Centuries*. Princeton: Princeton University Press, 1983.

Watkin, E.I. *Poets and Mystics*. London: Sheed and Ward, 1953.

Weeks, Andrew. *German Mysticism from Hildegard of Bingen to Ludwig Wittgenstein* Albany: SUNY Press, 1993.

Index

THEMES AND ISSUES
"Feminine" versus "feminist," 16n
Gendered discourse formation, 10
   questions of biological determinism, personal will, and cultural history, 10; see also literacy;
   syntax: word and image, 11
Gendered styles, 14–31
   a feminine style, 16–31; 43
   a male style, 16, 42–43; 153
   a mixed style, 18, 33, 41–42
   affinity for simile (feminine) vs metaphor (male), 42
   anti-exegetical (feminine) vs interpretive (male), 21, 38
   centrifugal (male) vs centripetal (feminine), 40–41
   linear (male) versus phasic (feminine), 36, 153
   hierarchic (male) vs fluid (feminine), 36
   paratactic (feminine) vs hypertactic (male), 36, 38
   synthetic (feminine) vs analytic (male), 25
   that such oppositions can only be heuristic, 43–44; extremes: beatitude or madness, 44
Literacy, exegesis, and education, a medieval interdependency, 23, 56, 62–63
   broadly and narrowly construed, 23–24, 64;
   and Hildegard, 25–26, 56
   and Julian, 26–30
   and Perpetua, 25
   and reading aloud, 24–25
Rupert of Deutz and the apocalyptic imagination, 50
Woman's voices, recovery of, 10
   male mediation of women's texts, 10
   scribal tradition, 10
   other male barriers, 12

PRIMARY AUTHORS AND WORKS
Hildegard of Bingen:
   and history, 46–47
   and the feminist issues of self-abasement and self-assertion, 56–61
   biographical sketch, 47–50
   double voicing, 60–61; polyphony and stereoscopy, 56; as image of incarnation, 69
   ecstasy, contempt for, 68
   flos cadit (the flower fades, falls), 85–87
   legitimacy of voice, 55–73
   modalities of reading biblical texts, 56, 61–66
   music and memory, 100–107
   phenomenology of vision and double sight, 56, 66–72
   summary of her feminine style of synthesis, 135
   works partially analyzed:
      Letters to:
         Christian von Buch, Archbishop of Mainz, 109
         Fredrick Barbarossa, 54–55
         Eleanore of Aquitaine, 53
         Eugenius III, Pope, 82–83
         Guibert de Gembloux, 64–72
         Hartwig, Archbishop of Bremen, 80–82, 93–94
         Henry II (of England), 53
         Henry, Archbishop of Mainz, 76–77
         Prelates of Mainz, 93–109
         Richardis von Stade, nun and abess, 84–90
         Richardis von Stade, Marchioness, 77–80
         St. Bernard, 56–58, 61–63, 66
      [Letters from:
         Christian von Buch, Archbishop of Mainz, 110
         Eugenius III, Pope, 72–73, 83–84

Hildegard of Bingen *(cont'd.)*
    Hartwig, Archbishop of Bremen, 90–93
    Henry, Archbishop of Mainz, 75–76]
    Liber Divinorum Operum
    (Book of Divine Works), 123–35
    final vision *(visio extrema)*, 129–35
    gloss of Verbum Caro Factum Est, 128–29
    the body in the seasons, 125–27
    structure, 123–24
    vision of Christ and St. John, 127–28
    Liber Vitae Meritorum (Book of Life's Merits), 119–23
    anti-feminist ploys, 121
    circular strategy, 122
    mirror of microcosm, 119
    pictura to *verbum*, 121
    poetics of middle, 122
    tally vs narrative, 122
    "Protestificatio" (foreword to the *Scivias*), 56, 58–61, 66
    Scivias, 111–19
    annunciation vs prediction, 119
    form as icon, 114
    general strategies, 111
    illustrations, 115
    tri-dimensional time, 118
    "seeing as," 119
    self-glossing, 115–19
    reader in a self-interpreting text, 114
    Vita, 62–64, 68, 74

Julian of Norwich:
  and *ad litteram* reading, 145
  and self-deconstruction, 145
  apophatic style, 146–47, 152
  biographical speculation, 138
  Christ's *kenosis*, 142–43
  compared to Hildegard, 136–38
  concatenation in, 152
  from sign to signifier, 141
  from vision to text, 138
  key phases (in commentary):
    He shewed me in party, 152
    Lo me here, 154–55
    He is oure clothyng, 158–59
    Quantity of a hazyl nott, 159–60
    eye of my understonding, 160
    Thre properties, 160–61
    Fallen to nought, 161
    We seke here reste, 161–62
    Nouhted for loue, 162
    Kynde yerning, 162–63
    He is the endless hed, 163

    To make many meanys, 166–67
    All of his goodnes, 167–68
    All the menys, 167–68
    The blessed kynde, 168
    His body is sperd, 168–69
    He commyth downe, 169
    Harte in the bouke, 169
    Our kyndely wyll, 169
    To seme left, 169
    With reverend drede, 169
    The clereness of fynding, 170
    The sekyng is as good as the beholding, 171
    I saw God in a poynt, 171
    Ne happe ne aduenture, 174
    sin is no dede, 174
    I leste neuer myne hande of my work, 175
    Art thou well payed? 176
    Endless lykyng, 177
    That yefte and that mede, 178
    Our lord looked into his syde, enioying, 179
    His swete looking, 179
    Loo how I loue the, 180
    See what lykyng and blisse, 180
    Behold and see, 180
    I am ground of thi besekyng, 184–85
    A louely thankyng, 185
    I make the to will yt, 186
    We take oure stede & wonyng, 186
    To be all onyd into him, 188
    Entende to his wooing, 188
    We die in longyng for loue, 189
    We shall see God face to face, 189
    Knit in this knot, 191
    The deepe wisdom is our moder, 191
    The substaunce & the sensualyte togeder, 193
    I it am that is to say I it am, 195
    I it am the . . . moderhed, 195
    To do the office of moderhed, 198
    Our precious mother Jesus, 198
    Jesus may lead us to his breast, 198
    By his lovely beclepping, 201
    A kyndely child despairs not, 201
    Suddenly thou shalt be taken, 202
    Thou shalt be fulfilled, 202
    As often as we may, & as long, 202
  manuscript tradition, 139
  note on her English, 150–51
  participatory readers, 142–43
  pleasures of continuance (anti-closural moves), 144–48, 152
  programmatic ambiguity figures hypostasy of Christ, 147
  reading Julian an *imitatio Christi*, 148

text as visionary analog, 144
Westminster *Shewings*, 139, 148–49

Vibia Perpetua:
authenticity of *Passio*, 33–35
biographical information is limited to *Passio*, 22
contributions to a feminine poetics of revelation that protects autonomy of the image (run-ons, weak subordinators, avoidance of metaphor, penchant for similes, reduced lexis, centripetal impulse, paratactic juxtaposition of images, etc., 18
visionary sequences of her *Passio* analyzed, 35–43
summary of her feminine poetics, 43–45

HISTORICAL AUTHORS AND FIGURES
Adelheid of Gandersheim, 77
Alexander III, Pope, 54
Andrew of St. Victor, 41
Augustine, St., 24, 143–44, 146
Bernard, St., 56–58
Bonaventure, St., 118, 142
Christian von Buch, Archbishop of Mainz, 109–10
Dante Alighieri, 11, 42, 59, 71, 89, 107, 143
Eleanore of Aquitaine, 53–54
Eugenius III, Pope, 82–84
Frederick I (Barbarossa), Emperor, 54–55
Guilbert de Gembloux, 52
Hartwig, Archbishop of Bremen (brother of nun and abbess Richardis von Stade), 80–82, 90–94
Henry, Archbishop of Mainz, 75–77
Henry II, King of England, 53
Hugh of St. Victor, 41
Jutta of Spanheim, 22
Paul, St., 65, 74
Plato, 107
Pseudo-Dionysius, the Areopagite, 137n1
Richard of St. Victor, 41
Richardess von Stade, nun and Abbess of Bassum, 73–94
Richardess von Stade, Marchioness, 73–94 *passim*
Rupert of Deutz, 50–51
Tertullian, 33
Timothy of Lystra, 74

MODERN WRITERS AND SCHOLARS
Auerbach, E., 18, 33, 211
Bakhtin, M., 40–41
Beer, F., 210
Bishop, J. 209
Blumenfeld-Kosinski, R., 211
Brown, P., 212
Bynum, C. W., 209, 212
Carlevaris, A., 209
Colledge, E., 26, 210, 211
Dodds, E. R., 33, 212
Dronke, P., 33, 37, 51, 209, 210, 212
Ellis, R., 211
Frye, N., 40–41
Fuehrkoetter, A., 209, 210
Gillespie, V., 26, 211
Glasscoe, M., 27, 210, 211
Habermehl, P., 33–35
Hart, C., 209
Hodgson, P., 211
Holloway, J. B. (Sr), 21n, 139–40
Hozeski, B. W., 209
Jakobson, R., 44n
Jauss, H. R., 16, 17n
Johnson, L. S., 28
Kurath, H. et al., 212
Liebschuetz, H., 210
Maisonneuve, J., 211
Minnis, A. J., 212
Molinari, P., 211
Newman, B., 51, 133, 209, 210
Nolan, E. P., 212
Owen, E. C. E., 18–19, 211
Pallphrey, B. 211
Peroud, R., 54n8
Petroff, E. A., 212
Robertson, E., 212
Robinson, J. A., 36n9
Ross, M., 26
Schipperges, H., 133, 209
Schrader, M., 210
Schwartz, E., 33
Smalley, B., 212
Spitzer, Leo, 37
Stock, B., 212
Szell, T., 211
Van Acker, L., 209
Van Beek, C. I. M. I., 211
Walsh, J., 26, 210, 211
Ward, B. (Sr.), 211
Watkin, E. I., 212
Watkins, J. M., 211
Watson, Nicholas, 26, 28–30, 210–11
Weeks, A., 212
Windeatt, B., 211